SMALL COUNTRIES, BIG LESSONS

Governance and the Rise of East Asia

Hilton L. Root

Published for the Asian Development Bank
by Oxford University Press

HONG KONG
OXFORD UNIVERSITY PRESS
OXFORD NEW YORK
1996

Oxford University Press

Oxford New York
Athens Auckland Bangkok Bogota Bombay
Buenos Aires Calcutta Cape Town Dar es Salaam Delhi
Florence Hong Kong Istanbul Karachi
Kuala Lumpur Madras Madrid Melbourne
Mexico City Nairobi Paris Singapore
Taipei Tokyo Toronto

and associated companies in
Berlin Ibadan

Oxford is a trade mark of Oxford University Press

First published 1996

This impression (lowest digit)
1 3 5 7 9 10 8 6 4 2

Published in the United States
by Oxford University Press, New York

© Asian Development Bank 1996

Published for the Asian Development Bank by
Oxford University Press

British Library Cataloging–in–Publication Data
available

Library of Congress Cataloging-in-Publication Data

Root, Hilton L.
Small countries, big lessons: governance and the rise of Asia /
Hilton L. Root.
p. cm.
"Published for the Asian Development Bank by Oxford University Press."
Includes bibliographical references and index.
ISBN 0-19-590026-X (alk. paper)
1. East Asia—Politics and government. 2. Democracy—East Asia.
3. Asia, Southeastern—Politics and government —1945- 4. Democracy—Asia, Southeastern.
I. Asian Development Bank. II. Title.
JQ1499.A58R66 1996
320.95—dc20   96-19242
                                                               CIP

Printed in Hong Kong

Published by Oxford University Press (China) Ltd.
18/F Warwick House, Taikoo Place, 979 King's Road,
Quarry Bay, Hong Kong

CONTENTS

Chapter nine

Chapter ten

List of Tables

List of Figures

A FRENCH FABLE REVISITED

The forests of Old France were once inhabited by wolves for whom survival during the difficult and lean winter months was a struggle. One particularly resourceful wolf pack was headed by Grisdos, renowned for overcoming any obstacle in the search for prey to feed his large family. The avarice of Grisdos is so legendary that even today young French bankers in a hurry are referred to as young wolves.

One day Grisdos learned that never again would his family ever have to fear hunger. A great El Dorado of wealth awaited them, if only they could cross the great ravine. "The inhabitants on the other side are so rich, they have everything, and their life is so easy, I have to take my family there." To find a way to cross the great ravine, Grisdos decided to go to the Old Owl. "Surely," he exclaimed, "a wise old owl like Veronique will know how we can get there." The Owl did not disappoint. She reassured Grisdos that the way was simple. "Crossing the ravine should not be a problem, all you have to do is turn yourself into a bird and you can fly right over it." Grisdos was relieved. "I knew you would have the answer, wise old bird. Coming to see you was so clever of me." He ran home and reported her advice. "We only have to become birds and fly across the wide ravine that separates us from great wealth." Grisdos's family of poor, famished wolves looked at each other dumbfounded. "But we have no idea how to become birds," they retorted. An embarrassed Grisdos replied, "It sounded so simple, I did not even think of asking how we could do it."

Grisdos went back to Veronique to report his pack's consternation at not being able to become birds. Again, the Old Owl told him not to worry. "There is a second best way. The alternative will mean getting wet, but all the same you will get where you want to go. All you have to do is turn yourself into a fish and you can swim across." "What a wonderful idea Old Owl, certainly we can manage that," replied Grisdos. And so he ran back to his family, delighted to report the alternative. "All we have to do is become fish and we can swim across the great ravine." Once again the wolves stared back in disbelief and asked: "How do we do that?" Grisdos, still undeterred, responded, "I was so delighted to learn there was another way I didn't think of asking."

So he went back again to the wise Old Owl, this time asking advice on how to become a fish. Looking down from the ancient oak tree the Old Owl dispassionately responded, "Wise Old Owls don't worry about how. We only give advice, provide the policy. Implementation is up to you."

Today, the parable of the wolves is reenacted by hungry young nations eager to acquire rich industrial economies. Their leaders entertain visits from experts of the development banks, their brightest students study economics at foreign universities. They, too, receive the same advice. "Just turn yourself into a market economy!" and the unsurpassed El Dorado of industrial wealth and technologically induced plenty will become yours.

How to execute this great transformation, however, is quite another story, one that has yet to be convincingly told.

FOREWORD

With the relationship between governance and development attracting increasing attention, the Asian Development Bank, too, is seeking to sharpen its focus on this important subject. After approving an operational policy on governance issues, it is now engaged in applying these guidelines in individual country assistance plans.

ADB also undertook a study of East Asian development experience, examining three specific aspects of governance: (i) bureaucratic capability for the implementation of policies, programs, and projects; (ii) the government/business interface for effective policy outcomes; and (iii) the principle of shared growth, from which all population stands to benefit.

As part of the inquiry, papers were prepared for the Governance and Development Workshop held at ADB headquarters in April 1995. The Workshop brought together development practitioners and academics from six of the high-performing economies of the region – Hong Kong, Indonesia, Japan, Republic of Korea, Singapore, and Taipei,China. This book distills the analysis emerging from the Workshop, as well as the series of in-country investigations that paralleled it.

We hope this contribution to the debate on governance and development guides the discussion along fresh channels, ones directly relevant to efforts by ADB's borrowing member countries to improve their management of the development enterprise. In bringing out this publication, ADB wishes to express its warm appreciation to the Workshop participants, as well as to those individuals interviewed in each of the countries concerned. If this volume adds to our understanding of East Asian development success, the credit is largely due to them and to Dr. Hilton Root, ADB's consultant.

S. Nishimoto
Chief
Strategy and Policy Office
Asian Development Bank

INTRODUCTION

This book distills the knowledge gained from dialogue between the Asian Development Bank and its borrowing member countries, initiated in the spring of 1994 in the hope of defining a Bank-wide policy on governance. The dialogue began with an effort to take stock of the Bank's extensive, but diffuse, experience in governance contained in hundreds of proposals, appraisals, and evaluations of projects undertaken in member countries. Discussion with top government officials in the major donor and borrowing nations followed.

The dialogue revealed considerable apprehension among borrowers that the governance policy would reflect donor preferences and experiences. Most of the existing definitions of governance, such as that espoused by the Organisation for Economic Co-operation and Development, seemed to reflect the experience and interests of Western donors without taking into account important components of the Asian experience.[1]

To dispel apprehension that the final policy would reflect such a bias, an in-depth probe of the relationship of governance to development in East Asia was conducted to inventory the best examples of contemporary development practice in the region. Bank-wide "ownership" of the final policy-relevant output would thereby be enhanced.

A technical assistance project was approved in December 1994 calling for a comprehensive analysis of governance and development in East Asia with the goal of defining lessons that

---

[1] For example, democratic elections are generally held to be the standard of accountability. But the Asian experience indicates that accountability for policy performance and political accountability are not the same and that accountability for policy outcomes is not guaranteed by the existence of elections.

could enrich the Bank's policy dialogue with other member countries. Papers were commissioned from more than a dozen country specialists for presentation at a workshop held at the Bank in April 1994. Visits to all of the countries participating in the meeting allowed the author to interview a wide range of government, private sector, and academic leaders. The concrete experiences of the architects of country development strategies in Hong Kong, Indonesia, Japan, Malaysia, the Republic of Korea, Singapore, and Taipei,China were probed. Key players from government and business gave abundantly of their time. Two follow-up visits and a series of four seminars with government and private sector leaders in the Philippines rounded out the project.

Three particular observations of East Asia's unique development experience were highlighted in previous studies. East Asian development stands out in the world for promoting growth with equity, for limiting bureaucratic corruption, and for successfully implementing interventionist industrial policies that often failed in other regions.

Contrary to historical experience and contemporary evidence in other regions, the high performing economies of the region registered high rates of economic growth while improving their social indicators (see Table 1). The positive association between growth and low inequality in the distribution of income in these high performing economies, and the contrast with other developing economies, is well illustrated in data collected by the World Bank, which ranks 40 economies in two ways: by the ratio of the income share of the richest fifth of the population to the income share of the poorest fifth, and by per capita real gross domestic product (GDP) growth between 1965 and 1989. Of the seven high growth, low inequality economies, six were developing economies in East Asia – Hong Kong, Indonesia, Republic of Korea, Singapore, Taipei,China, and Thailand – and the seventh was Japan (see Figure 1).

Table 1:

The Development Performance of East Asia's High Performing Economies

Economy	GNP per Capita Annual Growth Rate (1980-1991) (percent)	Real GDP Annual Growth Rate (1980-1991) (percent)	Life Expectancy at Birth (1991) (years)	Female Adult Literacy (1990) (percent)
Hong Kong	5.6	6.9	78	64.1 (1975)
Korea, Rep. of	8.7	9.6	70	93.5
Singapore	5.3	6.6	74	74.0 (1985)
Taipei,China	9.8 (GDP)	7.7	77[a]	84.0
Indonesia	3.9	5.6	60	75.3
Malaysia	2.9	5.7	71	70.4
Thailand	5.9	7.9	69	91.3
China, PRC	7.8	9.4	70	61.8
Low- and middle-income developing countries, all regions (average)	1.3	3.3	64	46.0

Sources: World Bank (1993b) and ADB (1993).
[a]Refers to females in 1990.

With the exception of Hong Kong, highly interventionist policies were adopted throughout the region, yet without the same deleterious consequences that occurred in other developing

Figure 1:

Income Inequality and Growth of GDP, 1965-1989

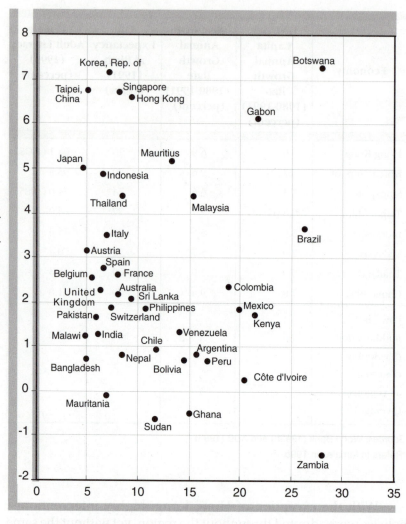

Income Inequality

Source: World Bank (1993a).

Note: Income inequality is measured by the ratio of the income shares of the richest 20 percent and the poorest 20 percent of the population. For a decade by decade breakdown, see Appendix B.

regions.[2] As the then World Bank President Preston conceded in his Introduction to *The East Asian Miracle: Economic Growth and Public Policy*, contrary to expectations, "In some economies, mainly those in Northeast Asia, some selective interventions contributed to growth" (World Bank 1993a). Yet similar policies rarely succeeded in other economies. To account for this discrepancy, the World Bank study highlighted the importance of learning more about the "interaction between policy choices and institutional capability", which is still uncharted territory.

A reputation for a relatively transparent and corruption-free business environment also set the high performers apart from their counterparts among developing nations. A number of independent surveys indicated that, compared to most developing countries, civil servants in the high performers were relatively free from political influence and corruption (see Table 2). Nevertheless, a popular conception exists of rampant corruption. Scandals involving politicians in Japan, Malaysia, and the Republic of Korea have been prominently exposed by the international media. We hear about a bridge that fell down in Korea, or cost overruns in building a subway in Taipei, but not about the many public projects throughout the developing world that were paid for but never built. In large part, East Asia's scandals become known because these countries have mechanisms for detection that occasionally work. Yet international journalists frequently fail to credit countries for identifying abuse of public trust and for making its redress a matter of public concern. Moreover, the international press fails to distinguish political from bureaucratic corruption. The distinction is important because bureaucratic corruption generally involves greater distortions to economic incentives than political corruption (see Chapter 10, "The Right Kind of Corruption: The Korean Paradox", page 163).

Another source of misinformation is the character of anecdote and public opinion within a country. Statistical surveys often tell a very different picture than that derived from personal reflection. For example, Koreans were especially concerned about income

---

[2.] This is particularly well documented for the case of the Republic of Korea by Jones and Sakong (1980), Amsden (1989), and Taipei,China by Wade (1990b).

inequality, but the data reveals less income inequality in the Republic of Korea than in most other developing countries. Those interviewed in Taipei,China expressed deep concerns about corruption, yet surveys report less corruption than most countries at similar stages of development.

Curiously, when asked directly to identify the primary cause of development, most government and private sector leaders emphasized strong, discretionary government; authoritarian leadership that could act swiftly and decisively, making difficult decisions while riding roughshod over the opposition.[3] Economic growth and law and order as achievements of authoritarian government are items of faith. However, this belief conflicts with the substance of what we heard, and it conflicts with the observation that the majority of authoritarian governments in the world did not promote growth, or confidence of the business sector.[4] Some modification of the relationship of authoritarian government to growth is desirable. Moreover, the differences between so-called authoritarian states are as great as what separates them from the democratic alternatives. For example, the standard distinctions between authoritarian and democratic aspects of political control are not helpful indicators of the predictability or consistency of the economic policy framework.

Those interviewed also tended to focus on what their nation's past experience meant for their current development. This concern differs dramatically from the Bank's concern with the universal and transferable dimensions of development management. The

---

[3] A corollary is that democracies have difficulty carrying out reforms that demand sacrifices because elected officials will not risk a loss of popularity. Authoritarian governments conversely are considered more capable of sustaining reforms. Thus the standard prescription – economic before political development. However, the assumption that authoritarian governments can more easily ignore the grievances of groups hurt by the reforms is based on a number of naive assumptions about politics.

Riding roughshod over special interests is overrated. Often authoritarian governments stand on narrow coalition foundations and therefore cannot risk to alienate key supporters. When social foundations are weak authoritarian regimes do not have the broad coalition support to sustain reforms, but instead must cater to volatile and highly mobilized groups. Therefore, authoritarian regimes are not necessarily able to consider long-term national interests any more effectively than their so-called democratic counterparts. A naive belief that authoritarian rulers are less dependent on coalitional support than elected officials underlies the fallacy that proreform coalitions will prevail more easily in an authoritarian regime.

[4] One of the book's referees bluntly put it, "Strong leadership is all, the rest is just rationalization".

Table 2:

Transparency International Corruption Ranking 1995[a]

Country	Score	Number of Surveys	Variance	Country	Score	Number of Surveys	Variance
New Zealand	9.55	4	0.07	Portugal	5.56	4	0.66
Denmark	9.32	4	0.01	Malaysia	5.28	7	0.36
Singapore	9.26	7	0.21	Argentina	5.24	2	5.86
Finland	9.12	7	0.07	Taipei;China	5.08	7	1.03
Canada	8.87	4	0.44	Spain	4.35	4	2.57
Sweden	8.87	4	0.11	Korea, Rep. of	4.29	7	1.29
Australia	8.80	4	0.54	Hungary	4.12	3	0.69
Switzerland	8.76	4	0.52	Turkey	4.10	4	1.33
Netherlands	8.69	4	0.63	Greece	4.04	4	1.65
Norway	8.61	4	0.78	Colombia	3.44	2	1.12
Ireland	8.57	4	0.61	Mexico	3.18	4	0.06
United Kingdom	8.57	4	0.17	Italy	2.99	4	6.92
Germany	8.14	4	0.63	Thailand	2.79	7	1.69
Chile	7.94	3	0.97	India	2.78	5	1.63
USA	7.79	4	1.67	Philippines	2.77	5	1.13
Austria	7.13	4	0.36	Brazil	2.70	4	3.11
Hong Kong	7.12	7	0.48	Venezuela	2.66	4	3.18
France	7.00	4	3.32	Pakistan	2.25	4	1.62
Belgium/Lux.	6.85	4	3.08	China	2.16	4	0.08
Japan	6.72	7	2.73	Indonesia	1.94	7	0.26
South Africa	5.62	4	2.35				

Source: Transparency International (1995).
[a] This index reflects the level at which corruption is perceived by business to impact on commercial activities, and is based on seven surveys. Only countries for which a minimum of two scores exist are listed. Three figures are given for each country. The first is overall integrity. A ten equals an extremely clean country, while zero indicates a country where business transactions routinely require kickbacks, extortion, etc. Column two indicates the number of surveys in which a particular country has been included. Column three indicates the variance of the countries. Variance was not significant for any of the East Asian countries included in the book. The study does not distinguish the kinds of corruption or what effect they have on business incentives. Thus, the survey establishes no direct links between corruption and development.

Bank's goal was to identify useful lessons for other developing countries and ultimately to learn how to transfer the benefits of the East Asian experience to other developing regions. Being able to identify the key institutional measures responsible for a country's economic take-off seemed particularly useful from the Bank's point of view because such lessons might help guide future technical assistance to borrowing countries. Therefore, the study analyzes only the trajectory toward sustained growth and middle income status.[5] The evolution of the economies after they passed the threshold of poverty to become middle income countries is another question that raises different analytical issues.

The study of governance in East Asia is intended to help the Bank and, indirectly, other organizations concerned with development to sharpen their ability to ensure that the quality of governance is appropriately highlighted in programs to assist developing countries. Lessons of the East Asian experience should guide Bank officials to improve their evaluation of the quality of economic management at the project level, including assessments of the institutional capacity of borrowing entities. The hope is to provide a governance framework in policy dialogue and in policy intensive lending operations and, ultimately, to introduce a formal capacity-building program in governance.

The policy implications derived from the exercise are summarized in Appendix A, which presents the essence of the governance policy that was adopted by the Bank's Board of Executive Directors on 3 October 1995. The lessons learned during the study of the East Asian experience helped shape the policy and win support from borrowing countries. Although still in a preliminary stage, a consensus emerged on a number of shared objectives, including rehabilitating the public sector, fortifying the legal foundations for development, and expanding participatory development by constructing a more transparent interface for public-private interactions.

---

[5] "Middle-income economies are those with a GNP per capita of more than $635 but less than $7,911 in 1991. A further division, at GNP per capita of $2,555 in 1991, is made between lower-middle-income and upper-middle-income economies" (World Bank 1993a, xv).

Despite the contributions of over a dozen scholars, a recognized measure that links governance directly to economic outcomes was purposefully not constructed. A standard measurement was not welcomed, in part, because member countries want their specific histories and stages of development to be taken into account. Differences in political history have provided a diversity of political systems and institutional cultures in the Asian and Pacific region. None of these can claim to have any comparative advantage in matters of economic governance. Many institutional alternatives permit sound development management. Members want their particular histories and levels of development to determine their institutional choices. Therefore any definition of good governance must take into account the region's vast political diversity and should not seek to impose the institutions of one country on another, regardless of how successful that country may appear to be.

Chapter one introduces the finding that one common thread through the region's growth experience is the successful implementation of economic and social policies. Two important institutional components of that capacity are bureaucratic capability and the existence of an effective state-society interface. An emphasis on the institutional framework integrates the descriptive country chapters that follow. The final two chapters and Appendix A discuss the general characteristics of the institutional matrix in East Asia that encourage productivity growth and flexible responses to changing economic incentives.

PREFACE

The Asian Development Bank is the first multilateral development bank that has a board-approved policy on governance – an achievement that took teamwork and discretion, and built on a long history of trust between the Bank and its members. At many junctures, the process could have unraveled. A number of individuals kept the project on target despite the hazards of possible misunderstandings among member nations that have dramatically different political traditions and cultural expectations.

As task manager, Karti Sandilya anticipated and prepared the author for every glitch along the way. On the road from Tokyo through Taipei, Seoul, Jakarta, Hong Kong, Kuala Lumpur, Singapore, and back to Manila, Karti was a valued companion and colleague. Shoji Nishimoto as Chief and Jan P.M Van Heeswijk as Assistant Chief of the Strategy and Policy Office provided the leadership within the Bank that crafted a consensus on the key issues. Their combined foresight and forbearance inspired the process of translating the initiatives of donors into programs and actions that are consistent with Bank practice and norms. Christopher MacCormac and Khaja Moinuddin provided key insights throughout the process.

Executive directors of Canada, Anthony Berger and Julian H. Payne; France, Daniel Besson; Germany and the United Kingdom, Han-Jürgen Stryk; Pakistan, Vicente R. Jayme; India, K. Venkatesan; and the People's Republic of China, Li Ruogu were essential in helping the author articulate the concerns of donors in a language that addresses the sensitivities of all stakeholders. Executive Director of the United States, Linda Tsao Yang, and Alternate Director Cinnamon Dornsife shared the author's struggle to find common ground between many competing and potentially conflicting visions among Bank membership. Their insights, suggestions, and personal support were critical throughout the fact-gathering and consensus-building stages.

Vice-President Peter Sullivan and General Counsel Barry Metzger both participated in and helped to guide the final outcome. Bank President Mitsuo Sato offered all participants the latitude to exercise their professional judgment, while keeping their attention focused on the long-term objective of deriving a framework that could provide stable and consistent direction to the Bank's policy dialogue with borrowing member countries.

The input of a number of country consultants and experts must be singled out. The participants at the Governance and Development Workshop held at the Bank, from 19-21 April 1995, included Kim Kihwan, Kathleen Lauder, Miranda Goeltom, John P. Burns, Hahn Young-Whan, Shiau Chyuan-Jenq, Kengo Akizuki, Yasunori Sone, Colin Sankey, Norman Miners, Yun-han Chu, Kwang Choi, and Ahn Choong-Yong. Key in-country interviews are noted at the beginning of each chapter.

Hoover colleagues Bruce Bueno de Mesquita, Ramon Meyers, Alvin Robushka, Henry Rowen, and Barry Weingast gave generously of their time and expertise as readers of the manuscript. Joyce Cerwin provided organizational and research support. Many thanks to Hoover Director John Raisian for affording the author long absences to complete the research that went into this project. Judy Banning edited the successive revisions and prepared the final manuscript for the printer. The author would like to dedicate this book to Robert Hartwell and Alan Kors in gratitude for clearing the path that made it possible for me to move on to projects such as this. The author takes full responsibility for any errors or misconceptions that persist despite such excellent council. The Asian Development Bank should not be identified with the views and opinions expressed in this volume. They are exclusively those of the author.

Hilton L. Root
19 February 1996
Manila

TERMS AND ABBREVIATIONS

ASEAN	Association of Southeast Asian Nations
BAPPENAS	National Planning Council (Indonesia)
CPIB	Corrupt Practices Investigation Bureau (Singapore)
EPB	Economic Planning Board (Republic of Korea)
GDP	gross domestic product
GNP	gross national product
ICAC	Independent Commission Against Corruption (Hong Kong)
IMF	International Monetary Fund
KMT	Kuomintang (Chinese Nationalist) government (Taipei,China)
NECC	National Economic Consultative Council (Malaysia)
NGO	nongovernment organization
NWC	National Wages Council (Singapore)
OECD	Organisation for Economic Co-operation and Development
PAP	People's Action Party (Singapore)
PRC	People's Republic of China
UMNO	United Malays National Organization (Malaysia)

Note: In this report $ refers to US dollars.

CHAPTER ONE

INSTITUTIONAL INNOVATION IN EAST ASIAN DEVELOPMENT

Conventional wisdom suggests that a key reason for the success of economic policy in East Asia is the authoritarian character of the political regimes. Comparison of the economic performance of nations within the region, however, indicates that a link between authoritarianism and successful growth should not be taken for granted.

Authoritarian regimes in Myanmar, Philippines, and Viet Nam, for example, consistently failed to make the tough economic decisions needed to sustain growth. The connection appears even weaker when the region's experience is compared to other developing areas, such as Africa or Latin America, where authoritarianism and growth rarely complement each other. Since regime type is a poor predictor of economic performance and the much vaunted dichotomy between democracy and autocracy provides little illumination on why economic policy succeeds, we must look to other explanations to understand the institutional foundations of East Asian growth.

In this essay, explanations popular among various academic disciplines and policymakers will be examined, followed by suggestions of alternative factors and relationships. Then, seven case studies will be presented in the hope of identifying generalizations about the role of government in East Asian development.

The Confucian Cliché

Confucianism is sometimes proposed as the cultural explanation for the success of Asia's high performing economies. But the values typically associated with Confucianism are not unique to the region.[6] Most are universal values, such as filial piety, held in reverence by cultures and belief systems throughout the world. Moreover, traditional Confucian values, such as family loyalty, can justify nepotism and thus stifle the development of modern government structures. For example, a national civil service requires performance-driven evaluations and adherence to bureaucratic norms.

While Confucian principles emphasize rule by persons of moral authority over rule by law, and paternalism over legalism, the success of the best performing economies in the region corresponds with a shift away from ascriptive standards. Even though Confucian thought links seniority to moral authority, leaders like the Republic of Korea's Park Chung Hee (44 when he took power) or Singapore's Lee Kuan Yew (35) were young men who seized power forcefully and then appointed other young men like themselves to positions of authority, disregarding their Confucian heritage.

Lee Kuan Yew expressed his non-Confucian disdain for seniority in July 1961, "I am in favour of efficient service. The brighter chap goes up and I don't care how many years he's been in or he hasn't been in. If he is the best man for the job, put him there" (Quah 1993b, 324). Similarly, under Park's leadership the age structure of the Korean administration changed, so that by the middle of the 1960s bureau directors were two years younger than their subordinates.

Another cultural obstacle to be overcome was that the Confucian elite did not highly value business activities. In traditional Confucian society, business must approach government

---

[6] Those who emphasize the role of Confucianism must explain why, compared to the industrial West, economic growth has only just begun in the Confucian Hong Kong, Republic of Korea, and Taipei,China, while the People's Republic of China and Viet Nam have remained immobile. Moreover, why does North Korea stagnate while the Republic of Korea prospers? A Confucian explanation offers little insight into the take-off of Southeast Asia's star performers — Indonesia, Malaysia, and Thailand — and it denies the region's success of any universal relevance.

as a supplicant. A respectable image of business had to be created to surmount this bias.[7]

The Role of Policy Selection

Economists, rather than relying on cultural factors to explain the success of East Asian economies, tend to emphasize the importance of choosing the "right" policy. However East Asians did not always choose the "right" policies – they did not always follow the recommendations of economists. For example, economic experts spoke out against the Republic of Korea's Seoul-Pusan Highway and the Pohang Comprehensive Steel Mill projects. Although considered inconsistent with national comparative advantage, these projects have been successful beyond any expectations.[8] Even Korea's highly leveraged chemical industry, condemned by economists in the 1980s, looks successful in the 1990s. And, in another instance, a World Bank report projected the rapid decline of Singapore after its separation from Malaysia.

East Asian leaders, like those of most developing nations, believed that national development and shared growth required executive interventions in the market. Among these interventions, land reform, significant investment in agriculture and rural infrastructure, encouragement of small- and medium-sized enterprises, and limits on inflation are promises often heard, but rarely implemented in developing countries. Slogans in most countries, these reforms were realities that brought considerable economic rewards. Mobilization of the domestic market and reduction of income disparities between the urban and rural sectors were outcomes that East Asian leaders could be proud of, and that could be used to garner support for their governments.[9]

---

[7] Curiously, the most successful country in the region, Japan, attributes less to Asian values, while the Philippines leads the region in asserting Asian values as a key factor of Asian success (*Far Eastern Economic Review* 1995, 37).

[8] During the Republic of Korea's high growth period, financial activity, including access to the banking sector, interest areas, and credit allocation, was heavily regulated despite the arguments of experts that the economy would collapse due to the assumed inefficiency of the financial sector.

[9] Rural political support mattered more to governments in East Asia than in most developing countries. Bangkok, Jakarta, Taipei, and Tokyo are less supportive of their respective national government than the country as a whole. Japan's Liberal Democrats, Indonesia's Golkar, and Taipei,China's Kuomintang depended heavily on rural support.

Measures to promote investment were commonplace throughout the region. Conscious industrial policy was practiced by a number of the high performers and most made subsidized and directed finance available to promote investment and infant industries. Even efforts to reconfigure the ownership structure of private firms were undertaken. These familiar tactics to promote strategic industries – avenues for rent seeking and bribe taking in most developing countries – were often effectively implemented in East Asia. Even the presumed shift by the high performing East Asians from import substitution policies, associated with Latin America or India, to export-oriented industrialization receives more credit than is perhaps warranted.[10]

Policies that presumedly worked in East Asia produced unsustainable levels of debt elsewhere, so that Latin American reformers typically respond to invitations for the renewal of state activism, "We tried it and were impoverished" (Jaramillo-Vallejo 1994). For instance, the articles of incorporation of Korea's National Development Bank are identical to those of Argentina's. They agreed on the same objectives: Fund those activities in which private sector spending is insufficient, select activities with high social rates of return, and prepare borrowers for private capital markets. That they worked in one country, but not the other, was thus not the result of design. This prompts us to ask: Does good governance emerge simply because of state "will" and official "power" or do these elements of development management need special encouragement and nurturing?

While they promoted exports, many East Asian governments maintained state-led import substitution into the early 1980s.[11] State-owned enterprises played a major role in Indonesia, Malaysia, the Republic of Korea, Singapore, Taipei,China, and Thailand. Although in most developing countries such enterprises

---

[10] The kind of interventions touted by East Asians resulted in corruption and other undesirable effects elsewhere (Summers and Shah 1992). Interventionism enabled governments the means to reward followers and consolidate political support.

[11] The real exchange rate index based on the gross national product deflator rose equally in Latin America and East Asia during the 1970s (Teranishi 1994). The Republic of Korea and Taipei,China targeted industries by selectively supporting exports without cutting import barriers. Thus, they combined import barriers with export promotion balancing incentives. In addition, Korea carefully screened foreign investments.

generally performed poorly, in the Republic of Korea, Singapore, and Taipei,China, they sometimes out-performed private sector firms. Along with import substitution, closed economies, tariff barriers against imports, large state sectors, and state-controlled banks were all common throughout the region. In addition, with the exception of Hong Kong and Singapore, restrictions on financial markets and selective credit policies also existed. Why, then, was East Asia spared the adverse economic consequences that resulted from highly interventionist policies elsewhere?

Few governments profess a preference for inflation, unlimited printing of money, or the promotion of income inequality between sectors, regions, and social classes. Many governments borrowed internationally for deficit reduction, rural development, and small- and medium-sized enterprise promotion. How did the high performers accomplish what so many others merely promised?[12]

One common thread to the region's growth experience, which helps distinguish it from the rest of the world, was the successful implementation of economic and social policies. This capability stands out as being so fundamental, it is the focus of this analysis. Two important components of this implementation capacity are bureaucratic capability and the existence of an effective state-society interface. Bureaucratic capability means that civil servants were subjected to performance evaluations while being expected to act as neutral referees in the development process. The existence of effective channels of communication with the government enhanced the private sector's ability to carry out policies successfully. In exchange for participation in the policy process, information provided by the private sector allowed governments to select policies that worked and to eliminate those that failed.

The quality of the dialogue between the private and public sectors did not reflect regime type. The region's democracies did

---

12. Many governments said they wanted to achieve what the high performers achieved. Many nonperformers even borrowed extensively from international sources using similar rhetoric, that is, the promotion of small- and medium-sized enterprises, and rural infrastructure. Ultimately, differences between nations are not in what they professed but in what they accomplished. The essential question then is: Why were certain East Asian countries able to carry out policy interventions more successfully than other developing countries? One clue might be the relative priority given to politics (ethnic nationalism or third worldism and geopolitical posturing) as opposed to economic development.

not promote participation in the policy process more effectively than countries in which national leaders were not elected. In fact, many of the countries that enjoyed the most extensive functional participation in the policy process, Hong Kong, the Republic of Korea, and Singapore, shared varying degrees of undemocratic means of creating a government. Yet, they rank high among all developing nations in the transparency, accountability, and predictability of the public sector. The attainment of high levels of accountability and transparency without the formal trappings of democracy is a dilemma that confounds simple assumptions about the relationship of regime type to economic performance.

Bureaucratic Capability

In most developing countries hosting authoritarian political systems, the state is an instrument for predation and public officials are among the principal beneficiaries. In such states, government interventions in the economy usually provide extensive opportunities for members of the civil service to misappropriate public wealth. Therefore, when the relationship between bureaucracy and development is examined, corruption typically is at the top of the list of defining features. In contrast, East Asia's rapid economic expansion presents a different face. More often, it is associated with successful state mobilization of national resources. Among the world's developing nations, East Asia's high performing countries stand out for their implementation of policies that limit the effects of corruption on investment.

Comparing the civil service establishments of the region's high performers with the laggards may offer important lessons about how to generate bureaucratic capability. What mix of incentives employed in the successful East Asian governments induces civil servants to use their private expertise and knowledge gained in office to promote long-term public benefits rather than short-term personal benefits? What mix of incentives makes the gains of cooperation greater than the gains of a single defection? What mix of institutions and leadership encourages officials not to run off with the profits? In effect, how are public officials persuaded that a smaller reward over a longer time period is more attractive than using information acquired through public office for rapid personal gain?

East Asia's example suggests that it is important for leadership to base its commitment to growth on firm political foundations.[13] An important signal of that willingness is the credibility of the regime's promise to share the benefits of growth widely (Campos and Root 1996). Most developing states offer such promises, but few actually deliver. Shared growth reduces the long-term danger that social movements will contest regime legitimacy and topple the government. The promotion of policies that offered broad benefits to the rural population was an important component of the commitment to shared growth.

In East Asia, the support of rural development featured policy choices that balanced indirect taxation on agriculture (overvalued exchange rates and tariff protection of nonagricultural goods) with rural infrastructure development. Unsustainable migration to cities was prevented by building rural infrastructure, including schools, and by increasing employment opportunities in the countryside. Relative to other developing regions (Latin America or sub-Saharan Africa), low levels of policy-based resource shifts from agriculture to urban-based industries meant that East Asia's urban population constituted a smaller proportion of the total population. Moreover, land reform (in Japan, the Republic of Korea, and Taipei,China), and public housing, an urban surrogate for land reform (Hong Kong and Singapore did not have land to redistribute), concretely signaled leadership's commitment to shared growth.

Thus, while in the 1970s governments in the developing world acquired insupportable debts as they bought the political support of narrow urban coalitions by subsidizing consumption, East Asian leaders, depending upon political support more geographically and sociologically spread throughout the population, avoided high levels of international debt. Broad

---

13. Governments consistently have to make difficult decisions. Whether sacrifices will benefit the general population or narrow interest groups depends on the regime's political foundations. The decision by Germany's Third Reich to murder Jews was difficult, significant resources were diverted to the task, but the outcome was self-defeating. Similarly, the murders during the Marcos regime were decisions entailing great risks, such as the possibility of revenge sought by surviving family members, but these were the wrong difficult decisions because government took risks from which few people benefited.

political foundations allowed East Asian governments to keep public sector deficits well below the averages of developing countries.[14]

The East Asian example suggests that the more convincing the government's commitment is to shared growth, the greater will be the value placed on long-term gains and capital investment by individuals and firms within the country. By undermining social support for parties that advocate revolution, equity-enhancing policies inspire confidence in the regime's survival. This in turn induces longer time horizons in the investment calculations of the private sector.

Another signal of the regime's commitment to growth was effectively conveyed by leadership's efforts to uphold standards of civil service integrity. Above all, this meant signaling that personal connections would not protect public servants from prosecution for wrongdoing and that the advancement of integrity would begin at the top. By making it clear that any confusion of private with public interests would not be tolerated at any level of the administrative hierarchy, governments signaled that officials would not confuse the profits that should accrue to entrepreneurial activity with the maintenance of public order. It was only once this assurance was clearly demonstrated that government could be accepted as a reliable partner in the development process.

When leadership shows an interest in capturing the gains of private sector development for itself, short-term thinking will be engendered among investors. Despite the extensive intervention of most East Asian governments in the economy, the ruling oligarchy did not monopolize access to the market. Therefore, that intervention did not lead to predation by those who controlled the political levers. If government officials are in competition with business for the rents or profits that accrue from economic activity, a partnership between the two groups in the interests of growth cannot be forged. By ensuring a distinction between the gains of political and economic management, government created a foundation for effective cooperation with business.

[14.] Hong Kong, Singapore, and Taipei,China consistently ran budget surpluses (Thomas and Wang 1992).

In the absence of an elaborate legal system, most East Asian high performers depended upon credible bureaucracies to enforce contracts. Hong Kong, Japan, Malaysia, the Republic of Korea, Singapore, and Taipei,China all took efforts to ensure that civil service appointments were based on job-related ability. In addition, recruitment within the civil service was supervised by relatively autonomous bodies that shielded the appointment process from direct political intervention.[15] A performance bond – years spent preparing for competitive and advanced degrees – had to be posted by would-be civil servants.

To measure and enforce performance, mechanisms to ensure the responsibility of technocrats for policy outcomes were constructed, along with devices to simplify the policing of defections by public officials. In the best cases, oversight mechanisms were complemented by internal grievance procedures. The Republic of Korea and Taipei,China created a structure that was flexible enough to allow officials to improvise in response to their local clientele.

The Role of Political Leadership

Leadership plays a critical role in inspiring bureaucratic performance. To induce the cooperation of the civil service, bureaucrats must first be convinced that leadership's commitment to growth is credible and that their expertise will be valued. At critical points, Park and Suharto defended technocrats from political opposition, signaling their personal commitment to reform. They understood that once lost, a reputation for sound management may be lost irretrievably.

Secondly, leadership must demonstrate a commitment to addressing wrongdoing at all levels of the administration, including the very highest. Leadership must establish and consistently enforce performance criteria for entrance and promotion, instead of using the civil service as a spoils system to reward political supporters. Finally, leadership must not exempt

---

[15.] The Asian experience is in accord with Western fundamentals. Max Weber noted "According to experience, the relative optimism for the success and maintenance of a strict mechanization of the bureaucratic apparatus is offered by a secured money salary connected with the opportunity of a career that is not dependent upon mere accident and arbitrariness" (Weber 1976, 208).

itself from the standards it hopes to inculcate in others. Expectations generated by positive perceptions of the government's institutional capacity to implement programs are necessary to inspire private sector confidence and cooperation. This realization led Park, Lee Kuan Yew, and Chang Kai Shek to address administrative reform immediately upon taking power. Lee Kuan Yew liked to reiterate Churchill's comment, "I worry more about my bureaucracy than about Hitler."

East Asia's most successful leaders undertook public sector reform before proposing administrative guidance of the economy. They understood that doubts about successful implementation would undermine citizens' acceptance of reforms. When uncertainty exists about a regime's ability to implement policy, citizens will defend the status quo against uncertain future benefits. Therefore, without an efficient public sector, growth is in doubt from the start. Such doubts will shift the investment horizons of the private sector away from long-term capital intensive commitments toward short-term projects with immediate payoffs. Investment also reflects private sector expectations that profits are secure. Such expectations depend heavily on the structure of the state's interface with society.

Participatory Development:
The State-Society Interface

Curbing the predatory behavior of autocratic states is one of the major conundrums of political development. This problem is acute in developing nations, especially those governed by dictatorships, which often have difficulty committing to secure property rights and rule-bound market systems. In the absence of a rule-bound regulatory framework, clientalism[16] and secrecy arise. Both detract from economic growth.

When leadership does not recognize the constraint of law, certain kinds of information sharing may expose firms to harm. Firms sharing information are exposed to political risk if the ruler

---

[16.] Clientalism refers to the personalized pairing of partners in recurrent exchanges. Particularistic ties are developed to cope with the costliness of contract uncertainty. Thus promises under clientalism are likely to be honored despite the absence of a public enforcement authority. Because the exchange is highly personalized, social or political rank will heavily influence the terms of trade.

uses information about the firm's assets to build political power or to punish opponents. Unable to prevent the use of information in ways that are prejudicial, leadership will generally receive too little information about the performance of policies from the groups targeted by the policies. To overcome these information failures, many of the region's governments, Hong Kong, Japan, Malaysia, the Republic of Korea, Singapore, and Taipei,China, encouraged the expansion of functional intermediaries, such as manufacturers' associations, to broker information needed by the government. Such intermediaries can collect and certify information and pass it along to the leader.

When the government's past behavior does not, by itself, inspire confidence, the flow of information exchanged will depend on the credibility of the intermediaries as brokers between government and industry. Since government depends on quality information for the formulation of effective policies, leadership will grant the industrial association some degree of autonomy. This will enhance the association's credibility. Thus leadership may encourage associations to appoint industrywide representatives to consult with government on an industry's behalf and to address the press directly. When viewed as a legitimate spokesperson for the industry, an association is a more effective partner for the government.

Even the rise of intermediaries does not suffice to overcome a more general political problem. Intermediaries are unlikely to share information if leadership can be expected to use that information opportunistically, at no political cost to itself. Therefore, mechanisms that impose costs on the political opportunism of leadership are necessary.

Consultative bodies were one such mechanism that emerged to "tie the dictator's hands" in a number of East Asia's polities (Root 1989). For example, deliberative councils in Japan and the Republic of Korea gave exporters a central voice in policy making relating to their industry. Although such mechanisms must be tailor-made to meet the special requirements of each society, certain fundamentals must be addressed. These mechanisms can provide a framework for the cooperation of economic actors by limiting the leader's ability to change policy arbitrarily and, hence, redistribute economic rents and wealth. By making the economic rules governing an industry more predictable and secure, the deliberative council format renders profits less prone to political risk. If expected returns from future development are secure, firms and individuals are more likely.

The council format facilitated bargains between constituent groups in exchange for information needed to formulate rational economic policies. The exchanges helped leadership evaluate policy performance and ensure policymakers accurate information about private sector assets and strategies. These council formats also facilitated, with varying degrees of success, the sharing of information between firms about markets, marketing strategies, products, and new technologies. In Hong Kong and Singapore, where minimal attempts at industrial policy had occurred, institutions to generate a continuous exchange of information between business and government on the consequences of policy were of less importance to the governments.

However, advisory committees do play a major role in the governance of Hong Kong, where they are used to bolster the legitimacy of the government and build a consensus in support of new policies. Consultation takes place between civil servants and advisory committees at all stages of policy making, beginning at the proposal stage. The committee will be asked to comment on draft legislation and, once it is enacted into law, the committee will be involved in the drafting of any subsidiary legislation or regulations that are needed for its implementation.

Why did governments not overturn decisions ex post or use knowledge gained opportunistically? Tying the fortunes of many groups to the continued use of the cooperative decision-making structures raises the cost of altering the system ex post. Once councils permeate an economy, a government that unilaterally imposes its will on an industry or sector will risk undermining the value of councils for other groups, thus subverting the entire system of cooperative decision making. Government, then, is unlikely to abide only by those decisions it prefers, overturning those it opposes. Increasing the transaction costs of policy making may also retard growth and, consequently, provoke challenges to the legitimacy of government. Thus, by institutionalizing deliberative councils, government reduces its discretionary power, but gains the confidence of business in the stability of agreed upon policies.[17] Councils are a means to attain predictability by tying the hands of government, but they are not sufficient to sustain transparency over time. As already noted, bureaucratic capability must be nurtured and leadership must resist the temptation to use control over the economy to build a narrow support base.

Channels for information exchange between business and government are essential if government seeks to play an activist role in economic management. The local and field-specific knowledge of economic interest groups will surpass the expert knowledge of the bureaucracy in any economy. Whereas the survival of business depends on exact knowledge of a particular sector or market, errors made by government officials rarely result in dismissal or the collapse of the state. State officials can generally find the means to compensate for mistakes through taxation or coercion.

In contrast, errors may jeopardize the very survival of private enterprises. Normally they cannot bail themselves out by accessing the public trough. Although competition in the marketplace induces business to gather accurate information, competition motivates business to treat that information as proprietary. Improper information disclosure may enable a rival firm to capture markets, imitate product design, or intercept strategies; or it might enable government officials to punish the political defection of firms and to impose conditions of political loyalty. To avert being outmaneuvered, business has a high incentive to keep vital information secret, which makes economic planning or coordination by the state difficult. To program or coordinate national development, government must be able to overcome these anxieties about the opportunistic use of information by providing assurances of relative policy and procedural transparency.

During the rapid development stage, leaders of most high performers called upon interest group participation in policy making to gain a comprehensive image of the economy. Regular continuous sessions in a formal setting with influential private sector leaders were needed. Occasional, intermittent consultations

---

[17.] A wide range of deliberative bodies were developed, such as political councils and village associations.

were rarely adequate. For example, the export promotion councils of the Republic of Korea placed the concrete experience of interest groups at the disposal of officials.[18] The credibility of these formal meetings depended upon bureaucratic neutrality to separate public from private interests in a systematic manner. By chairing the meetings, the government bureaucracy enhanced its authority, allowing policy to reflect the rational administration of trained officials.

Several East Asian regimes developed methods to share benefits with labor and induce labor to accept sacrifices in the hope of seeing broader opportunities. The Republic of Korea and Singapore, for example, developed methods to bring the general public into the policy debate and to increase public awareness of general policy concerns, through such strategies as the creation of a five-year plan and the imperative to balance the budget and control inflation. In Taipei,China, local participatory forums were used to generate a consensus for the support of government programs and to encourage broad involvement in the growth process.

The emergence of consultative forums that offer functional groups a high degree of participation in the policy-making process highlights a noteworthy generalization about information symmetry and government in Asia. A cross-country comparison of the Asian experience suggests that the standards of sound economic management are indifferent to regime type and are not the monopoly of any particular political system. Moreover, only a weak correlation exists between participation in elections and the transparency of economic policy.

Parliamentary government does not ensure accountable economic policy or procedures. In fact, regimes can use democracy as an excuse for their absence. Elections may determine the peaceful succession of one government by another, but, as the comparison of the subcontinent with East Asia suggests, multiparty elections do not necessarily ensure participation in the policy-making process by functionally relevant groups. A larger

---

[18.] Taipei,China was a partial exception. There, officials used state-owned companies to control the commanding heights of the economy (Wade 1990a).

lesson might be that under-institutionalized political systems can undermine economic development in autocratic and democratic regimes alike (Huntington 1968).

Participation in the policy process offers a clue as to why some countries intervene in the economy more successfully than others.[19] Interventions tended to succeed in nations that had effective frameworks for the exchange of information between the state and society. The East Asian governments that are conventionally viewed as authoritarian feature a high level of consensus building and are particularly effective at reducing information asymmetry in the economic policy dialogue. Their experience suggests that mechanisms to improve the quality of information provided by government, and ensure high quality information from the private sector, are critical for governments to guide the economy successfully.

Leadership in Japan, Malaysia, the Republic of Korea, Singapore, and Taipei,China was able to instill the lesson that the same rules apply to everyone. When this lesson is not explicitly adhered to by those who run the government, social discipline will break down, and compliance with rules will diminish. When the population can observe that rules apply differently according to one's status, then all bets are off. Curiously, although the theme seems to reflect fundamental democratic sentiments, adherence does not reflect regime type. The region's democracies are not the best exemplars of even the most fundamental egalitarian practices.

Policy Adaptivity: Measuring Institutional Change

One of the least noted lessons of the "East Asian miracle" is the importance of being able to change, including the ability to recognize when change is necessary. The region's development experience makes little sense unless acknowledgement is given to how mistakes were often recognized promptly and corrective measures were taken swiftly. Changes include the reversal of heavy industry initiatives in Malaysia, the Republic of Korea, and

---

[19]. The region's laggards cannot be distinguished from the high performers by measuring the level of government intervention in the economy. In 1955, the state sector of Taipei,China accounted for 51 percent of the country's total output, a higher percentage than that of the Indian state sector. Most of the countries in the region were highly interventionist by the standards of neoclassical economics.

Singapore. Korea and Thailand both privatized major banks before being told to do so. The role of the state sector diminished in Taipei,China from 51 percent in 1955, to 19 percent in 1990 (Dahlman and Sananikone 1993). Imbalances due to macropolicies were rarely allowed to persist in any of the high performers.

The ability to change in the face of new information, and the ability to collect that information promptly and reliably, reflects the existence of effective institutions. It suggests that being able to craft and adopt new institutions is as important as the ability to formulate new policies. The introduction of new organizations, new rules, and new procedures, however, is not reflected in calculations of total factor productivity growth. As a result, institutional change is systematically underestimated. Because institutional learning and adaptation is not captured in measurements of productivity, economists may complacently argue that "The real issue is whether policies fit the economy's capacity and environment" (Petri 1993).[20]

The East Asian experience challenges an assumption – institutions are given and are not subject to change – that has profoundly shaped the development field. The transformation of key institutions responsible for the formulation and implementation of policy is central to the success of East Asia's high performers. Corrupt bureaucracies were reformed, a dialogue between the public and private sectors was initiated, and single party governments developed firm foundations for democratic practice. All of these suggest the need to go beyond matching policies to institutions; rather institutional innovation must become part of the development agenda.

---

[20] Ignoring the role of institutional and organizational innovation, Paul Krugman has evaluated East Asia's achievement purely in terms of capital formation (total factor productivity), which leads him to underestimate the region's achievement and to ignore one of its principle sources of growth (Krugman 1994). Organizational capability is a form of social capital that is not easily acquired but is easily taken for granted. The emergence of capital markets, for example, involved the acquisition of new organizational skills.

Replication

Rapid growth in East Asia was often preceded by social upheaval, war, and, sometimes, revolution. Tragic events completely transformed Japanese, Korean, and Taiwanese societies. However, no one would want to recommend that countries consciously program social upheaval as a precursor or necessary precondition of growth. Violent social change can also be a major setback; it may take years for stable conditions to re-emerge. What, then, can be done in the absence of catastrophe or the threat of catastrophe?

Hopefully, a more open global economy will be a catalyst for progressive policy change. The globalization of world capital markets will benefit those countries that practice good governance – transparent, predictable, and accountable regulatory regimes. In fact, the countries in the region that practice good governance also have the highest percentage of per capita private sector investment. By practicing good governance, countries will remove the impediments to private investment. Those that persist with poor policies and poor governance will find themselves excluded from private capital markets and unable to finance their future infrastructure requirements. A focus on good governance will move the development process to its final stage – national independence and integration into the world economy. Attention to good governance will help position countries to attract private resource flows and escape dependence on development assistance.

CHAPTER TWO

THE REPUBLIC OF KOREA
PARK CHUNG HEE'S
'MODERNIZATION OF THE FATHERLAND'

The architect of Korea's modern industrial society, Park Chung Hee, was an institution builder.[21] He appreciated the need for leadership to have a vision that had meaning for all levels of society, as well as the need for institutions to make leadership accountable for that vision. During his 19-year rule, Park crafted the foundation upon which modern Korean society stands.[22]

Capitalism did not have deep roots in 1960s Korean society. To foster a consensus in favor of capitalist development, President Park introduced a nationalistic element that is captured in his slogan "Modernization of the Fatherland". This seemingly benign phrase aroused strong sentiment among Koreans who had once lost their fatherland. In the nineteenth century, they missed an historic opportunity to open their society to outside influences. Choosing the wrong policies – isolation and tradition – the "Hermit Kingdom" was invaded by the Japanese in 1910 and colonized.

[21.] In this paper, Korea refers to the Republic of Korea.

[22.] Based on interviews with Chang-Son Kim, director, Ministry of Finance and Economy; Soon Cho, The Bank of Korea; Yong-Duck Jung, Seoul National University; Young-Whan Hahn, Chung-Ang University; Chung-Yum Kim, Commerce-Industry Association; Kihwan Kim, of Kim & Chang, Seoul; and Yong Ahn Choong, Chung-Ang University.

Although Park never used the term *capitalism*, he insisted on regaining control of the nation's destiny through modernization. This meant that some groups would lose privileges, while others would gain. By making opposition to reform seem unpatriotic, the theme "Modernization of the Fatherland" prevented the polarization of society into winners and losers. Modernization became everyone's responsibility.[23]

The Plan

Park's program for industrializing Korea emphasized extensive government management of private firms. The government identified industries that had potential for growth and were essential for national industrial self-sufficiency. Improvements in the production process and cost cutting, therefore, were valued over product innovation and novelty. Recognizing that a top-down mobilization of the nation's resources called for a high level of bureaucratic capability, Park devised a central command system that required bureaucratic accountability for performance and mechanisms to communicate effectively with the private sector.

To gain broad private sector support for leadership's proposed administrative guidance of the economy, collusion or rent seeking[24] had to be reduced. Ensuring the quality of the bureaucracy was the first step. A bureaucracy capable of overseeing a state-administered modernization program needs proper incentives – both carrots and sticks. Officials were defended from the opposition their reforms aroused, and promoted on the basis of their performance – the carrots. On the other hand, those who slid back were punished and eliminated – the sticks.

Before Park, nepotism characterized government and private sector organizations. The primacy of family and regional loyalty

---

[23] Consistent with this experience, the government has adopted the phrase "Globalization" in 1995 rather than the more contentious term "Liberalization".

[24] Rent seeking refers to activities that consume resources to achieve a pure transfer of wealth from one sector, group, or individual to another. These activities are wasteful because they use up resources without creating additional value for society at large. Lobbying for a monopoly is a good example.

were tolerated, and were even ideologically exalted – society had no other method to organize loyalty and build trust. The government did not uphold impersonal, universal standards of conduct. However, fighting alongside American forces in the Korean War, the huge Korean military was exposed to modern managerial techniques and skills. A central goal of Park's reforms was to transform the familistic structure of society. The skills that the military had acquired in modern organization were put at the disposal of the larger society. Recognizing that the nation possessed only a handful of specialists in economics or commerce, Park concentrated that limited commercial and industrial expertise in a few centralized government ministries where they could be effectively utilized to benefit the entire nation.

In 1961, only two months after taking power, he created the Economic Planning Board (EPB) to promote his first five-year plan. Being a new organization, it could embrace new management techniques, and hire well trained personnel. Because access to information was needed to coordinate the economy, the Statistics Bureau was placed under EPB's authority. Budget power was transferred to the Planning Board from the Ministry of Finance, leaving that ministry with authority only for revenue. EPB was also given control of the flow of outside resources. And since EPB's leader was designated deputy prime minister, he also chaired the economic minister's council.[25] Control over subsidies, import licensing, discretionary enforcement of regulations, subcontracting, foreign exchange controls, and domination of strategic industries put EPB in a predominant position within the nation's economic administration. Budgetary clout – supervision over budgets and control over disbursement of funds to other ministries – allowed EPB to impose its viewpoint on other government bureaus.

[25.] The EPB's first mission – planning, budgeting, and statistics – was later expanded to include foreign-capital management and price management. Since most industries were oligopolies, the government determined price levels to protect consumers from collusion. This function was eventually dropped and the government only decided the price levels of public utilities. The EPB was also responsible for policy coordination, settling disputes between ministries and among government departments.

Park and the Bureaucracy

The staff of Korea's first president, Syngman Rhee, was picked from among friends. Political criteria, that is, being an anticommunist, mattered more than the manifestation of technical competence.[26] A study of Rhee's speeches between 1955 and 1959 revealed that only 12 percent of his words touched upon reform or modernization, as compared to more than 50 percent of the words in Park's speeches between 1964 and 1967 (Hahn 1995). Under Rhee, salaries were low, inviting widespread corruption. Especially notorious were the windows through which the government reached the general public: the processing of industrial licensing and the control of foreign exchange.

To transform the bureaucracy, Park conducted a clean sweep at the highest level. Mandatory early retirement was decreed for the entire top tier. Since low salaries tempted officials to engage in irregularities, it was easy to find fault with their performance. The saying of the times was "If you shake someone hard enough, there is no one in the world who will not give up dust".[27] When the dust fell, not a single member of the Old Guard remained.

A merit system, in which government officials had to document their expertise, was imposed. Even cabinet members were appointed on the basis of previously documented performance in government. Promotions were also determined on a merit basis, without reference to personal relationships.

In 1961, competitive exams for admittance into the civil service were introduced. All former bureaucrats had to report to retraining centers. In 1962 and 1963, laws were passed requiring these entrance exams and instituting a two-tier system. The ablest could take the civil service exams. Those who started at the routine level could rise from the bottom and the age level for high positions was lowered. While life tenure was secure and dismissal had to follow proper procedures, any civil servant could be fired for poor performance. However, salaries remained low. To remedy corruption, still visible at the contact points with the civilian population, Park introduced a pension system in the mid-1960s.

[26.] Competent administrators were found in the Bank of Korea, not the bureaucracy (Chung-Yum Kim interview).

[27.] Kihwan Kim interview.

The president thereby gained leverage over wrongdoers who, when caught, were fired and deprived of all privileges and pensions.

After his first five-year plan produced few results, Park introduced the New Year visits. These were 3- to 4-hour visits with his ministers to discuss specific goals, and strategies to achieve those goals. Each administration was compelled to visualize future performance. Heads of bureaus were asked for precise projections of goals and statements of how leadership could help.[28] Park returned the following year to review the promises, sentence by sentence, goal by goal. "Anyone who talked about complexities, or who mumbled, was pushed out".[29] After a couple of years, the full implications of these visits were understood. Only those who made progress according to the plans survived. "Those ministers who achieved 100 percent were saved, but those who failed to achieve 80 percent or more, lost their necks" (Hahn 1995). After two or three years, following Park's example, managers throughout the bureaucracy learned to do the same with their subordinates. Many initiated monthly visits.

Signaling the Commitment

Park has often been faulted for inconsistency. The constant reshuffling of ministers and portfolios is cited as evidence that ministers rose or fell according to the president's whim. However, inconsistency was not the perception of those who worked most closely with him, and who were aware of the strong opposition his programs encountered, both within the government and within civil society. Chung-Yum Kim emphasizes how the president's firm commitment was necessary to overcome resistance, reduce protectionism, and introduce competition by promoting exports.

Korea's first government had maintained a trade management system inherited from the Japanese colonial period and based on protectionism and the subsidy of sectors. Park

---

[28.] Park also sent military personnel to every ministry for a short period, as part of the emergency plan to coordinate activities and to provide him with objective goals. If the military officers preferred to maintain their civilian roles, they were retired from military service and assigned to the civil service.

[29.] Kihwan Kim interview.

directed Deputy Prime Minister Kee-Yang Chang (1964/67) to eliminate this colonial baggage. Chang's determination to implement the International Monetary Fund's recommendations on liberalizing trade, industry, and foreign exchange, despite strong opposition from the business community, earned him the reputation of being a "bulldozer".

Insisting that "the market must be implemented as a condition of my taking this position", Chang persuaded Park to allow him to choose his own people. He raised interest rates, liberalized foreign exchange rates, and then liberated general prices. Government ministers were instructed that windfall profits would not be allowed during the transition and that inflationary prices must not lead to speculation. Chang's five personal assistants stayed despite the reshuffling of officials who opposed the liberalization. Opposition of the finance ministers, and the social opposition of firms and government bureaus was fierce. Even the ruling party requested Chang's removal. Yet Park persisted, signaling his commitment to modernization by defending Kee-Yang Chang. Similarly, Duck Woo Nam (finance minister, 1972/74; deputy prime minister, 1974/78; and prime minister, 1978/80) received Park's staunch backing, although many of those who served under Duck Woo Nam were fired when they resisted the overall objectives.

The frequent reshuffling of ministers occurred precisely so that policy consistency could be maintained in the face of opposition. Park provided every possible means of support and defense from attack to his "bulldozers". His firm support of the ministers who carried out the reforms induced loyalty and integrity. This confirms a critical aspect of East Asia's successful transitions.

Technocrats must be persuaded that leadership will fully utilize their talents and stay the course when difficulties arise. When leadership does not manifest a consistency of purpose, the bureaucracy is more likely to use its expertise to increase its private wealth, rather than postpone private gratification and work for the national good.

Another mechanism to institutionalize the president's vision was the granting of special recognition to economic bureaucrats who provided exceptional service. The top talents were recruited into the Office of the Presidential Secretariat in the Blue House. This bureaucratic elite was then sent back to their home ministries, enriched by the opportunity of having observed the policy process from the national, rather than the narrow ministerial, perspective. The hope was that upon their return they could infuse their ministry with the president's ideals and vision (Hahn 1993). As a sign of the president's commitment to technocratic criteria in the appointment of key officials, Park took deliberate efforts to keep the military out of the government's economic decision-making apparatus. Only 7 (14.95 percent) of the 47 economic ministers were ex-military officers, compared to 26 of the 120 (38.3 percent) other ministers. No minister of finance was ever a former military officer.

Signaling the commitment to modernization also meant setting a personal example. Park did not take side payments or tolerate those who did. During his presidency, no government construction or public works project was ever marred by a scandal.[30] Once after attending a reception at the home of a senior official, and having observed that the home was equipped beyond the official's means, Park ordered photographs of the residences of top officials. Those who were seen to be living beyond their means were promptly dismissed.[31] After Park's death, foreign bank accounts were never found, his only property was his own house, which he owned before the military coup. The president's austere example was followed by the ministers who served him. Not one was ever found to have enriched himself while in office at the nation's expense. Park recognized that integrity was essential and that unless leaders are above suspicion their motivation may be impugned, thus putting reforms at risk.

State-Society Interface: Instilling Political Norms

To achieve industrialization with an emphasis on heavy and relatively high-tech industries, Park devised a system that relied on government discretion to guide private industry and to achieve policy goals set by government. For the plan to work, Park had to assure the private sector that government would play by the rules and not co-opt the profits that accrued to the private sector.

[30.] Chung-Yum Kim interview.

[31.] Young-Whan Hahn interview.

A mechanism was needed to ensure the credibility of government commitment to long-term growth. Discretionary government interventions had to be complemented by a predictable process or set of rules by which interventions were determined and implemented so that firms were assured their competitors were not recipients of favored treatment. Moreover, effective planning required institutions that gave incentives to firms to not contaminate the information they provided to the government. Therefore the process for determining the character of government interventions had to be predictable, even if the interventions themselves were determined according to need.

Much of the government's leverage over private industry came from its role in securing foreign capital for the nation's private firms – it provided the guarantee for foreign loans that were then disbursed to the private sector. Since the government had the responsibility to pay back the loans, it claimed the right to monitor the strategies and investment plans of private sector recipients. If business would fail, the government would also fail.

To motivate business leaders and gain their cooperation, the government set up communication mechanisms, both within the government and then with the private sector. The first step was the establishment of monthly meetings, called within the government and chaired by the president. Participants in these meetings – the Economic Trend Review – included the prime minister, economic ministers, major representatives of the government, party president, chairpersons of the commercial banks, the central bank governor, and members of the ruling party. The Trend Review meetings, held at EPB, were complemented in the mid-1960s by the introduction of the Export Promotion meeting held at the Blue House.[32] Participants included economic ministers and vice ministers; ruling party representatives; legislators; representatives of business, especially the conglomerates, trade associations, and the labor leaders of export-oriented industries.[33]

[32.] The Ministry of Commerce and Industry initiated the Export Promotion meetings.

[33.] Samsung never attended. At the time, they produced mostly consumer products, such as cloth and sugar.

Industrial associations were begun at Park's request. Although business association members chose their representatives, the senior executive officers were often former government officials whose leadership of the industrial associations put them in a position to coordinate business activities and to lobby effectively on the behalf of industry.[34] Park understood that for the meetings to carry credibility, the participants had to be independent representatives of their respective industries.

Every three months, Park conducted an additional review and analysis of major national projects. Representatives of business enterprises that were engaged in exportation were invited to the quarterly Export Expansion meetings, along with central bank governors, representatives of government-controlled industries, and selected professors. In the 1970s, during the shift to heavy industries, the president expanded the Review Council to include economic ministers and presidents of 82 defense-related companies.

At the various meetings, government programs were introduced. The participants all received the same quality of information at the same time. Thus the meetings were instruments for transparency. To ensure that the meetings would become effective vehicles for public officials to respond to the business community, areas of disagreement between the government and business groups were openly addressed. Park hoped a dialogue between the private and public sectors would resolve problems immediately. Thus, in the meeting, the president might suggest to ministers ways to resolve particular problems. The instruction, "Why don't you do this?" was given on the spot. Transparency was assured because problems were confronted before all of the relevant players.

Once the underlying rules were publicly known, it was more difficult for the government to practice favoritism. The format of monthly meetings provided information about the details of policy implementation to all members of an industry, making it difficult to conceal collusion between government agencies and preferred firms. To assure firms that favoritism was to be restrained,

---

[34.] Their service mimicked the Japanese "amakaduri" or descent from heaven.

President Park never handled political contributions and never held face-to-face meetings with local business representatives on an individual basis. Instead, he met enterprise leaders on a group basis, as leaders of their industry, not of their firm.[35]

To further establish the confidence of business representatives at the export promotion meetings, good performers were recognized with medals or other forms of military prestige. Companies that competed for recognition and citations were reported in newspapers. In fact, throughout Park's 19-year rule, the press was allowed to report on economic matters provided it did not directly criticize the government or meddle in politics. Park wanted to elevate the social status of the business class and change the public's perception, thus making business almost as honorable a career as government service.

To promote an export drive, Park had to cushion industry from the full scope of risks entailed by international competition. Government made subsidized credit available to firms that attained export goals. A policy of allocating credit to successful exporters (subsidized bank loans offered to firms without collateral on the basis of their exports) provided an objective criterion that was difficult to manipulate politically, and induced firms to provide auditable accounts. Thus, export promotion constituted a government intervention based on well-defined rules. Monitoring company performance was easy because the government controlled the banking system and could, for example, verify when a letter of credit arrived for orders. Three checking devices allowed the government to ascertain a firm's performance: (i) the letter of credit had to be confirmed and irrevocable; (ii) a clearing process checked items coming in and going out of the country; and (iii) the exporters and the banks had to document the firm's performance during the negotiation process for subsidized credits. Nonperforming firms were quickly dropped from the list of beneficiaries.[36]

[35.] Chung-Yum Kim interview.

[36.] A government claim-settlement body housed within the Chamber of Commerce was established to review claims of foreign firms for items exported by Korean firms. Foreign importers could register complaints or directly appeal cases to the claim-settlement body. Foreign exporters were also encouraged to register their complaints with the commercial attache in Seoul.

Another inducement was the reimbursement of import taxes upon proof that the firm had met an export criteria. A virtuous circle emerged that required the export-oriented companies to maintain good balance sheets, which could be audited by public accountants. In 1974, when President Park instructed his cabinet to make large businesses go public, the accounting procedures that were introduced to facilitate the export drive also facilitated the pricing of shares to be publicly traded.[37]

In short, the implementation of Korea's export-push policies offer a sharp contrast to the inward-looking policy environment of the subcontinent's import-substituting governments. In Korea, the terms for industrial licensing, credit, or access to foreign exchange were allocated on the basis of an export yardstick, not easily politically manipulated. Competition for credit followed rules that were established within deliberation councils so that the criteria were known to all players. The government, in effect, acted as a referee: export determined one's score. The winners were eligible for government-controlled allocations of subsidized export credits. Because the contestants had to provide accounts that could be audited by rival firms, this allowed them, eventually, to attract funding from private capital markets. Moreover, international trade exposed Korean firms to advanced management techniques. The regime maintained its control over the economy by giving priority to foreign loans over direct investment. This allowed the regime autonomy from both local and foreign capital, providing great leverage in discussions with the private sector.

A fundamental transformation occurred during Park's tenure – the national consensus on the primacy of growth eroded. As wealth increased, a multiplicity of interest groups emerged. Ultimately, Park's belief that democracy follows from prosperity, and that freedom from hunger is a prior condition to freedom of speech, seemed less relevant to a society that, by the late 1970s, became socially and economically diverse.

Not a single memorial to President Park graces modern Seoul. Today he is remembered more for his intolerance of democracy

---

[37.] Between 1956 and 1973, only 66 firms were publicly listed in the stock market. During the period of 1974/79, the number of publicly listed companies increased to 309 (Kim 1993).

than for his successful management of Korea's economic transition. The surge of demands from the interest groups that sprang into existence due to prosperity exceeded the institutional capacity of government to accommodate or even to listen. Even supporters criticize Park for staying too long, and for not recognizing that the development of multiple interest groups complicates policy making, requiring more complex institutional structures, and broader avenues for participation. In effect, the failure to acknowledge publicly Park's accomplishments reflects Korea's tenuous political consensus and the continuing conflicts over greater economic liberalization needed to consolidate the progress already made in opening Korean society to competition. But this absence of recognition is partly due to the fact that Park's record is marred by the rise of the *chaebols*,[38] and the importance of money to the political machine Park left behind.

Power was concentrated in too few hands. This was inimical to political development and that of civil society. Because of the rise of the chaebols, many Koreans have a negative view of capitalism, which to them means concentration of economic power in the hands of a few. This negative view often translates into hostility to further liberalization. It is reinforced by the Confucian bias against business, which is at the bottom of the functional hierarchy of Confucian society. Because business did not rank high in Confucian society, Park believed a respectable image had to be created. He gave business special recognition, including medals and dinners at the Blue House. But he was never able to eradicate this bias, which is especially prevalent among Korean intellectuals who view themselves as having the ultimate voice in evaluating the legitimacy of power.

The speed of the nation's economic take-off is another reason why Korea has not yet reconciled its present status as a newly industrialized country with its recent impoverished past. Collective amnesia and utopian visions of how the transition might have included simultaneous political development often prevail over sober assessment.

[38.] Chaebols are conglomerates, big business groups owned and run by a single family, such as, Daewoo, Hyundai, and Samsung.

Nevertheless, President's Park's 19-year rule is an outstanding example of what is meant by institutionalization or state building. Perhaps his outstanding contribution to Korea's modernization was the management of the transition from a society of personal networks to one of impersonal contracts, enforced equally regardless of an individual's or a firm's status. Although considerable vigilance is needed before a full-bodied legal system to support economic and civil rights will be secure in Korea, the social structure and the basic behavioral assumptions of civil society were transformed by a shift from rule by men or by moral authority, to rule by impersonal institutions, law, and authority vested in institutions.

Park's regime can be identified with the universal application of rules and laws. He insisted that if rules are bent, the integrity of the system will break down. By promoting the notion that the state must serve all equally and applying the same rule to one and all, Park helped to undermine patron-client relations and nepotism as the basis for social organization. In contrast, many of the region's economies remain systems of personal networks, not impersonal market economies functioning within a rule-based system of economic and civil rights. Network economies can substitute for the absence of law, as in Indonesia or in the Chinese world, but are unlikely to sustain the depth of capital markets or capital intensive investment that has characterized Korea's breathtaking transformation.

Good ideas and catchy slogans can be found throughout the developing world. But Korea's commitment to modernization persisted long after Park passed away because he was an institution builder who understood that ideas must not only be stated, they must penetrate society. Korean political culture has learned from Park the need to devise institutions that will make leadership accountable for achieving its vision. Park, in his first two years, created the Economic Planning Board. He restructured the bureaucracy, making promotion dependent on exams and documented performance. He called upon business to form industrial organizations. Routinizing meetings between business and the government, he thereby created sustainable administrative structures and processes, so that program implementation would depend not on presidential or party involvement, but on the actions and competencies of rank and file bureaucrats.

Thus Korea's experience teaches the importance of institutionalizing new organizations, new competencies, and new operational modes and processes. It refutes the idea that leadership should be satisfied with merely adapting policies to outmoded or ineffective capabilities. Instead, it builds on Park's message, "Change the capabilities and you can accelerate performance and growth."

CHAPTER THREE

TAIPEI,CHINA'S GREAT SEPARATION

The seizure of Taipei,China in 1945, by two million Chinese mainlanders, transferred to that country the capability to govern all of China. The power vacuum, created by the departure of the Japanese, allowed the Chinese Nationalist or Kuomintang (KMT) government to dominate easily the compact island of only eight million inhabitants, and to impose fundamental reforms without the encumbrance of local resistance.[39]

Being strangers without vested interests in the land ownership structure of the regime, KMT officials were able to decree land reform without sacrificing their political base.[40] By capturing the industrial sector created by the Japanese, the party quickly gained control of the commanding heights of the economy. Compulsory membership in business associations was then imposed on the remaining sectors. In addition to the industrial organizations, KMT maintained many connections with the private sector and actively promoted civic organizations of all kinds. In 1952, some 2,560 associations, both business and civic, were registered with over 1.3 million members. By 1987, 11,306 associations carried a membership of 8.3 million (Tien 1989). KMT

---

[39] In 1949, the KMT regime moved to Taipei,China, along with approximately 2 million soldiers, officials, and their dependents, increasing the island's population from 6.8 to 8.1 million.

[40] When invading parties are small, they sometimes choose to rule through control or co-option of indigenous elites.

consistently attempted to penetrate these voluntary organizations and to subordinate them within the party ranks (Tien 1989, 43-63). In fact, this oversized state could have monopolized every aspect of society, as well as government. Why, looking back at KMT's remarkable record of economic growth, was such a preponderance of power utilized in a relatively benign manner?

KMT was not in a position to take all, as a roving bandit in a single raid, and then move on to the next prey. Having just lost all of the People's Republic of China, it had no place to go after seizing Taipei,China. There were no other islands left to govern under the Chinese flag. To become a durable, stationary government, KMT drew on its considerable experience. After all, the party had a history it did not want to repeat. It remembered the hyperinflation that led to economic collapse and produced the social upheaval that destroyed the party's rule on the mainland. To avoid a similar catastrophe, KMT was willing to leave economic policy to the technocrats; it remembered the class bias that encouraged support for the Communists. This time, to avoid precipitating class conflict, the pretense of representing an all-class political alliance was fundamental to the party's legitimacy. Shared growth was promoted in the hope of avoiding social contestation (Campos and Root 1996). Leadership worked to reduce the dangers of social mobilization by promoting policies based on egalitarian access to business opportunities.

When memory failed, it could be jarred by the need to gain legitimacy in the eyes of the country's principle source of foreign aid, the United States government. The Americans, sharply critical of KMT rule on the mainland, only grudgingly extended support to the party, and were strongly committed to overcoming the Nationalist's reputation for corruption.[41] While supplying $1.5 billion in aid, the United States attempted to reshape the structure of the government and its personnel so that it could undertake socioeconomic reforms, including land reform, while formulating and implementing sound macropolicies. As a result of American persuasion, a number of administrative reforms were undertaken during the next decade to make the KMT administration capable

---

[41.] In 1949, a White Paper issued a comprehensive and devastating critique of the regime.

of sustaining an outward orientation. Although upgrading the public bureaucracy was a priority for both governments, the agencies that disbursed American aid were the first to be reformed. Administrative reform eventually extended to cover not only the organization of government but also the training and comportment of government personnel.

The Executive Yuan was restructured and streamlined (reduced from 15 to 8 ministries). Those ministries responsible for implementation of policy were kept functionally separate from the agencies responsible for policy formulation. Among the policy formulators, the Taiwan Product Board was set up in 1949; the Economic Stabilization Board in 1953. The Stabilization Board was responsible for industrial development planning, utilization of American aid, government budgeting, agricultural sector planning, and price controls. It was terminated in 1957, and the Council for United States Aid in the Executive Yuan was reorganized to handle planning. The Industrial Development Commission formulated the island's first four-year plan.

American influence on all of these bodies was pervasive, it even penetrated those economic agencies not directly concerned with disbursing aid. For example, the Industrial Development Commission, within the Economic Stabilization Board, held its meetings in English to facilitate communication with American aid missions and representatives from American consulting companies. As an important counterweight to the Nationalists, liberal-minded economic bureaucrats obtained a forum to influence the policy dialogue, and to advocate for the expansion of the private sector and the adoption of an export orientation.[42] The Nationalists tended to champion an expanded influence for state enterprises protected by import-substitution industrialization.

The need to gain American support ultimately led the government to accept a broad role for the private sector in the economy, more open economic policies, and, finally, an export orientation. One reason why these policy shifts were accepted was that they were formulated by individuals and agencies that did

---

[42.] Most of the bureaucrats who are reputed to be examples of KMT's commitment to technocratic autonomy are, in fact, associated with the American aid mission. Technocrats were not placed in prominent decision-making positions within the party hierarchy.

not have a vested interest in policy outcome. In fact, these were policy choices that had powerful opponents and challenged important interests. By separating those who formulate policies from those who implement them, there is less opportunity for vested interests to intervene and alter the policies that affect the global economy.

The reforms of Taipei,China's administrative structure were motivated by the idea that at the more tactical level where policy is implemented, it is necessary to distinguish sharply between the interests of policy as a public good from the private interests of those affected by the policy. To mitigate against the dangers of interest groups hijacking the national agenda, those who formulated policy were separated from those who implemented it. The goal was to ensure that the formulators would have no vested or private interests in policy outcomes.

Another important change, registered during the 1950s, was a shift toward competitive exams in the recruitment process. The goal was to introduce a merit system in personnel policies to replace the tradition of recruitment based on personal recommendations. The Americans pushed for a more technocratic criteria. Until 1962, the rate of recruitment by exam in the Executive Yuan was only 13.7 percent, and in the education system, a mere 2.4 percent.

The administrative reforms after 1960 elevated the role of competitive exams in the recruitment process. However, political loyalty remained an overriding consideration, especially where the promotion of senior bureaucrats was concerned. To reinforce administrative competence further, the American aid missions financed the study of public administration in the United States, and helped to establish departments and graduate schools of public administration. Position classification systems and management of information were all upgraded. To prevent elitism in compensation, the same pay scale structure was developed for individuals in the capital and in the field. To ensure that an officer in the field did not have an incentive to cheat, the party decided there should be no conspicuous differences in the private lives of those who served the public.

While a state bureaucracy independent of the party was not an option KMT was willing to consider, the upgrading of the technical skills of the party's administrative staff was. The most important innovation practiced by the party was the separation of the party from the business community. By giving up direct control of the economy, and expecting members of the government to divorce their private activities from public ones, the party orchestrated a fundamental transformation.

On the mainland, the traditional Chinese bureaucracy maintained patrimonial control over decision making in the economy. The distribution of patrimonial services and prebends allowed them to develop networks of clients. Ministers and their families typically reinvested the funds they collected as state officials back into government-run commercial monopolies. A system of bureaucratic capitalism emerged in which officials, on the strength of their political position, engaged in private enterprises. Bureaucrats typically used government office to benefit their private economic interests or to buttress those of their clients or friends. A digression from this pattern had dramatic implications for Taipei,China's industrial structure. It was fundamental to nurturing confidence in the island's industrial capability.

Controlling Corruption

The government's revamped administrative structure was not intended to be a substitute for a commitment to maintain the integrity of those who implement policy. To ensure that those who implemented the policy would not be beholden to those affected by the policies, the government enhanced its capacity to weed out corrupt officials.

Integrity was instilled in the civil service by a series of examples that early in the regime's history demonstrated leadership's intolerance of private opportunism by public officials. Further, to signal government's commitment to transparency, policies, such as open bidding for contracts and land purchases, were introduced. The use of insider advantages by officials was purposefully resisted with the creation of an independent board of overseers and an independent examination board to monitor recruitment into the civil service.[43] Given complete powers of

---

[43] Political appointments, although free of the examination criteria, are subjected increasingly to a qualification filter – the acquisition of an advanced degree from abroad – more than 80 percent of the cabinet in 1994 had PhDs from American universities.

impeachment and investigation over government officials, the Control Yuan was established to convey the necessity of civil service integrity.

Elected indirectly by the Provincial Assembly and the Municipal Assembly of Taipei and Kaohsiung, the Control Yuan approves the appointments of grand justices, as well as the presidents and vice presidents of the other branches of government, and members of the Judicial and Examination yuans. Its jurisdiction includes impeachment and censure of government officials, supervision of the Examination Yuan, and field investigations of all levels of government.

As a foundation for the regime's bid for legitimacy and political transformation, the Control Yuan's work began with KMT's capture of the island. Thirty-three impeachment cases occurred in 1949, and impeachments averaged 13 annually throughout the 1950s and 1960s. Most memorable, the successful impeachment by the Control Yuan of Wang Zeng-Yi, Chang Kai Shek's nephew, demonstrated that even the premier's closest relations were not exempt from the standards that applied to all public servants. Impeachment proceedings against such high-level officials as Premier Yu Hung-Chun in 1957, Taipei Mayor Huang Ch'jui in 1964, and Economics Minister Li Kuo-ting and Finance Minister Chen Ch'ing Yu in 1966 (Tien 1989, 151-5) highlighted the regime's continuing commitment to rooting out corruption at its source.[44] Complacency set in during the late 1960s when KMT awarded membership in the Yuan as spoils to loyal politicians.[45] The Yuan's relative inaction in the 1970s highlights how governance requires continuous attention and innovation.

Although the party's use of the Control Yuan is often criticized for not being extensive enough, it seems that usage effectively

---

[44.] Impeachment of the president or vice president requires the initiative of at least one fourth of the Control Yuan, plus a majority vote. After adoption, motions of impeachment are forwarded to the National Assembly for action. Censure of government officials requires an initial investigation and the concurrence of at least three members of the Yuan, followed by a trial before a military or civil tribunal. If censure is adopted, the offender's superior decides the appropriate punishment. The Yuan only makes recommendations, but punitive measures must be taken against guilty parties. Ultimately, the Control Yuan generally reflects the KMT's position on the issue (Tien 1989, 154).

[45.] Recommendations of punitive actions against government officials involved in the illegal financial activities of the Taipei Tenth Credit Cooperation in 1985 were ignored, illustrating the political stalemate that preceded the island's political liberalization.

signaled expectations governing the use of power by state officials. The salience of the corruption cases that were successfully prosecuted heightened public awareness of what to demand from those in government service.

State-Society Interface

Despite the autonomy of KMT from Taiwanese civil society, the party took a number of steps to institutionalize the ties that did exist, in particular, to the business sector. Nevertheless, establishing regime legitimacy took priority over satisfying the demands of business. The party justified its domination of the business classes by the need to avoid fomenting social and class conflict.

KMT was an institution builder in spite of itself. It formalized the private-public sector relationship by compelling all businesses to join trade associations dominated by KMT. State-sponsored industrial associations were created throughout the economy, and all firms had to document membership in at least one such organization. These compulsory, noncompetitive associations were endowed with regulatory authority.[46] They provided a formal structure for cooperation between the government and the private sector, and a stable structure for the exchange of information.

Dialogue with business was predicated on the government's belief that the cooperation of the business sector was needed to influence the flow of domestic investment and to direct the performance of the economy. Business organizations facilitated the exchange of views over time and across industries, thus enhancing the government's ability to take policy positions. Once the associations were created, the rules for gaining consensus from the business sector did not have to be renegotiated each time the government wanted to propose a new policy initiative.

Ideally, the associations were designed to transmit messages, mobilize political support, and implement policies for the party. Thus, to obtain coordination and consensus on economic policies, the party dominated the agenda-setting mechanisms of association

---

[46.] Three national peak organizations stood at the summit of the nation's industrial organization: the Federation of Industry, the Federation of Commerce (representing manufacturing and service), and the National Council of Industry and Commerce, whose membership included virtually all of the elite business groups.

meetings. Formal meetings or methods of reaching agreements were not legislated, thereby allowing the party to maintain leverage. By keeping ties on a particularistic basis, and promoting a decentralized industrial structure, KMT kept business in a subservient position. In this regard, KMT's strategy differed significantly from that of Park's government in the Republic of Korea. Bent on isolating potential opposition groups, the government set up strict guidelines to manage personnel and budgets of the associations. Nevertheless, participation in the councils was valued by business leaders, who actively competed for appointments on the boards of the business associations. The large firms were especially eager to participate in the hope of enjoying the audience of economic officials, as well as, having increased access to bank credit. Moreover, protection from foreign competition and collusive pricing might become available to firms that performed according to official goals and in harmony with official priorities.

To maintain the policy dialogue with business, KMT had to uphold policy commitments that were to bear fruit in the future. Because KMT valued private sector support, it adhered to the policy commitments staked out in the meetings with business associations. In effect, as long as the party had a tight grip on the reins of political power, this format allowed the party to strike effective bargains with critical private sector actors. Gradually, state-society relations attained a level of institutionalization that prepared the transition to the more formal consultative structures introduced in the late 1980s. Ironically, the institutions initially built to dominate society, later became battling rams against one-party rule.

As the party inevitably became vulnerable to the preferences of the sectors it had organized, the outlooks of the business elite began to influence the selection of policies by the government. The acquisition of autonomy in leadership selection and independent sources of funding allowed the associations to articulate preferences that sometimes ran counter to party policies. As social and economic differentiation and economic expertise outside of the government accumulated, the relationship between organized groups and political authorities shifted away from rigid party domination. By the mid-1980s, even officially created functional organizations began to reflect the social and political diversity of a wealthier society.

Although industrial associations helped channel information to the technocrats, the overall policy framework was the responsibility of technocrats, rather than the business leaders. Realizing that regime survival depended on growth, the party persistently deferred to the technocrats, allowing them to formulate policy with limited political pressure from the private sector. Party autonomy shielded the autonomy of the economic bureaucracy. Standing between the technocrats and the business leaders, the party took responsibility for all politically sensitive decisions. The autonomy of the technocrats was buttressed by their control over the banking sector and their guidance of the large state sector. This allowed the technocrats to shape the economy, compelling the business community to follow their lead. As Yun-han Chu put it:

> State owned enterprises as an independent power base provided the technocratic elite with the economic resources for building an array of satellite suppliers and subservient down-stream firms around the state enterprise sectors, thus constituting an army of economic constituencies in the pocket of planning technocrats. (Chu 1989, 134)

Most importantly, technocrats were not given authority to dispense economic privileges to business leaders of their choice. The party's deference to the technocrats may have created a cleavage between it and the business elite, who might have preferred to lead the nation's economic decision making.

The bargaining position of the Taiwanese business sector further improved vis-a-vis the state with the introduction of foreign direct investment and the option of overseas relocation. Firms that were not satisfied with government policies could defect with their capital intact. In particular, investment on the mainland, although initially illegal, gave business greater leverage in its relationship with the government. Eventually, the island's business elite attained a higher level of international prominence than its political elite. The island's economic leaders more easily could call on leadership in the industrial world than the representatives of KMT. As private sector wealth increased, the party's control diminished.

Although the party had a Leninist power structure, it eschewed central planning and did not desire to eliminate the private economy, instead it pinned its hopes on employing the native population in a strong private economy. KMT needed citizen support to stabilize and legitimate its rule. Bereft of natural resources, the party's only option for survival was to nurture confidence in the island's industrial capacity – this required a credible civil society. Although comprehensive control over any possibility of native political mobilization was easily achieved, the party needed to prevent civil society from being snuffed out and entirely eradicated.

Taipei,China's business community was invited into a partnership dominated by the party. This partnership emphasized political stability achieved through stable policy leadership and broad social consensus. While stiff penalties for corruption and an austere example set by upper leadership gestured a commitment to keeping the government out of the business of business, company laws allowed for the expatriation of capital, thereby protecting private sector profits from political opportunism. By credibly protecting the profits of the private sector, the regime fostered the economic elite's cooperation in the promotion of regime stability.

In effect, Taipei,China joined Hong Kong and Singapore to become the first Chinese societies to separate the political from the economic elites.[47] The credibility of KMT's leadership was explicitly tied to the party's continuous commitment to uphold this separation. With democracy, that separation has waned. Politicians need money, which often comes from exchanging political benefits for the funds needed to win elections. To cope with the evolution from single-party rule to pluralism, a more interactive consultative structure imitating Japan has emerged.

---

[47] The political neutrality of the bureaucracy is another issue and it was not encouraged. The political views of civil servants were monitored. Newcomers to the recruitment process had to pass the exam on Sun Yat-sen's doctrine and personal backgrounds were scrutinized for signs of disloyalty. Every executive organ augmented its regular personnel unit with a security division and a party cell to conduct loyalty and performance evaluations, which were taken into account during promotion reviews. Membership in the KMT was an explicit benefit to career improvement in all ministries.

CHAPTER FOUR

SINGAPORE
WHAT'S IN A NAME?

Keeping party and government clearly demarcated is the key to effective government according to Lee Kuan Yew. Thus, Singapore's leader from 1959 to 1989 took measures to ensure a distinct division of labor between the dominant People's Action Party (PAP) and the technocratic or bureaucratic core of his government.

The price for PAP's withdrawal from economic decision making has been considerable. Relying upon the party's capacity for political recruitment to win elections, Mr. Lee has allowed the party extensive leverage over the political system in lieu of giving economic privileges to the politicians. Satisfied that political opposition has been reduced to a minimal level, the party rarely intrudes on the turf of the civil service or the technocrats.

To institutionalize technocratic dominance in economic decision making, the independence of the bureaucracy from politics was codified. The rules covering hiring, promotion, and dismissal were based on three fundamentals: Keep politics out, keep performance accountable, and keep it clean. As a result, a bureaucrat must resign before becoming a member of Parliament, and party membership reduces the likelihood of a bureaucratic appointment. Civil servants are not allowed any relationship with the private sector. They cannot accept gifts or even lunch from private parties. Maintaining the separation also means denying requests of prominent business representatives who come to

Singapore and ask to see high-ranking political figures. Singapore is one of the few nations that will today consistently follow this practice. It is critical for a nation whose primary asset is its reputation for fair business practices to deny such requests despite international practice.[48]

The bargain that allowed Mr. Lee to keep politics and economic management separate was conducted to attract the foreign investment upon which the prime minister had pinned his hopes for the island's economic survival. Independent and semi-independent judicial bodies ensure that separation.

Free of Politics

A neutral recruitment system is essential if the separation of politics and the civil service is to be maintained.[49] The peaceful transfer of power from the British helped Lee Kuan Yew accomplish his mission. The Public Service Commission, responsible for the quality of the personnel entering the civil service, is modeled after the British Civil Service Commission. It was crafted to ensure impartiality; its members, all non civil servants, deliberate on recruitment and promotions (Quah 1982, 1993b). One way it ensures impartiality is by offering undergraduate scholarships, on the basis of competitive exams, to support study at both local and overseas universities. The recipients are then bonded to government service for a fixed number of years. The commission also competes for qualified personnel by conducting career talks with graduating students (Quah 1993b, 322).

Limiting staff size is another key to an accountable civil service. These limits result from periodic rationalization of departmental services, streamlining of work procedures, extensive mechanization, and automation. Review teams regularly examine

---

48. Tommy Koh interview.

49. In Singapore, the civil service consists of the Singaporean Civil Service, the statutory boards, and the government-linked companies. The public bureaucracy refers to the Singaporean Civil Service and the statutory boards. The Civil Service consists of 13 ministries with a total of 61,956 employees (1 January 1991). Forty-two statutory boards exist, employing 65,000 persons (Singapore 1991, 24). The assistant auditor general was quoted as saying that there were 14 ministries and 41 major statutory boards in Singapore (Quah 1991). Statutory boards are the major instruments used by the government to implement socioeconomic programs.

agency activities to improve personnel utilization and to assess whether bureau workloads are necessary or if activities can be accomplished at a lower cost. A zero growth policy introduced in 1988 was an outcome of these evaluations (Quah 1991, 1993b). But the limits would be ineffective if the civil service were used to create a support base for politicians. Keeping politics out of bureaucratic recruitment is critical for the government to restrain overstaffing.

Overstaffing of a civil service is usually due to politics. Bloated bureaucracies result when leadership rewards followers with official posts. These positions are valued more when they include opportunities to collect bribes and fees. Therefore politics often motivates governments to increase the size and activities of fee-collecting agencies. Whereas fees, levies, and opaque legislation characterize the investment codes of most developing nations, Singapore's one-stop shopping is heralded as one of the most efficient investment processes in the world.

When political motives influence civil service recruitment, reform from the inside becomes difficult. A regime that challenges its bureaucracy may lose support from its core followers. When official corruption cannot be restrained from the inside, the eruption of public discontent may undermine regime stability.[50] Not surprisingly, avoiding bloated bureaucracies is easier than reforming them.[51]

[50.] In comparison with the relatively stable expansion of Singapore's bureaucracy (its growth was proportional to economic growth), the administrative personnel of the People's Republic of China reached 31 million in 1990 from 13 million in 1980. "Conservative government estimates indicate that, in the early 1990s, excess personnel in party and government agencies reached 600,000, at and above the level of county administrations; and 2.1 million in township governments. Consequently, the state's administrative expenditures surged through the 1980s: in absolute terms, the government expenditures in 1990 were nearly eight times those in 1978, as a share of the central government's total budgetary expenditures" (Pei 1995). At the same time the provision of public goods (education, law and order, environment, and physical infrastructure) declined. The lack of a distinction between party and government allows a considerable amount of the nation's economic growth to be consumed privately by officials of the state.

[51.] Exemplifying this difficulty, Aquino of the Philippines attempted to clean up the bureaucracy by reducing its size, but the departed were replaced with friends of the regime, bringing the size of the civil service up to former numbers.

Accountable Government

In Singapore, government accountability has several dimensions:

- Fiscal accountability – responsibility for the management of public funds,
- Legal accountability – responsibility for obeying the law,
- Program accountability – responsibility for carrying out a program,
- Process accountability – responsibility for executing orders, and
- Outcome accountability – responsibility for results (Quah 1991).

Mechanisms to ensure each dimension of accountability require officials to document carefully the use of resources earmarked for the creation of public goods.

Accountability begins at the top. Ministers are accountable to Parliament for the decisions of their department. Civil servants are, in turn, accountable to their ministers. However, civil servants are not personally accountable for their ministry's policies. When errors occur, the ministers involved, not the civil servants, must retire.

Fiscal, legal, and outcome accountability is the responsibility of Singapore's auditor-general. The auditor's office attends to financial and compliance audits, value for money audits, and program audits. It controls financial and compliance audits to assess the efficiency of the internal regulation of revenue, expenditure, and asset liability. When conducting a value for money audit, the adequacy of personnel and equipment for the workload will be assessed. Also of concern is compliance with the law. Program audits determine whether procedures exist to evaluate program effectiveness and if results established by legislation are attained.

Singapore's Public Accounts Committee reviews the accounts of statutory boards after spending has occurred. It has the power under law to request any person to give evidence or to provide subpoenaed documents. Its jurisdiction covers all bodies entrusted with public monies (14 ministries and 41 statutory boards in all). Although its first concern is to ensure that public money is spent as Parliament intended, increasingly it addresses value for money issues. In anticipation of future problems, it often recommends measures to prevent waste or abuse. Comprised of eight members of Parliament, the Public Accounts Committee's human resources are limited. Lacking a full-time research staff it relies heavily on the auditor general. If these measures at auditing are not strict enough, members of Singapore's civil service have an additional reason to think twice before siphoning public resources for their own consumption.

Corruption Free

PAP's battle against corruption spearheaded its victory in the May 1959 general election.[52] Many relate PAP's first electoral victory to its firm stand against the widespread corruption preceding Britain's departure. The party has never digressed from its commitment to corruption control. Although an independent corruption agency, autonomous of the police, was created by the British in 1952, adjustments made by Lee Kuan Yew increased its effectiveness. The prime minister acted immediately to strengthen the original British institution by issuing the Prevention of Corruption Bill in 1960. This legislation articulated the government's belief that to translate its policies into action, efficient and effective administrative machinery is required.

The appeal of engaging in corruption was considerably reduced by the expansion of the Public Service Commission's powers to include authorization to "investigate any bank account, share account, or purchase account" of any suspected wrongdoers. Located in the prime minister's office, the Corrupt Practices Investigation Bureau (CPIB) members were even authorized to inspect the books of the wife, children, or agents of all civil servants. Amendments were added as needed. In 1963, CPIB officers acquired the right to require the attendance of witnesses and to examine them. An amendment in 1966 allowed conviction of participants who did not receive a bribe, but who intended to commit an offence. Moreover, those who committed offenses outside of Singapore would be treated as if the offenses occurred in Singapore. Even a deceased person is considered to have

---

[52] The PAP campaign against curbing corruption was initiated by revelations that the Labour Front's minister of education received political funds from a foreign power. The minister's confession sealed the party's fate.

benefited from corruption if "at any time since the beginning of the period of 6 years ending at the date of his death, held any property or interest therein disproportionate to his known sources of income, the holding of which cannot be explained to the satisfaction of the court."

With CPIB behind him, Lee Kuan Yew could forcefully punish any abuse of public authority. If the activities of officials attract the attention of CPIB, their careers will be compromised. One minister, Mr. Teh Cheung Wan committed suicide even before he was accused. The discipline imposed on government inspires sacrifice from the population, which understands that nothing is expected of it that is not also expected of those who run the government.

Another measure of the leadership's partnership with the civil service is based on sharing the fruits of growth. The prime minister keeps civil service salaries commensurate with those in the private sector. The parallel salary policy gauges whether civil service salaries are in tandem with the growth of the market and reflect national prosperity. Along with competitive salaries, Singapore offers accelerated promotion for high flyers (Quah 1984, 1992, 1993b). The prime minister has consistently asserted that adequate pay is essential to maintain civil service quality and to avoid hypocrisy. "Pay now or we pay later!" has been the government's motto. "Feed them peanuts and they will behave like monkeys!" is another often heard refrain. A firm believer in you get what you pay for, Lee Kuan Yew liked to note that as Asia's highest paid prime minister, he was also its poorest.

While the Singaporean bureaucracy is relatively free of corruption, rude and uncooperative behavior has been reported at the counter. To remedy the rudeness, a telephone hot line was introduced in 1991 to receive complaints from the public (Quah 1993b). The hot line was one of many services introduced by the Service Quality Improvement Unit (1991) designed to obtain feedback from Singaporeans to improve government departments and statutory boards.

In sum, institutions designed to prevent both the People's Action Party and the civil service from misappropriating public wealth are essential to Singapore's success. Keeping the bureaucracy functionally separate from the party prevents the privatization and consumption of public goods by officials of the state. Lee Kuan Yew's commitment to high salaries, extensive oversight, and merit-based recruitment is motivated by the belief that Singapore's most precious asset is an efficient government that maintains the island's reputation for a fair business environment. In Lee Tsao Yuan's words, "The prime minister realized that if the civil service is not capable, nothing can get done despite good ideas. Getting the policies right is only one half of the story. Making them work is the other half."[53]

Singapore's State-Society Interface

Singapore's leadership understood that without foreign investment the future would be dim. One attraction for such investment would be an efficient public sector, a rarity among the world's developing nations. But, compared to many of these, Singapore had few natural resources to offer. Its major resource – an industrious population – carried a serious incumbrance: labor relations were marred by strikes throughout the decades of the 1950s and 1960s. A solution to endemic labor unrest was needed to lure international investment.[54]

In 1972, a tripartite body, the National Wages Council (NWC), was introduced to overcome this impediment by facilitating bargaining between labor and management. Government is represented by the permanent secretaries of the concerned ministries, labor selects its own trade union representatives, and business has ten representatives: two from American multinationals, two from Japanese, two from German firms doing business in Singapore, and four representatives divided among both large and small Singaporean organizations.[55] The politicians, in strict Singaporean fashion, are not represented at the meetings but the party (PAP) will usually endorse the bargain after it has been negotiated.

[53.] Lee Tsao Yuan interview.

[54.] Companies investing in Singapore often identify political stability as the most important reason for locating there. Fundamental to that stability is the country's ability to strike a deal with labor.

[55.] Singaporeans often refer to one significant weakness in the country's economic performance. Domestic firms account for only one third of the island's output. Although it appears that risk taking by Singaporean firms is weak, and that local entrepreneurship requires additional stimulation to prevent distortions that may discourage international investment, the government does not provide special incentives for local firms. It believes that a level playing field is the best way to attract and keep multinational firms.

Two rules account for the success of the council, according to its chairman since its introduction, Professor Lim Chong Yah. NWC decisions must be unanimous and the negotiations must be confidential. Unanimity ensures that no two parties can gang up on the third party, and that agreements can be implemented without coercion. Because it is understood that a consensus is necessary for all decisions, people will tend to give in on small points. Confidentiality ensures the free exchange of views, allowing parties to change their minds without loss of face. These two rules, the only two the council has established, account for the self-enforcing character of council decisions. In fact, Professor Yah attributes the failure of similar councils in New Zealand to the use of the press by participating politicians to embarrass rivals publicly and discredit holders of opposing views. "Never discuss quarrels publicly. If everyone knows that you are in a quarrel you cannot patch it up." For these reasons, parliaments are not appropriate sites to conduct such negotiations. Without assurances of confidentiality, Professor Yah concludes the danger of losing face will eventuality undermine the council's value as a means of dispute settlement. In another case of failure, Professor Yah reports that the government of the Republic of Korea used the council format to impose wage settlements on labor, again undermining the institution's credibility, and hence its survival.

Should employees and unions fail to resolve differences over wages, NWC provides guidelines after conducting an audit of the economy. This audit takes into account the level of employment, international competitiveness, inflation, productivity, and equity. Although not mandatory, NWC guidelines are generally accepted. The council provides a format for consensus building in which no party is forced to accept an agreement against its will. Not a single major strike or lockout has occurred since this bargaining mechanism was introduced, despite the nation's early history of labor strife.

The tripartism fostered by NWC has allowed Singapore to become a showcase of successful human resource management. Among the council's achievements is the introduction, upon its recommendation in 1979, of the Skills Development Fund. The fund was designed to address an externality that bedevils human resource development in a number of competitive industrial economies. Firms inadequately train their workers for fear that workers will carry their new skills to rival firms. One solution to inhibit turnover is Japan's life-long employment system, but such a system might discourage the foreign investment upon which Singapore depends.

Under the Skills Development Fund, employers who train their own workers are eligible for financial support that can exceed a firm's contribution to the fund. Because the employers must pay a percentage and training is made available only upon the company's demand, the supply will not exceed actual demand in the economy. The fact that firms do not carry the entire burden of worker improvement enhances the attraction of Singapore to foreign investors who may choose Singapore in expectation of the constant availability of a highly trained workforce.

By providing a format for the attainment of flexible wage rates, NWC has also become a powerful protector against unemployment. Wage inflexibility contributes to the underutilization of human resources. A flexible system allows wages to be indexed to profitability or productivity, so that wage reduction becomes an option to retrenchment during downturns. As an alternative to unemployment, wage flexibility does not impair the investment climate.[56]

The tripartite formula enhances the possibility of wage flexibility because labor has assurances that cuts will be economywide and will not discriminate against particular firms or sectors. NWC also serves as a neutral referee that lends credibility to any request for wage adjustments. Another advantage of the council formula is that wage contracts can be short term, so that adjustments to changes in the economy can be swift to ensure that recovery from recessions is speedy and that the benefits of growth will be shared by all parties.

The success of the council is a strong argument for more direct involvement of governments and donors in the process of institutional innovation. NWC allowed Singapore to overcome labor unrest, thereby transforming a liability into an asset. Labor relations have improved to the point where firms can respond

---

[56] When wages are not flexible, firms must downsize during recessions. This, in effect, overprices those who remain in the workforce, passing the burden of unemployment to society. When government provides generous unemployment benefits, firms can more easily pass the costs of retrenchment to society. The government, however, must increase taxation to support the system. This contributes to budget deficits and reductions in foreign exchange reserves, which in turn lead to exchange rate depreciation.

efficiently to economic indicators without the typical strife that accompanies rapid economic transformation in both developing and mature economies. Moreover, the council is an outstanding example of how consultation can promote growth with equity.

CHAPTER FIVE

HONG KONG'S 'POSITIVE NONINTERVENTIONISM'

Hong Kong's prosperity is often attributed to laissez-faire economic policies.[57] This attribution assumes that such policies can be maintained independently of state power. However, sustained laissez-faire requires that a state is strong enough to resist capture by organized pressure groups.[58]

In Hong Kong, a British system of checks and balances – bureaucratic autonomy balanced by a rule of law – inhibits rent seekers[59] from penetrating the state's organizational apparatus. It also limits the misallocation and consumption of public resources by interest groups, including government officials. The civil service in Hong Kong has many opportunities to meddle in the affairs of the civilian population. Housing, customs, transport services, civil aviation, port regulation, worker training, and, more generally, the infrastructure for economic development are among its

---

[57.] A policy of low taxation and minimal regulation of businesses has led many observers to characterize Hong Kong's government as "laissez faire" or noninterventionist.

[58.] The government maintained its relative autonomy without resorting to the policy of playing one interest group against another. As an island of fishing communities when the British arrived, there were no entrenched interest groups to contend with in Hong Kong.

[59.] Rent seeking refers to activities that consume resources to achieve a pure transfer of wealth from one sector, group, or individual to another. These activities are wasteful because they use up resources without creating additional value for society at large. Lobbying for a monopoly is a good example of rent-seeking behavior.

responsibilities. And although Hong Kong's utilities are privately owned, the government controls rates and profits.

From the very beginning, the colonial government claimed ownership of all land; a right from which it derives considerable revenues. Government sells long-term leases to the public, and decides on the amount of land to be offered, as well as the zoning. To assist economic development, land can be offered to priority interests at low interest rates. By the early 1970s, the government also controlled rents for domestic premises, and restricted rent increases and evictions.

Equity became a theme of government policy after the eruption of riots, bombings, and violence in 1967. The room for meddling increased further when social services were dramatically expanded during the 1970s. Bent on dispelling the notion that an exploitative colonial government represented the interests of a wealthy elite against those of the workers, the government addressed a wide array of social concerns, beginning with inadequate housing. To improve working conditions, the government issued labor legislation. It upgraded medical and social welfare services, and sponsored construction in the New Territories. Another area for intervention opened up when in 1965 bank failures led the government to take over and liquidate two state banks. Other troubled banks have since looked to the government for support.

Today, the government houses 42 percent of the population and regulates transport services,[60] banking, and the stock market. The government also builds the roads and provides a police force of 30,000. In addition, the government-sponsored Trade Development Council actively promotes exports along with the Trade and Industry departments, while the Productivity Council promotes competition in the industrial sector. All such interventions provide ample opportunities for corruption, while the growth of social services makes supervision from the top more difficult.

To carry out its increasingly active role, the civil service includes 189,000 people or about 6.6 percent of the colony's

---

[60.] It regulates the bus companies and owns the mass transit railway.

workforce of 2.5 million.[61] As the largest employer in the territory, the government could have easily cultivated its workforce to provide political support to the government. But in Hong Kong new posts cannot be created without the documentation of a clear need to justify the expense. Even after the civil disturbances of 1966/67, new posts were not created at a rapid rate. It was only after 1972 that growth was allowed and the civil service grew from 94,816 to 168,298 by 1982 (Scott 1994). To prevent government from becoming a source of employment for regime supporters or the employer of last resort, special mechanisms were designed.

Accountability

Despite the functions added, the colony's preoccupation with balanced budgets and value for money prevailed. Government expenditures must be justified and are carefully supervised. Cost efficiency requires careful oversight, something that is often deliberately missing in the bureaucracies of developing countries. Hard budget constraints result in the careful selection of projects, which are likely to be estimated at close or near to cost, as overruns cannot be financed out of deficits. Since the marginal dollar must be accounted for, cost overruns must be avoided. Accurate cost estimates allow for closer auditing of a project from the outset.

Thus, accountability in Hong Kong means, above all, imposing a value for money criterion on the provision of government services. These hard budget constraints apply to all branches of government. To ensure that the government balances its budget, the Financial Committee of the Legislative Council and the Director of Audit examine all public sector expansion. The Finance Branch exerts pervasive control. It controls fiscal policy and regulates expenditures to ensure that they are continually internally justified and publicly defended, thus keeping operating expenses to a minimum. The money supply is pegged to the American dollar to prevent the government from paying for services it cannot afford by inflating the value of the currency.

[61.] A civil servant is defined as any office worker in a government organization employed directly by the Hong Kong government. Those employed in voluntary agencies or government-funded statutory bodies are not included.

Accountability also results from a command structure in which lines of communication are clearly specified. Hierarchy, discipline, and neutrality permit effective top-down implementation so that measures are quickly carried out. As an additional assurance that taxpayers get what they pay for, the "Serving the Community" scheme informs the public through performance pledges published by individual departments. The pledges outline the standards set for various services so that the public knows exactly what it has a right to expect.

Recruitment

Civil service employment has never been expanded to dispel social unrest. Even after the discontent of the late 1960s, those employees added were usually specialists trained to perform specific tasks. It is understood that when positions are created without a clear technical justification, mischief is more likely to occur; therefore, new positions must be technically justified using functional rather than political criteria. A new department head cannot simply hire devoted friends and followers. Institutions have been designed to ensure that recruitment is open, competition is fair, and merit is determined by universal criteria that apply equally to all appointments. This means employees are subject to common appointment procedures and similar disciplinary codes and conditions of service.

As in Singapore, the Public Service Commission is responsible for civil service appointments and promotion, and thus keeps politics out of the recruitment process. The commission, established in 1950, is an independent statutory body, whose members and chair are appointed by the governor – the seven serving members are selected from business and the professions. While the commission also advises on training and discipline matters, its principal mandate is to ensure impartial promotion and appointment of the 32,600 posts referred to it individually each year for advice (the heads of departments are also authorized to make appointments). The commission is consulted on changes in procedures and can initiate proposals at any time.

The Civil Service Branch is the government's personnel agency. It monitors servicewide personnel policies and manages general-grade staff. Issues of pay and structure inevitably involve the Civil Service Branch, whose responsibilities include staff management; staff relations; training; appointments; pensions;

staff planning, pay, and structure; staff housing; and management of the government directorate, administrative, executive, clerical, and secretarial grades.

Pay

Competitive civil service salaries are viewed as essential to ensure quality public administration. As in Singapore, high salaries give bureaucrats an incentive to identify their own interests with national economic expansion. Civil service salaries are determined by job qualifications and parity between the government and private sector. To compete with the private sector, a pay trend survey (introduced in 1974) is conducted annually to determine the trends of salary adjustment in the private sector in order to assess the level of adjustment needed for the civil service in the current year.

A system of checks and balances includes three independent bodies to advise the government on pay and conditions of service. Their membership is selected from the private sector. The Standing Committee on Directorate Salaries and Conditions of Service considers matters concerning the most senior civil service office holders. The Standing Commission on Civil Service Salaries and Conditions of Service, established in 1979, advises on principles and practices governing pay and conditions of service. The Standing Committee on Disciplined Services Salaries and Conditions of Service, established in 1989, advises on pay and conditions of service for all disciplined service staff, except the heads of the services under the purview of the Standing Committee on Directorate Salaries and Conditions of Service.

In a representative government, requests for alternative patterns of distribution are more likely to emerge than in Hong Kong. A legislature can propose entirely new sets of responsibilities and mandate new structures to serve those responsibilities. In Hong Kong innovation is more difficult. New directions of civil service involvement, such as the creation of entirely new departments with new functions, is unlikely. The process of competing for additional posts is motivated by conflicts of interest among the already existing groups that want to better their position, increase their staffs, and acquire new resources and avenues for promotion of existing staff.

Although not directly accountable to a legislature, the civil service is accountable on technical, performance, and expenditure criteria. Curiously, when legislatures have important powers over the bureaucracy, they do not necessarily impose similar technical, budgetary, or performance-based control. When the legislature is in control, it is necessary to design institutions that prevent political criteria from motivating the appointment of new positions.

Corruption Control

In February 1974, as a final measure to prevent agents of the state from privately consuming the colony's resources, the governor of Hong Kong transferred responsibility for detecting and investigating corruption from the police force to an independent organization, the Independent Commission Against Corruption (ICAC). The ICAC commissioner reports directly to the governor and is not subject to the purview of any other branch of the civil service. However, an advisory committee, chaired by the Executive Council, does review the commission's work. While Corruption Commission staff are paid higher salaries than equivalent civil servants, any suspicion of wrongdoing results in job dismissal without appeal. Opportunity costs to suspected wrongdoers in the Corruption Commission, therefore, are greater than to members of the civil service. To achieve its principal function of investigating cases of bribery and corruption, and to prepare cases for disciplinary action, the commission employs 1,172 individuals.

Government officials who wish to consume social resources privately must consider that the Corruption Commission has extensive statutory powers of investigation. It can authorize officers to examine bank accounts and safe-deposit boxes; and require subjects to verify property, expenditures, and liabilities, or any money sent out of Hong Kong on their behalf. It can question under oath persons other than suspects, and restrict the disposal of a suspect's property during an investigation, or apply to a court to restrict its disposal if it is held in the name of a third party. It can also obtain, through order of a magistrate, the surrender of travel documents while an investigation is in progress. In addition, investigating officers may arrest, without a warrant, suspects for other offenses disclosed during the investigation of a suspected offense. Suspects may be detained for 48 hours for the purpose of further inquiries.

The success of such stringent remedies requires a high degree of integrity at the level of the governor's office. Such powers improperly used could lead to "negative corruption", that is, charging political opponents with corruption. Between 1974 and 1983, 22,391 corruption complaints were received, 10,642 were investigated, and 3,033 prosecutions resulted. Over time, greater public participation has increased the Corruption Commission's success; the Annual Report of 1982 reported a 74.9 percent conviction rate. The first ten-year report boasts that

> The climate of corruption has radically changed. The large-scale group corruption – the big syndicates – no longer prey on the public. The public themselves would now not tolerate this. Although we cannot eradicate corruption, the corrupt now go about their business covertly in fear. The bravado of the early seventies has disappeared. (ICAC 1983, 17)

Having broken the back of large-scale syndicated corruption, the commission now focuses on more mundane pockets of corruption in both the private and public sectors. A wide range of public bodies, from education to fire services transport, have been reviewed allowing the commission to become expert in devising procedures to supervise accountability in a variety of government departments. Emphasis is now placed on the task of reviewing procedures and administrative routines in government departments to minimize opportunities for corruption.

The Corruption Commission is a typical Hong Kong success story, and is often consulted by private sector organizations, allowing it to supplement its budget.[62]

[62.] As an illustration of the growing public support enjoyed by the Independent Commission Against Corruption (ICAC), 59 percent of complainers in 1982 willingly identified themselves. This can be compared to 33 percent when the commission began its work. Four separate surveys were conducted to determine the public's assessment of corruption and the effectiveness of ICAC. The survey of 1982 revealed that 95.6 percent of those interviewed consider corruption less prevalent. Even more striking was that corruption is now regarded as a moral and social offense. This sharply contrasts with the early 1970s when corruption was regarded as a necessary evil and a normal business practice. The continued role of the commission is felt to be critical; 87 percent feared corruption would recur if the commission was disbanded.

The State-Society Interface

Although business groups are strong in Hong Kong, they do not dictate policy.[63] Consistently, the government has managed to keep business groups at arm's length, so that they do not capture the decision-making system.[64]

Hong Kong is run by its civil service; business cannot force policy upon the government. An explicit example of the government's independence is that although business opposes Governor Patten's confrontation with the People's Republic of China (PRC), it cannot prevent Patten's baiting of communist officials. In addition, government resists demands from business for lower cost public utilities. It has extended rent control to industrial premises, and provides a guaranteed market for some locally manufactured products (Burns 1994b, 137). To prevent capture, the government uses a consultative process. Until 1985, business elites could address the colonial civil service only through the appointed Legislative and Executive councils.[65]

Unlike in Singapore, the workforce in Hong Kong has traditionally been weak and poorly organized. Manufacturing is dominated by small- and medium-sized enterprises. "In 1971, 60% of manufacturing businesses in Hong Kong employed fewer than two hundred workers; by 1984, the figure had grown to 70%" (Burns 1994b, 131). Small businesses are usually family owned and managed.

[63.] Business representatives were appointed to the Executive Council in 1986. Communication with business was further enhanced by the growth of advisory committees that provided private advice and consultation. The consultative process allows government to speak in the name of a constituency. This process reduces public criticism as businesses gain prior knowledge of government decisions and have opportunities to influence outcomes. Representation in the consultative process diffuses sympathies among the business elites for more broadly representative institutions (Scott 1994).

[64.] The business associations include the Chinese Manufacturers' Association, the Employers' Federation of Hong Kong, the Hong Kong Federation of Industries, and the Hong Kong Chamber of Commerce. All of these appoint members to advisory boards and are represented on the Legislative and Executive councils. Until 1985, Legislative Council members were appointed by the governor and political parties did not exist. Final decisions are taken within the bureaucracy. These business elites are linked through interlocking company directorships and membership in business associations, like the Chamber of Commerce, and advise the government on education, labor, and transport. The directors of the Hong Kong Bank and the major trading houses are generally represented on the Executive and Legislative councils.

[65.] The Legislative Council remained entirely appointed until 1985 when 24 indirectly elected members were introduced. The 1967/68 riots did not result in any changes in the

The rules governing Hong Kong date back to 1843 when constitutional authority was concentrated with the governor, who rules in consultation with the Executive and Legislative councils.[66] The governor has the right to assent to any legislation, appoints all judges, and can give directives to the civil service or ignore their advice. If he chooses to exercise the full limits of his power, he could impose his will arbitrarily on any or all of the branches of government. On paper, the colony seems like an autocracy, yet, like most of East Asia's other high performers, consultation – the sharing of information between the government and private sector – is routinely practiced and is highly institutionalized.

The process of consultation in Hong Kong begins at the level of the Executive Council, which in 1986 consisted of five ex-officio high government officials – the governor, the chief secretary, the financial secretary, the attorney general, and the commander of the British forces – and ten nominated members who do not hold public office.[67] Although formally empowered to override advice given by members of the Executive Council, the governor is unlikely to do so as he depends heavily on the cooperation of nongovernmental council members for their contacts among the broader community. Moreover, the cooperation of the top business firms and leaders of the professions is necessary for a governor to implement programs. The Executive Council, as well as the Legislative Council, the urban or regional councils, the district boards, and the many advisory boards and committees appointed by the government all depend on private sector participation.

The Legislative Council is a good example of government by consultation. The council, which provides advice on the formulation of laws, reserves the largest block of seats for the

---

Legislative Council. Business interests continued to dominate the Legislative Council up to 1991 through the appointed members and most of the seats (12 in 1985/88; 14 in 1988/91; 21 in 1991/95) elected by functional constituencies. Since 1985, 2 seats in the Labour functional constituency have been filled by members elected by trade union officials. In the 1995 Legislative Council, 9 seats will be elected by those working in 9 sectors of industry, commerce, services, and primary production. In effect, the entire workforce will be given 2 votes, 1 in the 20 directly elected seats, and 1 in the 9 new functional constituencies. The Executive Council is still entirely appointed by the governor.

[66.] The governor is held responsible to the British secretary of state for the administration of the colony.

[67.] From 1948 to 1966, 6 unofficial members participated in the Executive Council; this increased to 8 in 1966, and since 1978 the number has varied between 8 and 12.

wealthiest sectors of the commercial, industrial, and financial communities.[68] It meets often and publicly debates proposals for future policy and public expenditure. The council has the right to question the government about matters of public interest. Any proclamation, rule, regulation, order, resolution, notice, rule of court, bylaw, or other instrument having legislative effect can be considered by the council. All legislation that can create offenses punishable by the courts must be presented before it. As a result, Hong Kong has no secret laws. The regulatory process is relatively transparent.

Committees form another element of the elaborate system of consultation that takes place between the private and public sectors. The Civil and Miscellaneous Lists of 1989 reported 264 committees, 154 of which were set up by ordinances. But these lists seriously underestimate the amount of organized consultation that may draw "unofficials" into the policy-making process. Norman Miners reported 393 advisory committees with a total membership of 2,106 citizens. Little is known about the activities of these committees as almost all are closed to the public and papers or minutes are confidential.

In the hope of encouraging popular support after the 1967 riots, the government set up new consultative institutions to improve social welfare. City district offices were charged with explaining government policy to the public and eliciting the support of local leaders. Local leaders were invited to serve on scores of new advisory boards and street associations, mutual aid committees, and district boards (Burns 1994b, 136). As a result of all of these measures, the system of government in Hong Kong is now dependent upon the participation of ordinary members of the public.

Touted as the "world's closest approximation to a free-market, private enterprise, capitalistic economic system" (Rabushka 1987, 145), Hong Kong frequently gives observers the impression that business operates on its own. One reason Hong Kong's economy

---

68. From 1844 through to 1985, all members of the council owed their seats to the governor. Twenty-four elected members were added to the Legislative Council in 1985. Elected members now slightly outnumber the 22 appointed members. The council meets once a week, instead of once every two weeks. Government proposals are closely scrutinized, speeches are longer, and debates more extensive than in the past.

seems so free of steerage devices is that organizations that carry out government policy are not always part of the government structure.

Hong Kong uses statutory corporations and other public bodies to complement the councils and to implement policies. Norman Miners explains the complexity of these devices, "All, some, or none of their staff may be civil servants; all, some, or none of their finances may come from government" (Miners 1992, 101). The actions of these organizations come in a bewildering number of forms. Some are statutory corporations established by the Legislative Council, others are private companies in which the government has taken an interest. Others are private institutions subsidized in whole or part by the government. Supervision may be exercised either directly by government officials or appointees, or indirectly through financial pressure, or by the threat of sanctions. This flexibility allows governance to escape narrow civil service regulations and can sometimes offer a cheaper method of control than subsuming an activity under direct civil service supervision. Moreover, the diffusion of fees and responsibilities allows the government to avoid blame for increased costs or administrative mishaps.[69]

Even the massive public housing program has a strong component of private decision making. The Housing Authority, which builds and manages public housing, blends both public and private management. The chairperson of the authority is a retired civil servant. Salaries of Housing Authority staff are reimbursed by the authority, whose revenue comes from the rents of the tenants housed in its properties. Although the Housing Authority freely determines management, the distribution of entitlement and rents, and the rate of construction is determined by the financial secretary. Building is financed partly by the surplus

---

[69.] Though often well disguised, big government has come to Hong Kong. In the fiscal year 1949/50, the Hong Kong public sector was 8.2 percent of the economy. By 1981/82, this had grown to 22.9 percent. It declined to 17 percent in 1986, and rose to 20 percent by 1988. In absolute terms, government grew throughout the 1980s (Ho 1979). Elected members now slightly outnumber the 22 appointed members. In the 1991/95 Legislative Council, there were 3 officials (chief secretary, financial secretary, attorney general); 18 members appointed by the governor; 21 members elected by functional constituencies; and 18 members directly elected in geographical constituencies. In the 1995/97 Legislative Council, all members will be elected, 30 elected by functional constituencies, 20 directly elected, and 10 elected by an election committee.

remaining from the government's Development Loan Fund. The implementation of Housing Authority decisions is made by another agency – the Housing Department, which is staffed entirely by civil servants. A service provided in this manner can be seen as either private or public depending on which lens one chooses.

The Vegetable Marketing and Fishmarketing organizations are also statutory. These organizations are quasi-private but employ civil servants to manage the transport of produce and the supervision of wholesale transactions. Both organizations are headed by a director and an advisory board representing the farming and fishing communities. Government has less direct control over the Productivity Council, the Trade Development Council, the Tourist Association, and the Consumer Council. Yet these organizations receive most of their income from the government.

Numerous statutory corporations engage in commercial activities, sometimes competing directly with the private sector. Yet again their equity is owned by the government, which can issue administrative directives. For example, the Export Credit Insurance Corporation markets its services on a commercial basis, but was set up with capital provided by the government, which also guarantees its liabilities. In 1977, the Industrial Estates Corporation was set up to attract high-tech firms. Part of its expenditure is financed by a fixed interest loan from the government. This blending of public and finance has allowed the application of commercial practices to the provision of public services.

The Role of the State in Hong Kong

The portrayal of Hong Kong as a noninterventionist state is a misrepresentation. Hong Kong's experience illustrates that even laissez-faire policies require a strong state to ensure that officials do not use the allocative mechanisms of the state to divert resources to their private consumption. The term "nonintervention" does not capture this aspect of the government's role.

A noninterventionist state must be able to prevent the intervention of those who would use the state to benefit themselves. The notion of a noninterventionist state assumes the state will provide basic law and order, the administration of justice, and the provision of public works. But a weak state cannot provide these. The state must constantly intervene to ensure there is no tampering with the rule of law. The bureaucracy must be carefully monitored to ensure that it is accountable for performing its tasks and for using public money effectively. The ability to limit private interests from capturing the state, while providing global conditions – a stable monetary and policy environment to foster investment – is Hong Kong's special achievement, for which its state institutions merit special credit.

The success of Hong Kong's "positive noninterventionism" means that firms do not require special assistance to establish themselves, as is often the case in many developing countries with opaque regulatory frameworks. Instead, the colony depends on ordinary market conditions to attract industries. Since international financial transactions are free, restrictions do not exist on foreign direct investment and direct investment abroad is possible for all Hong Kong residents. A legal system that protects property rights and contract law creates trust among anonymous trading partners and has allowed Hong Kong to become a major financial center (Lethbridge 1984, 235). That achievement is jeopardized by forces within Hong Kong that thrive on network trading within the PRC market. If the rule of law is threatened, Hong Kong is likely to become a base for cozy deals within the PRC world, and its status as an international financial capital is likely to evaporate.

CHAPTER SIX

MALAYSIA
THE WILL TO GROW

Malaysia came late, and through an unusual circumstance, to the status of a high performing Asian economy.[70] Its emergence as an industrial power, with a balanced economy and widely based industrial sector, curiously came on the heels of a financial crisis in the early 1980s that destabilized the policy framework built the previous decade to correct historic ethnic-based economic imbalances (see Appendix B, Figure 2). The drop in world commodity prices at that time threatened the availability of funds to sustain the economic costs of rigid ethnic quotas and could easily have led to destructive communal and intraparty conflict. Instead, the commodity slump motivated a relaxation of the quota system and openness to foreign investment, providing the opportunity

---

70. Based on interviews with Y.A.B. Tun Daim Zainuddin, executive adviser to the prime minister of Malaysia; Datuk Dr. Shamsuddin Hitam, deputy director-general, Economic Planning Unit, Prime Minister's Department; Encik Tew Swee Tong, principal assistant director, External Assistance Section, Economic Planning Unit; Tan Sri Ali Abul Hassan, director-general, Economic Planning Unit; Datuk Mohd Razali Abdul Rahman, chairman, Peremba (M) Sdn. Bhd; Tan Sri Azmi Wan Hamzah, chairman, Land & General Bhd; Datuk Syed Alwi Syed Nordin, director-general, Implementation & Coordination Unit; Encik Awadz Bin Mohammad, director, Administrative Reforms Division (MAMPU); Encik U. Menon, deputy director, Work Systems Division (MAMPU); and Alvin Rabushka, senior fellow, Hoover Institution.

to reconcile the policy of Malayanization with the conditions needed for Malaysia to become a player in the global economy.[71]

Squaring the Circle:

Patronage With Accountability

Malaysian development occurred despite allegations of rampant political corruption that reflected the extent of political party involvement in business. Although government and military ownership of profit-making firms exists throughout the region, Malaysia is distinguished by the extent of ownership and control that political parties exercise over business groups.[72]

Observers of Malaysian politics assume that economic decisions by the government are made on political and personal considerations (Gomez 1990). They claim the exploitation of government-owned enterprises in the interest of political parties, including the dominant party and its followers, provides ample opportunities for political patronage, conflict of interest, favoritism, and misappropriation of funds. Small, dispersed shareholders, it is also alleged, are losing out to the big, party-backed, industrial concerns. The little guys, we are told, are victims of the conspiratorial abuse of state power by a powerful and exclusive party elite.

Nevertheless, fears of undesirable social and economic consequences stemming from monopoly power have failed to materialize. Instead, Malaysia resembles the East Asian tigers – the Republic of Korea, Singapore, and Taipei,China – more than its immediate neighbors in the relative egalitarian distribution of wealth and in the integrity of its business environment (see Appendix B, Table 3, and figures 3a, 3b, and 3c). Like East Asia's other high performers, Malaysia grounds national unity in the

---

[71.] The Malaysian economy plummeted to its post-war low in 1985/86, when the world recession drove commodity prices down.

[72.] Party ownership has a history that goes back to the pre-Independence period. One political party, the Malaysian Chinese Association formed in 1949, started a welfare lottery in which only members could participate. The other parties pursued similar strategies to acquire the resources to run elections and to reward followers. In the late 1980s, the parties began to renounce direct engagement in business. The Malay Chinese Association, the first to begin, was the last of the major parties to renounce party corporate ownership.

economic equality of its citizens.[73] Despite allegations of patrimonialism, Malaysia distributes wealth more equitably than either the Philippines or Thailand, and its investment environment is cleaner than any of its Southeast Asian counterparts, except Singapore.

There is a compelling reason why the fusion of Malaysian economic and political elites has not resulted in the concentration of national wealth in a narrow band of regime cronies. Gross economic inequality would conflict with the government's commitment to egalitarian development – a commitment that is fundamental to the country's political stability and to the survival of the ruling coalition.[74] Patronage may result in concessions, licenses, and government subsidies, but it does not extend to inefficiency or excuses for poor management.[75] Although public tenders for government contracts are not routinely used – government prefers to pick management teams – companies that do not perform risk being cut off from future contracts despite ties to party leaders.[76] Instead of detracting from growth, alleged party control over the corporations it sets up in the private sector has imposed expectations of effective management on those placed in positions of corporate responsibility. The reputation of the party, its top leadership, the Malays as a group within the Malaysian

[73.] As Dato Seri Dr. Mahathir Mohamad writes in *Malaysia: The Way Forward (Vision 2020)*, "We must aspire by the year 2020 to reach a stage where no one can say that a particular ethnic group is inherently economically backward and another economically inherently advanced.... A `full partnership in economic progress' must mean a fair balance with regard to the participation and contribution of all our ethnic groups.... It must mean a fair distribution with regard to the control, management, and ownership of the modern economy" (Mahathir 1991, 10-11). Compare gini coefficents of the Philippines and Malaysia to see the dramatic differences.

[74.] Another reason is that Malaysian firms are generally managed by a modern bureaucracy of trained officials rather than by families. In the long run, the adaptation of international norms of corporate governance will increase the liquidity of Malay firms in comparison to their Chinese rivals.

[75.] The two most common charges of abuse are the absence of public tenders and the use of trusteeships to legitimate party business ventures. While different, these two concerns are closely related. As Gomez has written, "Appointments as trustees have been a form of patronage wielded by the party's elites as a reward for loyalty. As trustees, these persons have been largely dependent on the patronage of the government to ensure business success and protection from economic competition which might otherwise curtail the growth of the party's corporate investments. Such patronage involves concessions, licenses, monopoly rights, government subsidies and more" (Gomez 1990, 11).

[76.] For example, "To help businessmen whose problem genuinely stemmed from the recession [of 1985], those who no longer had projects but had good management teams

polity, and the reputation of Malaysia as a player in the world economy all depend on effective economic management.

The creation of the Implementation and Coordination Unit, which reports directly to the prime minister, signals government commitment to efficient management. It monitors the deadlines of all development projects to determine that costs do not overrun estimates, and that quality is maintained.[77] Extensive rationalization of public expenditure prevents individual politicians from using public funds to build private patronage networks within the party. Effective public management benefits the party proxies as much as Chinese, Indian, and international investors. On the need for effective management, the top civil servants see eye-to-eye with the politicians. Both groups understand that growth is what prevents ethnic rivalries from producing destructive conflict. Therefore, incompetence must not be allowed access to government largesse: projects must be successfully implemented, and foreign investors must be handled with professionalism.

An analysis of Malaysian public sector management will reveal how Malaysia has squared the circle of patronage with accountability. Two components of that ability are the neutrality and integrity of bureaucracy, buttressed by strict rationalization of public expenditures, and effective public-private sector information flows attained through the design of mechanisms for communication of all government branches with the private sector.

---

were awarded government contracts" (Cheong Mei Sui and Adibah Amin 1995, 84). Daim Zainuddin explained that knowing the management capabilities of those chosen was critical. Open competitive bidding has limits when projects are complicated. How could bureaucrats with little knowledge of the private sector accurately evaluate whether prices cited in bids were realistic? Neutrality in the bidding process could only be assured if the public sector knew as much about the private sector as the private businessmen. But in the 1980s, the bureaucracy did not have the background to assess bids accurately. Thus, they could be easily fooled and above all they could not evaluate the managerial capacity of individuals who were bidding (Daim Zainuddin interview). This was why Daim preferred to choose those with known abilities.

[77.] The Implementation Unit monitors failure of contractors and corrects poor planning. Subunits exist at three levels of government: district, state, and national. The units are concerned with implementation according to schedule, and monitor shortfalls in development expenditures. All agencies must submit quarterly reports to the unit of both financial and physical performance. When shortfalls or delays are found, the minister concerned is called. Any blockages must be eliminated, including those due to red tape.

Structural Continuity

The strength and continuity of state structures has been essential to the development of a diversified economy in Malaysia. The major economic and social reforms implemented since Independence have occurred without a major structural crisis or state breakdown. The political system, that is, the elected governments, have achieved the necessary policy alternatives. No military coup d'état was needed to bring about reform, and, as a result, the military's role in economic policy making is limited. Similarly, changes within the civil service have occurred without constitutional changes in the character of the civil service – the intent of the constitution has been respected. The Malaysian British Civil Service Commission, maintained and improved since Independence, was eventually transformed into a force for the liberalization of the economy and a catalyst for the dramatic economic progress of the years after 1981.[78]

The degree of state involvement in the economy has varied since Independence in correlation with the strength and configuration of domestic political coalitions. The peaceful transfer of power from the British was based on a bargain between the three major political parties, the United Malays National Organization (UMNO), the Malayan Chinese Association, and the Malayan Indian Congress. Thus, ethnic affiliations dominate party identification. The Malays have never been able to turn their political dominance into hegemonic force without risking undermining the basic reciprocity among the communal groups that is needed for growth. However, the balance of political and economic power within UMNO has shifted over time, dictating a number of major changes in economic policy.[79] Rivalries within Malay leadership led to the altered policy agenda of the 1970s. Coalition building and resource allocation within the party similarly influenced industrial policy choices resulting in another policy shift in 1980.

[78.] The British structure, however, was not suited to managing the vast investment stocks of government-founded companies, which required the ability to run a state enterprise for profit. Semi-autonomous agencies were created to administer the holding companies established by the government.

[79.] Leadership within UMNO is considered to be determined popularly and is highly competitive.

During the first period after Independence (1957-1971), a market-led approach to growth prevailed,[80] followed by a mixed market approach during the 1970s. Aggressive state-led industrialization introduced in 1980 was followed in 1983 by the seemingly contradictory theme of aggressive privatization.[81] Appointed to office in 1981, Prime Minister Mahathir did not see any fundamental inconsistency between the two themes. The state enterprises, the prime minister believed, would be privatized as soon as they were profitable.[82] By creating heavy industry units, the prime minister expected to prompt a dramatic expansion in private sector activity. To ensure the positive linkages between state investment and private initiative, the prime minister asserted the primacy of "clean and efficient and trustworthy government". His success was built on the principle that "Corruption and the establishment of an efficient, modern and high technology society are incompatible". In 1991, Mahathir introduced "Vision 2020", which essentially ended two decades of quota-driven development in favor of a more liberal framework for attaining full industrial and developed nation status.

Getting the Politics Right

Coping with ethnic polarization has been the basis of Malaysian politics since the end of the colonial period. Extensive immigration was encouraged by the British colonial government. As a result, the population, once entirely Malay, became a potentially explosive mixture of Chinese, Indians, and Malays. As early as 1901, the Malays were a minority in the federated Malay states, and by 1931 they had become a minority in the whole

---

[80.] Extensive state intervention in the rural sector improved the economic conditions of the predominantly rural Malays. Public expenditures during the first five-year plan allocated 23 percent to rural development, infrastructure 52 percent, and industry only 1.3 percent (Bowie 1991, 69). The government relied almost entirely on the private sector for commercial and industrial development.

[81.] The government's commitment to the heavy industry drive was roughly comparable to the entire annual budget for all social programs. The activist economic policies were motivated by impatience with the pace of industrial development and with weak attainment of the New Economic Policy's initial goal of 30 percent Malay corporate equity.

[82.] The industrial drive opened up areas that had the potential to displace Chinese operations. Existing capabilities were often ignored so that dependence on Chinese expertise could be avoided.

of Malaya (Puthucheary 1978, 8). After Independence, a consensus reached among the elites of the various ethnic groups prevented the deep ethnic and cultural cleavages from destabilizing the new state. A national alliance of the three main ethnic parties satisfied the British conditions for granting independence.[83] The Malays dominated government in exchange for granting Chinese and Indians full citizenship and commercial freedom. Since 1957, artificial antimajoritarian devices, the rule of proportionality, and mutual veto have been used by the political leaders of the different subcultures to maintain intercommunal political harmony.

Thus, the political equilibrium of the first decade after Independence rested on a negotiated intergroup arrangement: the Chinese in business, the Malays in politics.[84] In 1969, the Malays owned 1.5 percent of corporate equity compared to 22.5 percent by the Chinese and 62.1 percent by foreign interests (Bowie 1991, 88). This separatist formula, however, was torn down by the race riots of 1969, which overturned the notion that the Malays were only interested in politics, the Chinese in business.[85] According to Mahathir, who emerged as one of the most articulate of the country's new Malay nationalist leaders, the challenge was to prevent the "complete Sinocization of the economy of the country". Malay leaders asserted that the goal of national unity was compromised by the unfortunate economic status of the Malays and the possibility of total Chinese ownership of all nonlanded wealth. The economic foundation of national unity, they argued, must be economic balance between the races and the reduction of racially based economic disparities. As Mahathir put it, "There can be no economic stability without political and social stability". The new raison d'etre would be full Malay participation in the economy as a precondition of Malay equality with other races.

---

[83] The British wanted to avoid leaving government in the hands of just one community for fear of igniting the kind of ethnic violence that resulted in the partitioning of India and Pakistan in 1947. Their major political concern before departure was to prevent one group from taking over the process of creating an independent state, which might have triggered violent ethnic polarization.

[84] A formal ratified agreement documenting the postindependence communal settlement does not exist.

[85] Race riots broke out in Kuala Lumpur on May 13, 1969, and radical Malay nationalists called for the expulsion of non-Malays. The riots resulted in the suspension of

A new alliance contract was negotiated that allowed for the formation of a grand coalition government based on a consensus that the profound economic inequality would be overcome (Yusoff 1992). The Malays were promised access to business opportunities through preferential treatment that included quotas and privileges. To alter the level of Malay participation, and particularly ownership in the economy, the new political arrangement called for an altered relationship between the state and the economy. Aggressive state action designed to increase Malay participation in the economy included the formation of state-owned corporations established as proxies for Malay enterprises. The agreement reaffirmed equal citizenship, political participation, and office holding, as well as tolerance of the religion, language, and cultural institutions of the minority ethnic coalitions. Introduced in 1971, the New Economic Policy has provided the political stability upon which the country's subsequent dramatic economic development depends.[86]

The New Economic Policy, however, resulted in the domination of the political over the economic realm, putting at risk the neutrality of the civil service system. As a result, extra precautions were needed to protect that essential British legacy. These include the Development Administration Unit, introduced in 1972 as a center for administrative reforms, and the National Institute of Public Administration, set up to enhance the expertise of public sector employees. The Federal Establishment Office was reorganized as the Public Services Department, responsible for human resource development. In 1977, the Malaysian Administrative Modernization and Management Planning Unit was established under the prime minister to lead and monitor administrative reform of the Public Service.[87]

Parliament until 1971, and are generally viewed as a watershed in Malaysia's postcolonial political history.

[86] In the 1960s, Malaysia grew by an annual 5.1 percent; in the 1970s, growth averaged 7.8 percent annually; and in the 1980s, the annual growth declined to 5.9 percent. Over 30 years this has meant an average growth of 6.3 percent (Mahathir 1991, 12).

[87] Responsibilities of the Malaysian Administrative Modernization and Management Planning Unit were extended when it became the Secretariat for Malaysia Inc., set up in early 1983 by Prime Minister Mahathir. The Planning Unit is also a member of the National Development Committee and issues an annual report on civil service improvement.

The Organization of Government

The Prime Minister's Department

Functions and Organization

The Prime Minister's Department in general oversees and coordinates the policies of the government and their implementation. Its main divisions and units are

Divisions
- Administrative and Financial
- Cabinet
- Development of Federal Territory
- Islamic Affairs
- Management of Government Buildings

Units
- Economic Planning Unit
- Implementation and Coordination Unit
- Malaysian Administrative Modernization and Management Planning Unit

Other Miscellaneous Bodies
- Advisory Board
- Atomic Energy Licensing Board
- Klang Valley Planning Secretariat
- Islamic Centre
- Malaysian Micro-Electronic Systems Institute
- National Population and Family Development Board
- National Security Council
- Protocol Bureau
- Public Complaints Bureau

Cultural Transformation and the New Economic Policy

Deeply rooted cultural obstacles had to be overcome before modern public sector management could emerge. In 1971, long before becoming prime minister, Mahathir identified the cultural transformation that was needed before the Malays could be fully integrated into a national, and ultimately a world, economy.[88] In *The Malay Dilemma*, he established what was to become his agenda for fundamental change upon becoming prime minister in 1981 (Mahathir 1970). He explains:

> Because Malay value concepts and codes of ethics are different from those of the West, it is unlikely that mere changes in environment will bring about the necessary changes in Malay values to such an extent that they will be able to compete with the drive of other communities or races. In other words, without a radical change in their code of ethics and value concepts, the efforts to effect a mass cure of the ills afflicting the Malays will merely increase the general frustration of all concerned, as the results obtained would be minimal (161-2).

He adds that for "the most part the Malay social code is . . . anachronistic and can only lessen the competitive abilities of the Malays and hinder their progress" (171). "By and large, the Malay value system and code of ethics are impediments to their progress," he concludes (173).[89]

In short, Mahathir believed that for the Malays to benefit from ethnic quotas, their cultural norms, values, and beliefs had to be molded to suit national development. National development

---

[88.] Mahathir was among the most outspoken of a new breed of Malay politicians who challenged the traditional Malay leadership for not adequately responding to Malay grievances and for accepting Chinese interests at the expense of Malay birthrights. Mahathir's challenge (1969) resulted in his official expulsion from the party and the threat of imprisonment without trial. Exile allowed Mahathir the time to write *The Malay Dilemma*, which presented an eloquent account of the origins of the domination of the Malays by other races.

[89.] Among the behavioral constraints that beset Malay economic development were "fatalism" (Mahathir 1970, 158), "inability to accept the inevitable" (114), "failure to value time" (163), attraction to immediate benefits (109), "inability to understand the potential capacity of money" (167), and "failure to appreciate the real value of money and property" (169).

justifies aggressive rejection of subjective components of the nation's value system: personalism, familism, and particularism must give way to political neutrality, merit, and competence.[90] Under the motto, "Lead by example", Mahathir, once he became prime minister, made reform of the Civil Service the proving grounds of the effort to forge a new national value system in which abstract responsibilities to the state would dominate over traditional values predicated on loyalty to family, kin, and ethnicity. To signal his intent to impose work habits on the Civil Service, he appointed Daim Zainuddin, a self-made millionaire, to deliver private sector discipline and know-how to the Finance Ministry.

The Bureaucracy as a Microcosm of Society

The Malaysian Civil Service is beleaguered by two sources of uncertainty concerning its political neutrality. One source of concern is the economic role of Malaysian political parties. Most have used ownership to reward followers and to pay for the cost of elections.[91]

The second potential challenge to bureaucratic neutrality is the dependence of political leadership on bureaucratic participation in policy making. Since Malaysian Independence, when the leaders of the independence movement were drawn from within its ranks, the Civil Service has worked closely with top political leaders in the formulation of economic policies. This close cooperation has led to the view of the Civil Service as highly politicized, in the sense that its mission has not been simply to implement the wishes of politicians but also to help formulate the policies.

Classic definitions of bureaucratic politicization assume a clear distinction between implementation and formulation, which the Malaysian bureaucracy fails to achieve. This clear separation of policy formulation and implementation, however, rarely applies

---

[90.] The theme "Excellence in public service" drew its meaning from the assertion of neutral, merit-based criteria for providing and assessing public service as contrasted to the ascriptive criteria of race, ethnic, or family origin.

[91.] It seems this kind of business engagement is tolerated as long as its political leaders avoid direct profit taking for personal gain (Gomez 1990).

to developing countries where, following Independence, trained personnel are typically limited, and activist government economic programs require close collaboration of the political and the administrative elites.[92] Malaysia and Singapore were not exceptions. Even before Independence, the Malaysian Civil Service was often responsible for the direction of policy and thus accustomed to regular contact with the nation's colonial rulers. What began with native participation in routine administrative work, ended with the Civil Service taking a political role and fighting alongside the emerging political leadership in favor of independence. Independence created politicians out of former civil servants and required continuous mutual commitment toward defining common goals. After Independence, the key policy decisions were generally made by political leadership in close consultation with a core of senior administrators of the Civil Service. Their advice is usually consulted on the choice, design, and management of projects.[93]

Nevertheless, the dangers of politicization were multiplied by the introduction of the New Economic Policy, which implicitly expanded the political role for a bureaucracy charged with attaining racial quotas. In fact, it has been criticized as a means for the government to dispense patronage on a grand scale.[94] The privatization policy introduced in 1983 had similarly been criticized for providing politicians with the means to dispense patronage to businesses controlled by parties or by proxies of prominent politicians (Gomez 1990).

A number of constitutional measures serve to limit the politicization of the bureaucracy and to protect the principle of civil service neutrality. Appointments are made on the basis of

---

[92.] The experience of the Philippines should help illustrate the futility of the standard definition. In the Philippines, the Civil Service has had a limited role in policy making, but is considered to be highly politicized by the extensive penetration of patronage politics into recruitment and resource allocation. Politicians use their purse-string influence on projects and their control over appointments and promotions within the bureaucracy to direct resources to their supporters.

[93.] In Malaysia, the Prime Minister's Economic Planning Unit is the central planning agency of the government responsible for formulating policies, strategies, and programs for short- and long-term economic development. The unit draws its personnel from career civil servants.

[94.] "Politically well-connected businessmen and politicians with business interests have begun to dominate a scene where they are the main beneficiaries of business

merit, and qualifications are prescribed under documented schemes of service. Political acceptability applies to very few posts in the bureaucracy and there is limited evidence of political interference in the recruitment process. Only the minister of a department is a political appointee. Ministers answer to Parliament, but department secretaries do not. Normally, ministers trust names recommended by the promotion board chaired by the chief secretary.[95] Ironically, the business investments of Malaysian political parties offer alternative means of rewarding supporters, besides positions in the bureaucracy, thus reducing the pressures for direct politicization of the bureaucracy.

Another restraint on politicization is that Parliament does not exercise discretion over project level budgets, including those of big projects. The Economic Planning Unit, not the Parliament, has final say on all project approvals. Members of Parliament may use information to please their constituency but they may not intervene in management.[96] The Parliament's influence on policy is also limited; policy is decided by cabinet in consultation with the Prime Minister's Department. Politicians are told by the prime minister not to intervene in administrative decisions.[97]

As a further measure to reduce parliamentary control over project level budgets, all public accounts must be audited and reported on by the auditor general. The auditor general's mandate is to see that public money is spent only for the purposes authorized by Parliament or by the state legislature. He and his officers scrutinize the books of every ministry and department, as well as every state government. He submits his report to the House of Representatives. To protect his impartiality, his remuneration is charged to the consolidated fund and cannot be altered to his disadvantage during his term of office. He cannot

opportunities provided by the government, ostensibly to reduce interethnic economic disparities and, more recently, to promote privatization. This has also meant that part of the ruling elite has benefited personally in the process, since most politically-aligned businessmen appear to be proxies of powerful politicians" (Gomez 1991, vii).

[95.] One senior civil servant interviewed reported he could not remember any case in which a minister objected to the appointment of a secretary.

[96.] Politicization is reduced by laws that prohibit union leaders from holding political appointments or from publicly taking sides on policy.

[97.] Financial accountability for all aspects of government spending is ultimately to the Parliament, including all development expenditure bills. As a means of checks and

be renamed, except in the same manner as a judge. The auditor general is disqualified from any further appointment in the federal or state public services as another measure to prevent him from currying favor with members of the public service on whom he makes a report (Suffian 1976, 200-1).

As stated in the constitutional mandate, the Civil Service is to serve the government irrespective of personal judgments or preferences of the personnel. To achieve this, the civil service laws of Malaysia require that impersonal merit is the basis for recruitment, appointment, and promotions in government service. Mechanisms such as promotion boards and promotion appeal boards exist to protect civil servants from arbitrary decisions. Positions are classified and salary ranges are standardized on the basis of examinations and efficiency ratings. To ensure the demarcation between public service and private profit, clearly established guidelines prohibit public officials from pursuing private business engagements. The neutrality of the Civil Service is complemented by an independent judiciary. The importance of an upper civil service that leads by example is constantly reiterated in training and is asserted to be the basis for promotion.

To lead the economy through a number of major policy transformations, Dr. Mahathir Mohamad, upon becoming prime minister in 1981, undertook a major campaign to improve the bureaucracy's attitudes, skills, and ways of dealing with the public.[98] Beginning with imposing the punch card on civil servants, many of whom he believed were not at their jobs, he proceeded to introduce the job manual, because he suspected that many did not know their jobs (Khoo Boo Teik 1995, 182). In a speech on 25 June 1981, officials were bluntly told they must end their disinclination to work and stop treating government posts as

---

balances, the Audit Department does not report to the secretary general but to the Parliament, giving opposition party members an opportunity to scrutinize expenditures and to call the secretary general to discuss how money is spent. The Audit Act of 1982 specifies that the auditor general must report the findings of all investigations to the Parliament's Public Accounts Committee, which acts as the highest control on public expenditure. Each legislature has a public accounts committee that reviews the auditor general's reports and calls for explanations from heads of all ministries and departments concerned. An anticorruption agency, chaired by the deputy prime minister, deals with allegations of abuse of funds.

[98.] Mahathir came to power with a two-thirds majority.

sinecures at the risk of public humiliation (Khoo Boo Teik 1995, 309). Nevertheless bureaucratic performance continued to be lackluster. Much more fundamental reform was needed. The occasion came in 1991 when Mahathir announced the end of the policy of direct state intervention on behalf of Malay interests.

Mahathir's "vision" called for a fundamental rethink of functions and values of the bureaucracy. Privatization of government functions would allow for the reduction of salary outlays. Service and procedures were streamlined to attain new goals. Guaranteed employment was disavowed. "Right-sizing" means positions were maintained only if they were functionally justified. Mahathir's reforms responded to a common complaint heard in developing countries that information kept by various government agencies must be accessed separately and that the information or regulations may overlap or contradict. To overcome this problem a manual, "Dealing With the Malaysian Civil Service", was compiled. It lists the services and requirements of each government agency. The Citizen's Charter was introduced, which specified what is expected of each agency. This has meant removing bureaucratic constraints, by making it easier to apply for business licenses and permits, and the introduction of one-stop licensing centers. The Civil Service Link provides profiles of government agencies, rules and regulations relating to various incentives and the issuing of licenses, and an explanation of the laws governing taxation, business, and trade.[99]

Efforts to introduce the public sector to the work culture of the private sector include training programs and even joint sports events. Attachment programs were introduced in 1983; selected officials trained first at the Institute Tadbiran Awam Negara (National Institute of Public Administration) are attached for stints of three to four months to multinational corporations for exposure to corporate management techniques. Now many civil servants join the private sector after retirement with the government suggesting the name of the official to join the private company.

[99.] The Civil Service Link, established in 1994, is a database of information on a range of civil service activities that could help the private sector facilitate its planning.

In 1992, a new remuneration system was introduced involving pay scales, incentive schemes, and improved performance evaluations. Civil servants who incorporate newly idealized norms and practices based on official responsiveness to citizens' needs are rewarded with merit increases. Those who render service to citizens in the form of personal favors can be censored. Selective raises were introduced to increase the premium on competence. Triple increments per year, introduced in 1992 over union opposition, are allotted to the best 2 percent. The Efficiency Service Award was created to recognize outstanding government agencies. Under the new system, static increments can be applied to the inefficient without disciplinary action. A new retirement scheme, introduced in 1992, allows individuals to retire at age 40 and receive benefits at 50, thus encouraging them to join the private sector.

Accountability for providing value for money was augmented by the introduction of a Micro Accounting System designed to access the costs of outputs produced under various government-sponsored activities. In addition, by the end of 1993, 17 ministries set up internal audit units that provided independent observations on their agencies activities (Malaysia 1995a, 131).

The Constitution dictates that ministers should expect loyalty from the Civil Service without reference to the ruling political party. Interviews confirmed that this expectation is maintained on both sides. One reason the pieces fall so easily into place is that top civil servants and politicians continue to see eye-to-eye on major policy objectives.[100] However, because one political party, UMNO, has been in power since Independence, the Civil Service has not been truly tested to see if it understands the difference between loyalty to the government and loyalty to the political party. One positive sign is that the bureaucracy does not seem factionally divided into cliques based on loyalty to political figures. In a survey taken in the late 1970s by an independent academic of

---

[100.] Top civil servants share the belief of party officials that a shift to the private sector was possible because the New Economic Policy had successfully equipped the Malays with qualified individuals to manage globally competitive, private sector firms.

the relative efficacy of the Civil Service structures, civil servants ranked the three most important criteria for promotion as seniority, past performance, and qualifications. Belonging to the right family or right ethnic group, they indicated, matters less. Civil servants perceived themselves to be chosen on the basis of traits exhibited at the selection board interview (Puthucheary 1978).[101]

The institutions designed to prevent abuse in the Malaysian Civil Service work because they are strongly backed by political will. The politicians expect bureaucratic efficiency to contribute to economic growth, the basis of the party's success. The equation is simple but full of implications for the reasons why some countries have done better than others: In Malaysia, political legitimacy depends on growth, which in turn depends on a competent bureaucracy.

Social Equality and the Malaysian Bureaucracy

That the public administration is not comprised of economic or social elites is an important aspect of the government's success in its campaign to inculcate new values. In Malaysia, the official-citizen relationship does not reflect fundamental inequality in society. When a democratic ethos imbues the civil service, the role of the citizen as supplicant is not reinforced. Thus, glaring social inequalities between those who exercise power and the subordinated citizenry, as in the case of India or the Philippines, were not reproduced in government-to-citizen relations. When the action of a public official has no connection to the officeholder's status as citizen, favorable action from the bureaucracy minimizes personal debt for the recipient. The citizen's charters standardize counter services by publicly specifying exactly what an agency does and how long it takes to do it. This established criteria for customers to evaluate civil servants reinforces the importance of rules that apply to all citizens. Equality of social coalitions is also important for rational legal authority to emerge as the basis of relationships within the government. Members of a bureaucracy

---

101. Only about 20 percent expressed dissatisfaction with the treatment they had received in government service.

must not owe obedience to each other as individuals, but to the impersonal order. The law, not the person, must be obeyed.

Business-State Interface

The Mahathir difference was based on his ability to unite public and private into a sense of common destiny and partnership. The institutionalization of global policy level discussions in all government ministries was one tool he used to create a sense of shared mission with the private sector. Called consultative panels, the meetings began in 1983. They are introduced as part of "The Malaysia Incorporated Policy" (Malaysia Inc.) in order to unify public and private perspectives in the definition of national objectives.[102] As one of the major strategies for national economic growth, this policy requires that "the public and private sectors see the nation as a corporate or business entity, jointly owned by both sectors and working in tandem in pursuit of shared corporate goals" (Malaysia 1995b, 105).

The bureaucracy had to be persuaded that government should be probusiness because the good fortunes of business can generate taxes and a constituency for government. The bureaucracy and the business community both had to change their ideas about each other. Mahathir instructed the bureaucracy to "ensure that no undue hindrance is put in the way of the private sector". In turn, "the private sector must understand national policies, objectives and procedures in order to facilitate their dealings with the Government. A sovereign state cannot be a business company," Mahathir clarified, but "it can . . . be run like a corporation, with the national enterprise and the government laying down the major policy framework, direction, and providing the necessary back-up services." He also wanted no confusion between the government's involvement in business and the Malaysia Inc. concept (Khoo Boo Teik 1995, 132).

[102.] Malaysia Inc., introduced in 1983, created a framework for public-private sector cooperation and consultation. Designed to achieve national economic goals, the principle features of Malaysia Inc. were mechanisms for public-private dialogue, which led to an improvement in bureaucratic services.

Biannual meetings of the Malaysian Business Council, introduced as part of Malaysia Inc., were ways to get that message heard.[103] At all levels of government, consultative panels held annual dialogues with the private sector.[104] Improvement in the efficiency of systems and procedures for public sector delivery of services has been the focus of those discussions. The meetings were opportunities for the private and public sector to solve problems, cut red tape, and reach a mutual understanding of private sector rights. The meetings have tended to concentrate on identifying bottlenecks, inefficiencies, and slowness in the provision of government services. Formulating a general vision of where the country should go was left to top political leadership. In the councils, one businessman explained, "Quality of dialogue is set by the government sector, they lead, not the private sector. Front line economic ministers participate and the discussions often focus on the issues confronting immediate delivery problems. The details are handled by Malaysia Inc. working committees that are constructed to look at specific issues with the help of various chambers of commerce."

More extensive dialogue was necessary for the concept to penetrate every branch and subdivision of government. When Mahathir introduced "Vision 2020", he again emphasized the importance of institutionalized dialogue with the private sector. Vision 2020 expanded the participation of the private sector in public policy making by creating the Malaysian Business Council, inaugurated 28 Feb 1991, with Mahathir presenting his "Malaysia: The Way Forward". The Council brought together 62 captains of commerce, industry, and government. It was chaired by the prime minister to provide a forum for dialogue between captains of industry and the government.

To ensure that consultation with business was conducted through organized and relatively transparent procedures,

---

[103] Malaysia Inc. Officials Committee, chaired by the chief secretary, was set up in 1993 to replace the Malaysia Inc. Panel. The new committee consists of 12 senior government officials and 18 representatives from the private sector.

[104] As a response, the Ministry of International Trade and Industry solicits views through its annual trade and industry dialogue with trade associations. The Ministry of Finance holds an annual budget dialogue with the private sector to assist the formulation of the annual budget.

government supported the creation of peak business organizations. In May, 1992, a national Chamber of Commerce and
Industry was created by the government to serve as a forum for
consensus building on major policy issues. The government
encouraged the Chamber to become the premier business
institution representing the broad spectrum of the nation's
businesses – of all sizes and all sectors. As an apex organization,
the Chamber was encouraged to represent the complete economic
configuration of the nation and to act as a partner with the
government in planning for economic growth.

Results of Dialogue

Consultations between the public and private sectors often
concerned the determination of criteria for government decision
making. As a result, improvements occurred in systems and
service delivery. Obsolete laws were abolished, permits and
regulations were amended, and one-stop licensing centers offering
composite licensing were introduced. The management of public
complaints was upgraded. An informal component resulted from
the consultations. Various training and attachment programs were
introduced with the assistance and participation of the private
sector.[105] Government officials have been encouraged to mix with
private sector counterparts in a wide range of social activities.

There was a larger, more general outcome of creating this
consultative mechanism – a recognition emerged that policy based
on consensus benefits all parties. Strengthening the structural
mechanisms for interest group interaction in policy making
increases awareness of how narrow interests correspond to those
of national development. Mahathir hoped a more nationalistic and
unified political culture would emerge from the dialogue by
teaching competing parties to view their private interests in terms
of national or public goals.

[105.] Beginning in 1983, senior government executives now participate in an attachment
training program in private firms as a result of a program initiated by the Public Service
Department and the British-Malaysia Industry and Trade association.

The Change in Attitude

A comparison of Mahathir's National Development Policy of 1990 with the New Economic Policy of 1971, when policy formulation was cloaked in secrecy, reveals the emergence of a more consultative process. Before 1983, the government bureaucracy dominated all policy inputs before proposals were offered for public debate. For example, the New Economic Policy was formulated with virtually no private sector inputs. It originated in the Economic Planning Unit, although UMNO politicians are rumored to have had access to it before the plan was made public. Debate on the New Economic Policy began in the mid-1980s and centered on its continuation; five years of public discussion occurred before the National Development Policy was a concrete plan in 1990. Interest groups publicly took positions during the 1986 elections when public opinion was courted by all sides.

The transition from random, ad hoc, and highly divisive debate to a more productive and consistent exchange of views was facilitated by the creation of the National Economic Consultative Council (NECC). The Council, headed by an influential bureaucrat and consisting of 150 members, was launched on 19 January 1989. Membership ranged from officials, politicians, experts, and interest group representatives, to opposition groups, chambers of commerce, government officials, corporate leaders, economists, professionals, and minority groups.[106] The government side hoped the Council would legitimate and extend the scope of the New Economic Policy; however, the bargaining took on strong racial and adversarial tones. This very divisive issue kept cropping up despite the government's position that racial quotas as a concept were not negotiable.[107] In the second stage, five working groups were organized focusing on data standardization, poverty elimination, restructuring of society, internal economy, and human resources.

---

[106] The Council's secretariat was the Economic Planning Unit of the Prime Minister's Department. Opposition parties had 12 seats, the National Front 40 seats. Twelve parties were represented. DAP had six seats but they boycotted the meetings because some of their leaders were in jail.

[107] The accuracy of government data on the performance of the New Economic Policy was doubted with non-Malays claiming that the targets were met.

Each subcommittee debated the structure and details of the proposal. During its two-year life, 19 members dropped out of the Council raising questions about the unanimity of decisions.

Nevertheless, the prime minister announced the National Economic Consultative Council as "a sincere effort to get as many people as possible to be involved in determining the destiny" of Malaysia (Ho Khai Leong 1992, 213). The proposals of the Council were taken into consideration by the cabinet, which met to formulate the new policy. Although the cabinet decided the final policy, the Council mediated the range of policy proposals that went to the Parliament by outlining a general line of thought, fusing the process with ideas, bringing academic experts into contact with the politicians and private sector leaders, and compelling interest groups to see themselves in a larger perspective.[108] However, at no time did the Council challenge the Prime Minister's Department prerogative over Council matters. Although, the prime minister's office set the goals and defined the issues, an important difference resulted from the earlier pattern of policy making.

The Council was criticized for not having enough clout as it lacked independent power in policy making; many viewed it as a forum used for public relations. But as one observer put it, "The public visibility of the NECC emphasized the apparent importance of overall national interests and presented an illusory image of interest groups bargaining with each other, giving special importance to the non-Bumiputera interest groups. It allowed some, albeit limited, scope for the systematic mobilization of interests" (Ho Khai Leong 1992, 223).

[108.] The Council's report, issued on 9 February 1990, requested a nonpartisan commission to monitor implementation of the racial quotas, an idea that was rejected by the cabinet.

Mental Revolution

Forging a positive consensus regarding the principles that should guide the future course of national development is the hallmark of Mahathir's achievement. The New Economic Policy was essentially a negative consensus, conceived to correct the perceived inequities of the past. Mahathir's guiding vision focused on the positive, forging the future, rather than dwelling on past inequities. His strength as a leader is derived from a relentless drive to ensure that the vision is communicated into implementable projects. His unified vision of development was promulgated in policies such as: "Clean, efficient, and trustworthy", "Look East", "Malaysia Incorporated", "Privatization", and "Leadership by example", culminating in "Vision 2020". These themes were linked by the concept "that the private and public sectors [should] see themselves as sharing the same fate and destiny as partners, shareholders, and workers in the same corporation, which . . . is the nation."

In *The Malay Dilemma*, Mahathir observed, "Malay leaders have been known to say that Malays are not suited for business or skilled work. They are agriculturalists. Money does not mean the same thing to them as it does to the Chinese. They do not have the wish or the capacity for hard work and above all they cannot change." However, Malaysia's experience demonstrates that even such presumed cultural predilections can change. "Politics have shown that the Malays can change. It is difficult to imagine a race more disinterested in politics than the Malays were before the War." A complete reversal occurred after Independence. "The change in Malay political interests has confounded people not only by its vehemence but also by its permanent quality" (Mahathir 1970, 59).

Mahathir's commitment to the notion that dysfunctional belief systems can be discarded led him to insist upon a complete transformation of the ethos and functions of the Civil Service. While retaining its constitutional structure, the bureaucracy learned to use new tools. Its organizational capability was transformed by the redesign of management systems, communication flows, and methods of compensation. Public participation was enhanced by consultation with the private sector to achieve a consensus on the broader issues concerning the future direction of society.

Malaysia's transformation exemplifies the limits of cultural stereotypes such as the notion that Western models of civil service neutrality cannot be applied to a "patrimonial Eastern Culture".[109] The universality of Western bureaucratic norms and practices were asserted as goals of nation building and development without diminishing national self-respect. Western bureaucratic values of rationality, efficiency, and effectiveness along with those of responsiveness, equity, and participation were embraced in Malaysia, but the typical Western separation of policy formulation and implementation was ignored. The government's vision of excellence in the delivery of public services built upon the traditional framework of competence established by the British Civil Service tradition. But it was complemented by the prime minister's "Look East" policy and the adaptation of certain decision-making styles of East Asian origin, including a highly institutionalized business-state dialogue. Rejected was the notion that "indigenous cultural traits" excuse the absence of modern administration or the capacity to benefit from the examples of others.

The maintenance of civil service traditions while accommodating changes in values, functions, and technologies makes Malaysia's experience particularly relevant to other developing countries, highlighting the notion that cultural values need not obstruct collective learning. Historical and cultural factors can be overcome, organizational modes can be deliberately crafted, and social propensities can be molded. The belief in the possibility of cultural change has motivated Mahathir's success as a politician and leader of Malaysia. All Malaysians, not only the Malay subset, benefit from the mental revolution Mahathir inspired.

Convergence Malaysian Style

Malaysia presents a puzzle; on one hand, evidence of patrimonialism abounds, yet it coexists with accountability. This apparent contradiction is explained by Malaysia's will to grow.

[109.] For a more general discussion of what East Asian societies have gained from the West, see Hofheinz and Calder (1982, 41) and Wei-Ming Tu (1989, 92). Wei-Ming Tu argues that Eastern value systems, including Confucianism, have been revitalized by internalizing and domesticating the modern Western Enlightenment.

All political commitments depend on growth. Ethnic quotas depend on growth to avoid destructive communal conflict. State-run industries depend on growth to avoid heavy charges on the treasury, allegations of cronyism must be neutralized by proof of prosperity that benefits all. Effective public sector management unifies all these pieces to produce the political stability that in turn drives business confidence and investment.

CHAPTER SEVEN

INDONESIA
INFORMALITY TRIUMPHS

At Independence, Indonesia, a very large country, had a very small economy and more organizational disadvantages to overcome than most countries in the region. Unlike its neighbors – Hong Kong, Malaysia, and Singapore – where the native civil services absorbed much of the British tradition, overall civilian organization in Indonesia was weak. Colonialism did not leave the country with a class of large landowners, an indigenous business class, or a native bureaucracy with modern management skills.[110]

Even today, Indonesia's civil service still fails to meet the social demands of the country. The legal system is considered to be dysfunctional, a point that is emphasized in the sixth five-year

---

[110.] Based on interviews with Jannes Hutagalung, director, Ministry of Finance; Buly Oscar Surjaatmadja, deputy chairman, International Cooperation; Suryo Utoro, Chief Bureau, Multilateral Economic Cooperation; Suhadi Mangkusuwondo, Economics Faculty, University of Indonesia; P.T. Sarini Tokyu, Abdul Hakim Garuda Nusantara, director, Institute for Policy Research and Advocacy; Mohammad Sadli, chairman, Indonesian Chamber of Commerce & Industry (KADIN); Mari Pangestu and Hadi Soesastro, Centre for Strategic and International Studies; Rizal Ramli, managing director, Advisory Group in Economics, Industry and Trade (ECONIT); Ali Wardhana, adviser, president of INO; Kwik Kian Gie, Dorodjatun Kuntjoro Jakti, dean, University of Indonesia; Emil Salim,

development plan. It includes an entire chapter on the "unsatisfactory quality and capabilities" of legal institutions.[111] "The fact that colonial regulations, as well as national regulations no longer in tune with the current situation, are still being applied means that the legal structure underlying certain areas is not optimal." The report goes on to note that the commercial legal code of Indonesia is outdated. Not only is the substance of the law questioned, but the "institutional framework for legal functionaries" was considered to require wholesale improvement. The head of the Jakarta-based Business Advisory Indonesia (McBeth and Sender 1996, 52) reports "The rule of thumb is to stay out of court in Indonesia. The outcome is long-term and very unpredictable."[112]

Indonesia's weak civil institutions have meant that the functioning of the economy is more dependent on social institutions than any other East Asian economy. It is this backdrop – Indonesia's unique development experience – that allows us to focus on the question of how traders cope with contract uncertainty caused by a weak institutional and legal framework.

The separation of ownership and political officeholding, which is responsible for the sound economic coordination exhibited by the East Asian tigers, does not contribute to

---

chairman of Board of Trustees, KEHATI Foundation; Radius Prawiro, ex-state minister, coordinator for Economic, Financial and for the Supervision of Development; Widjojo Nitisastro, adviser, president of INO; Aburizal Bakrie, chairman, KADIN; Jusuf Anwar, secretary general, Ministry of Finance; Achmad Rochjadi, bureau chief, Planning and Foreign Cooperation; James Castle, Business Advisory Strategies; and Miranda Goeltom, deputy assistant minister, Coordinating Ministry for Economy, Finance and Development Supervision. These interviews were conducted by Hilton Root and Karti Sandilya, 9-16 February 1995. A number of meetings were held with private sector leaders who have requested anonymity.

[111] "As a consequence of Article II of the Transitional Provision of the 1945 Constitution, Indonesia today still maintains a number of colonial laws and regulations written in the Dutch language, without official translations into the Indonesian language. Among these are laws that are not only obsolete but also do not support development measures. Although steps have been taken, law development has not yet been able to formulate a national legal system. Approximately 400 colonial laws and regulations and a number of national laws from the past must be replaced and revised to become national laws that are imbued with the spirit of and based on the Pancasila and the 1945 Constitution" (Indonesia 1994, chapter 39, 3-4).

[112] The *Far Eastern Economic Review* reports that "lawyers can't cite a single instance in which a foreign bank succeeded in enforcing a mortgage claim in the face of resistance. As a result, few foreigners even bother working through the courts." Most use diplomatic channels or simply give up (McBeth and Sender 1996).

Indonesian development. The polity depends upon the military to ensure unity. The military acts as a political party and, at the same time, has an important stake in the management and growth of the economy. In addition, institutions to make leadership explicitly accountable for economic performance or to help gain national consensus are weak.

The importance of shared growth as an Indonesian value resulted from the strength of communism during the first decade of independence. It prompted the military to tolerate a band of economic technocrats to design and execute macroeconomic policy.[113] Requiring only the consent of top leadership, effective macroeconomic policies did not require wholesale reform of the bureaucracy. Instead, the technocrats were tolerated to garner the confidence of international donors. As long as the microeconomy was in the hands of the generals, technocrats were no threat to the dissemination of spoils. Even in the 1980s, during economic liberalization, reform came from the top with little concern for upgrading the performance of lower level officials.

Rent-Seekers' Heaven

Under the New Order government (1965-present), a regulatory framework was established that facilitated the exchange of economic assets for political loyalty. Decrees brought products of all kinds under various forms of administrative control. High import duties, import bans, and subsidies to capital importation made some enterprises profitable while penalizing others. Because administrative control over the economy was so extensive, investors and policymakers could not measure the economic impact of regulation. For example, in 1985, 1,484 items were restricted to holders of approved import licenses. These items accounted for about 26 percent of the total import value and 32 percent of domestic value added, with the exclusion of construction and services. While licenses were restricted to approved traders, imports were informally controlled through approval of the annual import plan by the Department of Trade.

[113.] Technocratic influence has not been continuous, but crisis driven. Suharto plays technocrats off against other political groups as his interests dictate.

Import licenses were another administrative mechanism used to allocate the economic assets of the country to political supporters of the regime. Of the 1,484 items under approved import licenses, less than one quarter were subject to formal quotas (Bhattacharya and Pangestu 1993).

Investment licensing allowed administrative rents to be allocated politically. While investments of any size, foreign or domestic, were screened by the Investment Board, private investments were subject to rigorous licensing procedures according to a schedule of priorities determined by the regime. The proliferation of provincial and local regulations, along with a restricted investment and capacity licensing system, extended control over foreign investment. Entrance of both foreign and domestic investors to specific industries was limited by the investment priority schedule, which identified areas for possible investment and indicated the number of projects for which licenses would be given. It even specified the capacity that the industry or activity was allowed to achieve. In addition, cumbersome land and labor laws, and the absence of updated corporate law kept the profits of economic development in the hands of those who were administratively chosen by the regime (World Bank 1991b, 79).[114]

Foreign firms wishing to invest were subject to tougher laws than domestic firms. These included restricted investment licensing criteria, minimum initial requirements for local ownership, specified phasing for the transfer of the company from foreign to local ownership, a ban on domestic trading of output and marketing of Indonesian exports, restrictions on what domestic inputs could be purchased, limitations on land lease, and limited access to domestic capital, including export finance. Virtually all aid credits were dispersed through the planning system. Tariff protection and tax favors gave the administration

---

[114.] "Until 1988, domestic and foreign investment was restricted to certain areas: there were capacity limits and ceilings on the number of permitted projects. Before starting operations, even approved indigenous firms had to obtain import and export licenses, a domestic trading license, land rights, a permanent operating license, and storage and location permits. All this often took two years. Total factor productivity fell by 2.5 percent in the mid-1980s" (World Bank 1991b, 79).

the capacity to ensure profits for those enterprises it preferred. With these restrictions in place, access to the economy was controlled to ensure priority to those whose loyalty to the regime could not be questioned.

Reducing opportunities for the development of financial capitalism was another important means used to control the exercise of political power. The regime's suspicion of financial capitalism reflected a fear that powerful private interests might challenge the government vocally or exit with their capital. As a result, the government did little to foster a powerful private sector, unlike the case in Japan, Philippines or the Republic of Korea.

Control over the banking system reduced the threat of defection, while allowing the central government to implement its spending programs – sometimes borrowing in excess of 30 percent of Treasury reserves. Government control over the central bank also influenced the country's financial development by extending credits to government-related nonfinancial institutions. This meant that the central bank went beyond the lender of last resort function to become a financial facilitator of government programs. Subsidized credit was available to projects mounted by government favorites. Interest groups, such as the sugar plantations or construction firms, could count on generous nonmarket credit allocations.[115] In 1978, state enterprises received 52 percent of all credit; in 1982, 37 percent. Extensive reform of the financial sector was precipitated by the second major external shock in 1986. This prompted the need for discipline. Liberalization of the financial sector began in 1988, and continued until 1992.

Still, in 1995, the effective rate of protection was much higher in Indonesia than in comparable Southeast Asian economies.

[115.] "The state banks were charging 25 to 50 percent per annum, depending on the class of loan, which implied a subsidy of virtually the entire amount of the loan, because within a year's time the real value of the principal virtually disappeared. In short, the state bank rates were meaningless, except as an indicator of the size of the subsidy to the privileged few in the private sector who had access to such loans at that time" (Glassburner 1978, 36).

One official pointed out:

> Indonesia has been less successful at bringing down
> protection due to the licensing and quota system.
> Licensing allows oligopoly to proliferate. Only certain
> importers are allowed to import certain products.
> Licensing was difficult to control because it affects
> individual companies allowing them to make private
> deals with officials. But controlling the budget was
> easy because cuts were not given to particular firms.

Budgetary austerity has been critical to keeping rent seeking
from the kind of excess that occurred in the Philippines.
Constitutionally imposed budgetary controls provide protection
from political pressure to agencies responsible for formulating
macroeconomic policy. Laws that mandate a balanced budget, low
ceilings on the extent of public debt, and institutional review
processes subject to parliamentary rules and oversight, all inhibit
direct meddling with the budget.

The monitoring of development is another reason
development funds have been used effectively in Indonesia.
BAPPENAS, the national planning organization, oversees the
utilization of all money for development projects by monitoring
costs, overruns, the accomplishment of performance deadlines,
and quality.[116] It is empowered to take corrective measures when
necessary. BAPPENAS has considerable monitoring clout over all
executing agencies that handle donor assistance. The agency holds
quarterly meetings with international donor agencies active in
the country. Although the Ministry of Finance is responsible for
disbursements, it depends on the technical expertise of
BAPPENAS for project evaluation. This highly centralized pattern
of project monitoring penetrates to the local levels. The agency
routinely sends agents to monitor project performance throughout
the country. In consultation with donor agencies, BAPPENAS does
not offer new proposals until it is sure that implementation
problems of similar ongoing projects have been solved. New

---

116. BAPPENAS does not centrally manage the economy, it evaluates petitions from
government agencies for investment funds channeled through the budget. It is not an
Indonesian Gosplan.

projects are conceived with reference to previous experience. The agency routinely upgrades the technical skills of its staff. Considering the high level of international assistance Indonesia has received, BAPPENAS has been critical to the country's good standing with donors.

Compared to other high performing East Asian countries, the development of Indonesia has been based on the exploitation of natural resources; 60 percent of output and 90 percent of exports in 1977 were resource based. Even as late as 1988, the proportion of resource output constituted more than 50 percent of exports, the remainder were primarily labor-intensive goods. While the share of the labor-intensive sector is increasing, capital-intensive investment is still weak and the share of engineering goods is increasing much less than in other East Asian economies (see Appendix B, Figure 2). As a result of an inconsistent regulatory system that nurtures rent seeking and encourages leakage, a dollar invested in Indonesia has produced less output than a dollar placed in the Republic of Korea or Taipei,China.

Something for Everyone

Nevertheless, Indonesia, since 1965, has been heralded as one of the most dynamic economies among developing countries. Despite various commodity "booms" and "busts", the rise in international interest rates, and currency realignments in the mid-1980s, the average annual inflation rate was controlled at 17.5 percent in the 1970s and 8.6 percent in the 1980s, while the economy grew at an annual average of 7.7 percent in the 1970s and 5.5 percent in the 1980s. Since the mid-1980s, the economy has diversified, the role of the private sector has expanded, and the reliance on oil is decreasing. The annual rate of growth during the Fifth Five-Year Development Plan (Pelita V), 1989/90 to 1993/94, is likely to exceed the target of 5 percent.

While those closely associated with the government have had many opportunities to accumulate wealth, there has been something for everyone in Suharto's development scheme. To win the support of the wider population, efforts were made to increase per capita income, primarily by focusing on agricultural development. Rapid growth, combined with gradual declining population growth (from 2.2 percent in 1980/85 to 1.8 percent in 1985/90), resulted in rising annual average income per capita by 5.5 percent in the 1970s and 3.3 percent in the 1980s (Nasution 1995).

Indonesia took less than a generation in the 1970s and 1980s to reduce the incidence of poverty from almost 60 percent of the population to less than 20 percent (World Bank 1990, 1). Despite a per capita income of $650 (1992), the *World Development Report 1990* (World Bank 1990) cited Indonesia for the highest annual average reduction in the incidence of poverty among all of the countries studied since 1970.

Bureaucratic Capability

At the policy-making level, Suharto's choice of economic advisers has won praise from all parties. Because Suharto welcomed the advice of his advisers, even when tough domestic opposition was at risk, the donors have always come to the country's aid. With the so-called "Berkeley-trained mafia" at the helm, they know whom they are dealing with, and what to expect. The technocrats promoted confidence among investors that macroeconomic management, prices, and exchange rates were secure. Because the institutions were less predictable than those in Indonesia's high performing East Asian counterparts, much depended on the continuity of personnel – many of the original advisers were still there 20 years later.

The president's commitment to his technocrats has passed several critical tests. Upon taking power, he followed their advice and took measures to end the 500 percent inflation of the Sukarno years. In 1967, a balanced budget amendment was inserted in the constitution. When the national oil company, Pertamina, was badly managed by a close supporter and powerful member of the officer corps, Suharto did not protect company management.[117] A new technocratic law was established to manage Pertamina; monitoring was to be by a board of supervisors, and Pertamina had to hand over all revenues directly to the government. In 1983, when depressed oil prices threatened to create wide-scale hardships, the president again took the advice of the technocrats and began a process of deregulation and investment openness.

[117.] The crash of Pertamina's empire of 50,000 employees in 1975 ranks among the great peacetime losses incurred by a country. The company's debts totaled over $10.5 billion equivalent to 40 percent of the national income (Milne 1987).

The arguments for freer trade continue to come from technical advisers, not from industry. Because of the extent of regulation, liberalization has had political consequences. In the late 1980s, when trade liberalization was introduced, the authority of the military and their role as partners with private sector investors was threatened, especially in the export sector. Nevertheless, Suharto took the politically difficult move suggested by his advisers.

Although economic policy remains largely insulated from outside pressures, the implementation of policy was often subjected to societal pressures. Bruce Glassburner writes that implementation is handicapped by "bureaucratic inertia and low levels of competence, entrenched by decades of overhiring and indifference to administrative skills" (Glassburner 1978, 34). One official remarked:

> Usually the policy-making bodies were kept clear of politics. However once the policies are made, implementation is left to the bureaucrats. It was at the implementation stage that political pressure emerged. At the policy level, government officials are protected from political influence but not at the implementation level.

Another senior official explains:

> Macrostability is easier than microadjusting, because small groups make macrodecisions and execute those decisions. Reforming governance requires a broader consensus. Monetary policy can be executed by less than 10 persons. Governance requires hundreds.

The role of the civil service in Indonesia resembles that of civil services in developing countries that have failed. Many of the bureaucrats are part of the political party, Golkar, and are selected for their political loyalty. Integrated into the political party, the civil service provides an important part of the voting population. Civil servants, such as village heads, campaign in the villages and mobilize the party's political support throughout the country.

Whereas high-level technocrats are encouraged to believe their ability to solve problems will be appreciated, the same appreciation is not extended as consistently to rank and file civil servants. The expectation that one's expertise will be utilized and that one can be promoted on the basis of achievement is often disappointed. One official noted that while the government can dismiss individuals who do not perform well, there is no stated criteria or procedures for dismissal. Demoralization is rampant because of the absence of a well defined, competitive career path with the possibility of rewards for a job well done. One civil servant explained recruitment by the civil service

> .. is often with no standard of needs. . . . It is easy to recruit and I would say we can cut more than half of our civil servants and the work is still going on in Indonesia, that is a very hard word, but that's the fact. The fact that they are not working eight hours as they should is also showing how inefficient they are working. And, of course, in this environment one would expect that there will be a competition for somebody to go to a higher rank because there are so many people. But that's not the case in Indonesia, because many other political factors come in, I should say, whether you are belonging to one group or you are friends or you are relatives of the higher ranking positions is necessary to get promoted, so there is not an incentive for the civil servants to prove themselves to perform well to get to a higher ranking. And that is very inefficient, so I would say that one task that has to be done in Indonesian civil service procedure is to create some incentives, not only in terms of financial reward but more on the surety of getting to a higher rank.

This systemic weakness has meant that government programs of high priority, particularly the regime's agricultural strategy and the attainment of self-sufficiency in rice, need direct and constant supervision by the president. These long-term trends reflect the high priority that Suharto's government places on winning the support of the majority of the population. Also an aggressive family planning program required direct monitoring from the center.

Policy objectives are attained if the president wants them to get done and if he gets involved. The *Far Eastern Economic Review* survey of Indonesia concludes, "All key decisions are made by one man" (McBeth 1995, 48).

Business-State Interface

The state-society interface in Indonesia is less formal, less institutionalized, than that of other nations in the sample. Business associations exist, but they play a more passive role than elsewhere. One official expressly said there is "almost zero private sector input in policy dialogue." Abundant oil revenues ensured that government was not beholden to individual business groups and thus never had to develop an institutional structure to cooperate or communicate with the private sector. The weak formal links between the private sector and the government are particularly apparent during the planning process.[118]

A representative of the ministry of planning, BAPPENAS, explains:

> There was no official contact with the private sector on the formulation of economic planning nor was there any effort to engage public opinion in the process. Radio and media were not used to help generate consensus on the plan. All infrastructure was conceived without consultation with the private sector.

But the government's mandarin style is changing. On the change, one government official noted:

> We have two ministers who were previously businessmen now which has never happened before. Ministers in Indonesia traditionally had to be civil servants. Now we have one minister for manpower

---

[118.] A representative of the Indonesian Chamber of Commerce, KADIN, reported that the chamber was not influential in policy dialogue with the government. Only after the budget is presented is the chamber invited to meet with the finance minister, usually about 100 representatives are chosen. The national chamber dialogues on macro issues. Sectoral issues are discussed with sectoral ministers directly during periodic consultations at the minister's request. This lack of consistency is one reason why one official reported, "Generally, regulations emerged from private discussion with individual firms," while one from another ministry reported that private sector inputs were kept out of policy making.

who is the owner of the big department store and conglomerate, the other one, the minister for environment is the owner of a real estate conglomerate which never happens before in Indonesia. There is a tendency that the tripartite thing (business, government, labor) worked not very well in the formal form like in Japan. But the ministers are inviting the businessmen to get some inputs of the problems they are having. Previously no way this could happen, the businessman has to ask five months in advance to be able to see the ministers. Nowadays the minister invites them and asks whether if we implement this policy what will happen to you.

Uncertainties about bureaucratic performance reflect the absence of an effective state-society interface. When business cannot trust the bureaucracy to be an unbiased referee, it is unlikely to believe that information shared with the government will be protected.

The Military

The absence of bureaucratic capability, coupled with a weak business sector, created a power vacuum that was filled by the army. Since at Independence, there were virtually no independent organizations other than the army, Indonesia's leaders have learned that any effort to govern must begin with the officers.[119] The military has an additional charm. It was indispensable in the battle for independence and, again, it was essential in the battle against communism that preceded the rise of Suharto. Thus, the president does not question the need to share power with other military leaders by giving them ministries and influence in the regions. The president takes their role so seriously that he feels it is incumbent to be familiar with his officers down to the battalion level in the Jakarta command. Important personnel decisions within the armed forces require the president's personal approval.

[119.] Some have argued that the military can play a similar role to the bureaucracy in India, as the cement of national unity.

Dwifungsi (dual function) allows the uniformed branch to play a major role in Indonesian politics. And despite efforts to reduce the political visibility of the military, the essentials of its political power are still in place 35 years after independence. The number of retired or serving military officers who fill bureaucratic and other civilian positions has dwindled from 25,000 in 1967, to 20,000 in the early 1980s, to about 14,000 today (McBeth 1995, 17). Nevertheless, as of 1995, 1,500 key posts in the central and provincial administrations and parliaments are reserved for active duty officers.[120] The number of military appointees made to the 500-seat House of Representatives was trimmed from 100 to 75 in May of 1995. A retired general is often chair of Golkar and cabinet ranking is always assured to a high-ranking officer, along with control of a territorial apparatus. This allows military influence to permeate down to the village level. In addition, the military remains the final arbiter of any political crisis.

Initially the military not only received a large share of the power, but also had considerable freedom to exercise it, penetrating virtually every function and level of government. Because political power translates easily into economic power in Indonesia, officers have been able to acquire a large share of the proceeds of the country's growth. If the government controls it, as in the case of the banks, or state enterprises financed by oil money, the military is assured a share.

Because government ownership and control is so extensive, aspirants in the private sector value connections to the military. This has allowed the military to extend its patronage throughout the business sector. One lawyer explained, help is needed to gain preferential treatment in three essential areas, from "(i) tax collectors; (ii) agencies that spend money, especially those that hand out government contracts; and (iii) agencies that issue licenses." Those who lack a facilitator will find that the individuals empowered to make these decisions can request considerable side payments or may act in an unpredictable manner.

[120.] "In 1984 a study found that fourteen of the thirty-seven cabinet ministers had military backgrounds, and that nearly half of the 106 sub-cabinet positions (secretaries-general, directors-general, and inspectors-general) were held by seconded officers. The same study found that the armed forces provided "about three-quarters of the twenty-seven governors and a small majority of district headships" (Liddle 1985, 72).

Labor relations is one area in which the military has been particularly visible. Military officials often appear on the boards of private firms as directors of labor relations. Their hands in this area can arouse controversy, as one lawyer asserted, "The military is placed on the boards of firms to intimidate workers and to crush strikes. In many strikes, the military incited violence to use force to suppress labor."

Military organization means that the dissipation of the wages of corruption is much less of a problem in Indonesia than in most developing countries. Military order ensures clients get the service they are paying for. Top people get their shares and corruption is not whittled away at the bottom by a hundred takers. Concentration at the top, where it can be controlled by the actual decision makers, provides assurances to the client that agreements will be carried out. Despite their sometimes very controversial role, observers agree that the military has been indispensable for the preservation of national unity and political stability.

A Very Special Relationship

As noted earlier, when access to government regulation, contracts, or relief from extortionary taxes is needed, a representative of the military can be useful. As one civilian official explained:

> Often, military officials are on the board of private sectors. To improve relationship with the government, they were offered key position on the boards because they were useful to the companies because of their connection or former associations with the government officials.

Another official confirmed this, "The military plays the role of facilitator in getting those signatures for private transaction to pass the review by a senior."

Highly personalized relationships with business often develop. Shares in the profits of enterprises are often acquired, particularly those owned by the domestic Chinese who need goodwill to gain necessary permits. There is even a special word, *cukong*, for arrangements between the military and Chinese firms.

A huge and inefficient state sector, sustained by funding from oil and other natural resources, dominates the modern Indonesian economy. However, beneath this high cost, low productivity sector is a dynamic private sector in which contracts are enforced on the basis of repeat play among Chinese families. The state sector is too large to allow the Chinese to dominate the economy, but they do dominate the private sector in which relations with the government tend to be informal: The Chinese pay, the military facilitates. The takings are viewed as benign by some, justified by others. As one official explained, "The military extracts its share mostly from the Chinese, not from the multinationals. The Chinese do not pay taxes, whereas the Westerners pay 90 percent of what they owe." Noteworthy about this statement is that although they carry Indonesian passports, the Chinese are typically referred to by their ethnic origin.

The undercurrent of prejudice that prevents the Chinese from attaining the full status of citizens is one reason the wealth of the Chinese is politically accepted by the military. Domination of capital by the Chinese does not challenge the political authority of the military.[121] In contrast with Thailand, where sharing power with the Chinese has always been a real threat to the military, in Indonesia, economic power does not threaten the military's political power as long as wealth is in the hands of the Chinese.[122] The military can rest secure because no civilian native rival is in sight. Thus, social prejudice toward the Chinese actually enhances their value to the military. "Everything depends on the resentment not getting out of hand, and the maintenance of secrecy about who gets what."

Although often discussed, the relationship between the Chinese and the military is too sensitive to be the subject of impartial documentation. When asked for concrete information

---

[121] In Indonesia, the Chinese make up 3.5 percent of the population and control 73 percent of private nonland wealth. In the Philippines, the Chinese are 2 percent of the population, but own 50 percent of the private nonland capital. In Malaysia, Chinese, at 29 percent of the population, own 61 percent of private nonland wealth. In Thailand, making up 10 percent of the population, the Chinese own 81 percent of private nonland wealth. Only in Singapore is the percentage of ownership proportionate to population size. There, 77 percent of the population are Chinese, who own 81 percent of the private nonland capital (see Australia 1995).

[122] In Malaysia, the Chinese interests are sufficiently strong and politically influential. They can influence the outcomes of elections, so they can stand up against the Malaysians. The Chinese in Indonesia had little political strength, so they depend heavily on the indigenous bureaucracy.

about the ownership structure of their firms, private sector owners resist. But often with the caveat, "We are paying too much for the protection we are offered." Officials tend to downplay the amounts requested, but few denied that informal payments are common for Chinese firms to gain the goodwill they need. Because the military's own directly managed commercial operations ended in commercial failure, they rarely question the importance of Chinese management in running profitmaking activities.

Today, the links between the Chinese and the military are declining. The utility of military officers is reduced for firms engaged in exports, as minimal regulations for export-oriented industries mean fewer permits are needed. In general, as the effective rate of protection declines and sectors are open to free competition, the role of facilitators wanes. But why are the Chinese so skilled, compared to the native population in running a business for a profit?

A Network Economy

On the seeming comparative advantage in trade and finance enjoyed by the Chinese, one Indonesian official explained:

> Some of the population have big resentment because they see that most of the rich are Chinese, but they are also aware and have to admit the fact that the Chinese are born to be businessmen. Indonesians are not born that way, we are trying to train ourselves to be a businessman but we are not born as a businessman. And we can see the same small workshops owned by Chinese side-by-side with the one owned by Indonesian. The Indonesian workshop will stay like that forever; the Chinese workshop in two-year time growing faster.

This explanation is not adequate. Consider the colloquial observation often made in jest that, "The Chinese are rich everywhere except in China; the Jews, except in Israel; Indians in Africa and the United States, but not in India."

Ethnic homogeneity allows the Chinese traders in Indonesia to personalize or particularize exchange relations. Among the Chinese, deals depend heavily upon social mechanisms, such as exclusion or ostracism from the community – those who violate trust are excluded from future transactions.[123] Members of a persecuted ethnic minority who are ostracized from their kin group will have nowhere to turn – acceptance by the mainstream population is unlikely. Besides more money can be made within the minority community than outside of it. Embedded kin or ethnic-based relations are a functional equivalent to the law of contracts. Ethnic ties economize on the costs of contract enforcement and information costs when the legal structures to support anonymous trade are weak. Among a minority, tightly knit kinship structure is a surrogate for other forms of contract enforcement mechanisms. This is illustrated by the fact that Chinese middlemen use credit in transactions within their own community, but only cash with indigenous merchants (Landa 1994).

Traders in this network economy depend on nonprice signals of the potential reliability of partners. Trade is based on moral rather than contractual relations or what is sometimes referred to as the Confucian moral code of ethics. Both are surrogates for legal uncertainty and both reflect the failure to base growth on institutions. These trade relations receive less emphasis where the Chinese are the majority.

Compared to Thailand, it is more difficult for the Indonesian Chinese to move out of their enclave and be accepted by the majority population. Because the Chinese cannot substitute ties to the ethnic majority, they value their ties within their own community more highly, and are less likely to act in an opportunistic manner with ethnic partners. Ruptured ties cannot easily be replaced. Thus the walls that separate Chinese firms from the general economy ensure a high level of compliance to social expectations within the community. Since leaving the enclave is not an attractive option, members place a premium on the value the ties make possible through membership. At the same time, ties to the Chinese overseas economy reinforce entrepreneurial activity, enhancing the value of membership in the closed

---

[123.] The same logic applies to the Chinese in the Philippines. Of the top 120 local import substituting industrializing companies, 54 companies or 45 percent are controlled by Filipino-Chinese families. With the exception of six firms, 48 or 89 percent were established after World War II (Rivera 1994, 161).

community. The informal social controls that operate among the Chinese provide a level of economic performance that the majority population cannot match. The result is a great gap between the performance of the majority population in commerce and trade and that of the Chinese minority. As a result, Indonesia's economic development has disproportionately benefited the Chinese minority.

Unfortunately, the prosperity of the minority increases the premium placed by members on maintaining homogeneity. This, in turn, nurtures prejudice. As economic opportunities increase for the group, they are likely to put higher priority on the value of the rights they hold in the personalistic market where ethnic origin confers the privilege of trade. However, when ethnic minorities do not tolerate deviation, they risk inciting the social jealousy of outsiders.[124]

The Majority

The poor economic performance of the native population drives home the need for an efficient public sector and a functioning legal system to monitor contract enforcement and economic transactions. Without a credible regulatory or judicial environment, the expectation of contract noncompliance is high among the majority population. When it is difficult to know who will be trustworthy and will honor contracts, anonymous trade will be considerably reduced. The problem facing future Indonesian development is that in the absence of effective legal sanctions, impersonal market forces will not dictate the appropriate pairing of trading partners. As a result, many economically feasible trades will not occur. Because of contract uncertainty, political connections will become economic capital. They, however, lack the liquidity of ordinary capital and cannot be traded.

The kind of impersonal and highly liquid capital markets found in advanced economies come into existence slowly in the Indonesian setting. The regulatory hurdles have a tendency to

---

[124.] This is especially true if both groups live in the same manner. When one group has a conspicuously different lifestyle, they may not arouse hostility, but when competition is for the same secular objectives, conflict is more likely.

discourage all but the well connected, and even these individuals cannot be assured that their deals will hold up when disputes arise. When legal sanctions are uncertain, traders will reluctantly choose partners from society at large, which is why legal institutions are critical to sustain broad-based trade. Then social relationships become the basis of intertemporal trade – a few well-connected large firms owned by a small circle of intermarried clans end up dominating commercial and industrial transactions of significant scale. In such a network economy, low cost, ethnic-based, or connection-based screening devices are valuable. However, the absence of a framework for abstract ties will ultimately affect the formation of capital markets, which depend heavily on anonymous market forces and high levels of institutional trust.

Family First

In a society where family comes first, the first family comes before all others. In fact, on Suharto's succession, a widely discussed issue is the share of economic opportunity controlled by immediate members of the first family. Although a number of lucrative assets acquired by the family can be described as purely gatekeeping, such as toll roads and supply services, the shares it has acquired in major companies reflect a systemic weakness in the business environment.

The First Family has used their position to dominate contracts with multinationals and with the development banks, because as partners for foreign firms seeking to invest in Indonesia, the family can add value. Their appearance on the board provides assurances within an insecure legal environment; capricious treatment by low level bureaucrats will be less likely. Since investors have reason to expect contracts, concessions, and investment approvals run by or involving family members, this explains why firms, like Japan's NEC and Sumitomo; America's Hughes Aircraft, Ford, and Union Carbide; France's Alcatel; Germany's Deutsche Telekon; and Switzerland's Nestlé, have all formed partnerships with the president's relatives.

The family can also help investors by reducing the costs of gathering information. Investors' confidence is augmented when the family gets involved, because they can expect that the family has information about the economy or about forthcoming political decisions that competitors lack. Protection, the reduction of information and transaction costs, and assurances against expropriation or bureaucratic caprice are all reasons why value is created for investors when the family gets involved. But that involvement nurtures resentment among those left out.

The Way to the Future

Indonesia is moving to a more civilian-based polity. The army still controls politics, but more discreetly than in the past. Within the military, divisions exist between the rich old guard and the new more technocratic young officers who find career paths are blocked and who are not sympathetic to the gains of those now at the top. These internal divisions augur change.

Globalization holds the key to a more open economy and a reduction of rent seeking, which is now being openly discussed and criticized. Presently, Indonesian conglomerates sell very little abroad, except for wood products. As one official stated:

> It is very important for Indonesia to enter into international covenants that force domestic industry to accept international standards. Through international commitments you force domestic firms to accept a more liberal future. Which is why the president placed such importance on hosting the meetings of APEC [the Asia-Pacific Economic Cooperation Group].

Indonesia continues to worry less about its reputation for a clean business environment than, for example, Singapore.[125] When investment is primarily in resource extraction, confidence in the country matters less. That, too, will change as Indonesia's industrial development becomes more dependent on attracting foreign capital. The critical issue for the country's future is to replace particularistic exchange networks with impersonal contract-based exchange. If better public facilities are provided

---

[125.] In a study by Transparency International of how executives perceive the integrity of business transactions, Indonesia scored lowest of 14 of the largest countries in Asia. Singapore and New Zealand scored highest with a rating of 9.7 out of 10, whereas Indonesia scored 1.9, below India at 2.6, Philippines at 2.5, and Pakistan and People's Republic of China at 2.1 (Regional Briefing 1995, 13).

there will be lower costs to the Chinese who break out of their ethnic enclave, and a chance for the majority of the population to catch up.

The great challenge for Indonesia is to create an appropriate structure for intergenerational growth and resource management. Development implies that individuals and groups must save and sacrifice today for benefits that will accrue tomorrow to be enjoyed by strangers. But sacrifice requires trust. Whereas basic trust exists in the family or kinship group where members know their role and what is expected of them, development requires a more abstract basis for trust. It requires a predictable institutional interface to mediate relations between individuals who do not have personal relationships. For intertemporal deals to coalesce between strangers, the rules of the game must be specified in ways that everyone can understand. Potential partners must be assured that the rules are the same for everyone and, if disputes arise, they must be assured that they can resort to a reputable third party.

An important difference between Indonesia and its more successful neighbors to the North is that such a framework has not evolved, instead a network economy prevails in which investments are determined by personal relationships. The inadequacy of institutions created a significant functional role for the first family to play in the emerging economy. That role will soon reach its limits. Because no one wants to compete with the family, the economy will not reach its potential. In addition, increased social jealousy could have political consequences. Resentment will focus on individuals who used the political system to accumulate their wealth. Moreover, doubts about the succession of a friendly party may undermine the family's appeal as a business partner. A rival could dismantle the family empire simply by revoking licenses or changing laws.

Basic family-based trust exists in all societies, not only those of East Asia. But it must give way to trust sustained by institutions if an economy is to attain its technological potential. Such institutions will, no doubt, also limit the scope of personal power enjoyed by the leader. Suharto's New Order Government transformed a deeply troubled polity into a model of equitable income redistribution during the early stages of modernization. If government continues to create credible public institutions, capital intensive development will follow the resource intensive development that has already begun.

CHAPTER EIGHT

THE PHILIPPINES
THE NEW STATE OF PATRONAGE

Debt-Driven Growth and Its Aftermath (1972-1986)

Many Filipinos welcomed the declaration of martial law in 1972 as an alternative to the fractious elite democracy that had paralysed government since independence in 1946. Marcos promised that *authoritarian constitutionalism* would foster technocratic efficiency and dispense with the pork-barrel politics of a Congress dominated by elite business interests. Park Chung Hee and Lee Kuan Yew were cited as examples of *developmental authoritarianism*, which represented an Asian way to foster economic well-being. However these leaders were institution builders, who established foundations that stood after they departed. Marcos was an institution wrecker, whose victims included the Congress, the judiciary, the civil service, and business. Alongside the political and economic supremacy of the traditional elite, he created a new elite based on his ability to use state power to disseminate economic privileges. Instead of the creation of new institutions, the personalization of authority and the role of patronage in politics attained new peaks.

Institution Wrecker

Upon declaring martial law in 1972, Marcos undertook a number of administrative reforms making the president the country's sole legislator, responsible for all lawmaking and all important administrative decisions.[126] All government expenditures needed executive endorsement and judges served at the president's approval. This concentration of power in the center actually deinstitutionalized state authority; power vested in institutions was placed in the hands of the president – to be exercised personally.

As traditional government institutions were either abandoned or undermined, personal relationships, not formal institutions, laws, or procedures, served as the basis of economic and social relations. The president offered compelling justification for the personalization of power. For the first time since Philippine independence, the ruler had the capability to promote rapid political and socioeconomic change, having removed the encumbrance of a Congress dominated by elite interests. Yet instead of building broad-based support through fundamental social reforms, the government choose to create an alternative elite. A political order based upon personal loyalties was created supported by an economic order similarly controlled by the ruler's whim.

The new regime's political sustainability was predicated on the ruler's ability to create clients by distributing economic favors. Deinstitutionalization, and the concentration of power in the hands of the ruler's family, laid the foundations for economic cronyism. In the name of technocracy and social equity, Marcos had created a new state of patronage. A Congress of many patrons was replaced by a centralized system of disbursement dominated by a single godfather.

However, the president's inability to dismantle entirely the old system was to be his downfall. In the end, the clients of the "New Society" were too concentrated and too isolated to protect their patron from the ire of those still entrenched interests they attempted to supplant. Interelite rivalry toppled the Marcos

---

[126.] Heavy government spending during the 1969 election campaign precipitated a balance of payments crisis that led to the emergency decrees of 1972 and the imposition of martial law. "Marcos must have spent between 800 and 900 million pesos, including 160 million pesos from the barrio improvement fund, 60 million from the medical fund and 200 million from various public works funds. The debasement of the vote into a market commodity is illustrated by reports that Marcos distributed individual 2,000 peso cheques to barrio captains" (Doronilla 1992, 117).

government and determined the shape of the polity that replaced it.

Asia's First Democracy

The Philippines had a long tradition of democratic self-governance that featured a system of checks and balances on the exercise of executive authority – an independent judiciary, a Congress, and a professional civil service. By 1916, constitutional arrangements included an almost fully elective bicameral legislature (only literate males could vote). Defense, foreign affairs, and education were the only exclusive American prerogatives. Thus effective colonial domination of Philippine policy ended before 1920, giving the Philippines the longest tradition of self-governance of any country being considered in this study. A predominantly Filipino local administration existed by 1921, when less than 6 percent of civil servants were American, and by 1927, 99 percent of the country's teachers were native (Wurfel 1988, 8-9).

As part of Marcos's assumption of power, political parties were eliminated and independent institutions, such as the Commission on Elections, were brought to heel. But perhaps the most striking component of the president's personalization of power was his control over the budget. The sacking of Congress in 1972 ended its line-by-line scrutiny over the budget. Thereafter, it became the president's private affair, shared with only a few of the highest members of the government so that drafting of the budget was synonymous with its enactment. Although broad categories of spending were made public, the president could transfer funds from one category to another without a trace. This concentration of budgetary power in one individual, unchecked by institutions, was unique among the countries considered in this study. The baneful effects of personalized rule could not make sense without this authority. Institutionalized hard budget constraints is one reason why leadership in Indonesia was more accountable for economic performance than the Philippines.

The Courts

Marcos had to overcome the most reputable court system in East Asia. It blended elements of American common law with

Spanish civil law traditions. "Keen legal minds and incorruptible jurists helped build the considerable prestige of the higher courts." (Wurfel 1988, 11) However, judicial independence was undermined shortly after the calling of martial law in 1973, when a compliant Supreme Court declared there was no judicial obstacle to its implementation. As a reward for their probity, Marcos ordered all judges, except those of the Supreme Court, to submit letters of resignation. All sitting judges now served at the president's pleasure. These letters were held until the Judiciary Reorganization Act of 1983. Judges lived for a decade under the pervasive threat of removal. The president placed himself further above the courts as the only authority to release individuals detained under presidential detention authorizations. When unsatisfied with outcomes of the civilian courts, he reserved the option of referring cases to the military courts. Thus *constitutional authoritarianism* came to mean rule by persons rather than by law, thereby undermining belief in the legitimacy of the judicial system to act in an impartial manner. Massive skepticism of the judicial process resulted.[127]

Elusive Technocratic Neutrality

Marcos inherited a well-defined and, by the standards of the region, modern government machinery. As noted, the American colonial administration depended on the local elite to run the colonial government, so that the departure of the Americans did not result in a vacuum of competence. The Philippine Constitution stipulated that merit should be the sole criteria for appointments to the civil service, "to be determined as far as practicable by competitive examination." Employees were banned from partisan political activity and could be suspended only "for cause as provided by law." The Civil Service Commission regulated the system. Nevertheless, despite the existence of what on paper seemed to be a constitutionally effective design, patronage politics took over and dictated a logic in which bureau directors and chiefs received appropriations from the legislature in exchange for the

---

[127.] Marcos made a number of changes to the constitution through amendments and plebiscites whenever it suited him.

appointments of friends or clients of Congress. The legislators used the weapon of budget cuts to capture the bureaucracy and undermine its independence. One method to shorten the leash controlling bureaucratic decision making was the tendency of Congress to keep it on a system of day-to-day financial support.

By 1964, civil service standards had decayed, 80 percent of the staff had entered without competitive exams, usually on temporary appointments. Of the higher level civil servants, 57 percent bypassed the exams. Congressional meddling was widely recognized as perverting the intentions of the constitution and as undermining the quality of those who served. Electoral politics were seen as the culprit and many quarters welcomed an end to the manipulation of public administration by politicians.

Like Park and Lee, Marcos's reform of the bureaucracy would be the centerpiece of the "New Society" he envisioned. The first major reform legislation, following the declaration of martial law, was in the area of public administration. Presidential Decree No. 1 ordered the Integrated Reorganization Plan, a wholesale reform of the nation's administrative structure. To enhance the technocratic component of policy making, the number of agencies reporting to the president were reduced, departmental organization was standardized, and a unified national planning agency concentrated all economic planning and implementation.[128] Its director-general, an economist of international prominence, became a key cabinet member. However, the promise of symmetry and simplicity was short lived. Twelve departments existed in 1970, 14 by 1972, 18 by June of the same year, and 23 by 1979, with the addition of three ministers of state without offices. The creation of new executive departments reduced the importance of bureau secretaries, while increasing the number of those who reported directly to the president.

At the outset of martial law, the Cabinet Coordinating Conference was convened by the executive secretary, and the president routed more than 90 percent of his decrees through it. But by December 1975, the office was abolished, forcing cabinet

---

[128.] Taipei,China avoided the concentration of formulation and implementation for reasons discussed in Chapter two.

officials to carry their proposals directly to Marcos, increasing his control at the expense of increasing his workload.

To instill fear of the regime, official rhetoric announced a campaign against corruption, backed up by the hanging of one Chinese drug dealer. The threat of summary dismissal had the effect of placing the bureaucracy on the alert, corruption was muffled, but the beneficial effects did not last long. Two major purges occurred under the authority of Presidential Decree No. 6 (early in 1973, and again in September 1975). In both cases, the dismissals affected all levels of the administration. Two thousand officials were listed in the September 1975 purge, including cabinet members, the auditor general, and the director of the Bureau of Internal Revenue. However, many of those who were fired were already retired or dead, while others were exonerated and the charges were dropped. Ten months later, many implicated officials were still at their posts. Those who were reinstated had learned to whom they owed their authority. The criteria for the purges appeared to be random, some of the best, some of the worst, and many in between were on the lists. The random character of the hunt for the "notoriously undesirable" encouraged fear and indifference rather than excellence (Cariño 1992). The lesson drawn was that connections mattered more than performance. The regime's credibility fell further when it neglected its promise to follow up on military corruption. But even more deadly to regime credibility was the growing suspicion that the worst offenders were sitting in the president's palace. By 1976, the corruption reached a level that was to surpass all previous experience. Rumors of the president's squeeze on private firms and of corruption at the level of the cabinet removed inhibitions at the lower levels.[129]

A massive increase of government personnel occurred during Marcos's term. Employment in the national government skyrocketed from 427,036 persons in 1971, to 976,489 in 1985 (Sto. Tomas 1994). Reorganization provided greater hiring authority to line organizations, reducing the direct control of the Civil Service

---

[129.] Dozens of interviews with private and public sector representatives cite 1976 as representing a decisive turning point in the level of civil service corruption.

Commission, and allowing high-level officials to hire supporters and build a personalized power base, while bypassing the commission's supervision.[130]

Although Marcos was often criticized for creating a bloated bureaucracy, the numbers alone do not support this accusation. Despite the expansion during his rule, the size of the Philippine bureaucracy is not exceptionally large relative to the nation's population. The wage bill, about 30 percent of government expenditure, is considerably less than averages typical of Latin American countries. The Philippine civil service compares favorably to Singapore in terms of the ratio of civil servants to total population. Nevertheless, the capability for effective policy implementation varies significantly between these two countries. The perception of a bloated bureaucracy is perhaps a reflection of the fact that in the highly politicized Filipino bureaucracy, appointments and functions often arise strictly because of political considerations.[131] The reforms undertaken by Marcos, and later by Aquino, neglected embedding performance-based incentives and evaluations into the system.

Despite the expansion of personnel, increased efficiency did not occur because of ad hoc organizational innovations. The overall structure became functionally incoherent as Marcos created departments without reference to task performance, often duplicating the tasks already assigned. Reporting systems and

---

[130.] In 1961, the government had 361,000 employees, 182,000 employed by the national government. In 1984, there were 1,310,000 employees, 667,000 at the national level (de Guzman et al. 1988, 186).

[131.] President Aquino, who followed Marcos, did not alter the political logic of civil service appointments. She allowed her secretaries to appoint undersecretaries on the basis of personal loyalty, in disregard of proper recruitment procedures. As a result, the problems in 1996 are the same. The politicization of the bureaucracy can be measured in the high percentage of career versus noncareer, permanent versus nonpermanent positions. Permanent appointment holders today constitute 94 percent of the career bureaucracy. Six percent of the career bureaucracy hold temporary appointments, often because they fail to meet the professional requirements for their jobs. The role of political appointees is greatest at the level of senior management. Senior officials are generally not career bureaucrats, which suggests the low stature of careerists as compared to political appointees. Only 46.6 percent hold permanent positions. In the national government, 90 percent of all managers are temporary appointments, so that the bureaucracy is essentially led by appointees who hold office at the pleasure of the political leadership (Sto. Tomas 1994). Most are patronage appointments made independently of any functional or performance-based criteria. This directly affects the capability of the bureaucracy to pursue professional objectives. Another weakness of the system is that the brightest have no incentive to pursue a career at the local government level where salaries are the lowest

lines of communication between ministries were weakened, diminishing accountability. Red tape increased, providing expanded opportunities for graft and side payments. Cumbersome procedures offered ample room for capricious interventions. Overlapping or redundant responsibilities and bottlenecks created many opportunities for political interventions, bribe-taking, favoritism, and lobbying. Anomalies could crop up at any level so that the most routine activities needed the support of a facilitator, the most effective being the president or a member of his family.[132]

Technocratic Cosmetics

Like the other East Asian leaders, Marcos tried to identify his regime with technocratic capability by appointing a number of Western-educated economists who had no political base of their own. These economists were critical for inspiring the confidence of international lenders and for brokering loans from international sources.

But unlike his counterparts in the Republic of Korea, Singapore, and Taipei,China, Marcos did not protect the technocrats from partisan interests. The technocrats were freed from congressional meddling only to be exposed to the more direct wheedling of regime insiders who wanted economic decisions to benefit their particular interests. Since the technocrats had no social constituency, and the regime itself enjoyed little autonomy, officials could count on limited protection from social opposition or the opportunism of regime insiders. Their vulnerability became evident when Executive Secretary Alejandro Melchor was

---

and promotions are unrelated to performance. Political accountability overrides functional accountability to a far greater extent than among the region's high performers.

Until December 1993, the Civil Service Commission, responsible for processing all original appointments and promotions, had incomplete statistics concerning the number employed and the size of the budgets. It did not require departments to establish performance evaluations of employees and lacked an accurate picture of how many vacancies had been filled. The Department of Budget and Management, responsible for authorizing the creation of positions, could not accurately report the number of positions. Government agencies routinely misrepresented their numbers to their administrative supervisors so that figures never tallied. An actual head count was not undertaken until December 1993. Previous statistics were based on estimates and samples.

[132.] One study estimated the country's annual loss to graft or corruption at 10 percent of the gross national product (de Guzman et al. 1988, 197-8).

dismissed in November of 1975 under pressure from Imelda Marcos. Despite the fact that the technocrats were increasingly bypassed, the regime maintained the confidence of the international business community and donors.[133]

The donor organizations hoped the absence of social constraints on policy making would mean more rational policies. They ignored the fact that technocratic policies had only a weak foundation in Filipino politics. Despite the weak coalitional foundation of the technocrats in the broader society, the International Monetary Fund (IMF) relied on the technocrats to promote their economic models. Although not able to surmount the opposition of big business interests to their policies, the technocrats remained players in policy debates, as useful allies of IMF and the World Bank.

In no area was Marcos more disappointing than in freeing decision making from political considerations in order to attain technocratic objectives. In the end, unlike his East Asian counterparts, Marcos did not motivate competence or honesty in the civil service. As a result, the regulatory environment lacked credibility – he had crafted a machine to mete out patronage and collect bribes.

Demoralization occurred after 1975 when it became clear that the president's intention was not to punish graft, but to ensure the loyalty of those in his service. Once their loyalty was ensured, Marcos looked the other way, and allowed his followers to use public office for private enrichment. A bureaucracy that grew according to political patronage criteria was kept weak by the prevalence of political over technical imperatives. Because of the regime's narrow social foundations, policy implementation was not a source of regime legitimacy. This failure is due in large part to the government's need to find a social constituency. Marcos focused on counterbalancing the power of the oligarchs by creating followers. His goal was to place the entire political community in his debt, from the richest oligarch to the poorest village captain.

[133.] Many technocrats took up seats on the boards of the distressed firms taken over by the government — they could draw handsome honoraria (de Dios 1988, 105), thus further compromising their neutrality.

Friends in the Most Unlikely Places

While the proteges of the Marcoses became the richest people in the country (for example, Roberto Benedicto and Eduardo Cojuangco, Jr.), mechanisms to create friends in the most lowly units of local government were also developed with the creation of 42,000 neighborhood organizations (barangays) only three months after declaring martial law. With the intention of breaking up traditional patronage networks that tied the small people to their local oligarchs, the president's local government reforms allowed him to disburse monopoly privileges down to the lowest level of government, providing him with little cronies down to the village level.

For example, in March 1979, President Marcos ordered the barangays to supervise the price of essential consumer goods. "But the barangays were an inappropriate mechanism to control prices because economic interests of many officials who ran grocery stores (sari-sari stores) were affected. Yet, the sari-sari stores were the main target of price controls. This placed the barangay officials in a situation where they had to control themselves, while at the same time they obtained powers to harass their competitors" (Rüland 1986, 26). Between 1977 and 1979, about 5 million pesos were misallocated in the city of Manila alone. When funds were distributed to the barangays before the national elections of 1984, they were generally used, not for development projects, but to buy votes by paying off local leaders who had access to vote blocs. Thus patronage at the local level allowed the president to manipulate even the grassroot political process. The occasional distribution of funds and control over scarce items allowed barangay officials to use their office to acquire and disburse spoils.

The necessity of consent from superior government officials made it difficult for communities to dismiss unsatisfactory barangay captains. Because dismissal was difficult, the population knew they had to come to terms with the appointees. With little threat of being dislodged, once in place these appointees could spin their network of patronage. Longevity in office made it possible for the chiefs to spin lasting webs of influence. The reorganization of local government, thereby, allowed the regime to consolidate its local rule by eliminating the influence of traditional elites and by tying the fortunes of the local captains to those of the regime.[134] But the same reforms had circumvented the possibility of locally based deliberative politics among civicly engaged citizens united by a shared social consensus.

New Clients for a New Society: Creating a Social Base

A Master Sloganeer

In public statements, Marcos knew what both his people and the donors wanted to hear. However, the populist slogans, emphasizing shared growth and an end to the old oligarchs, were rarely backed up by deeds to increase the welfare of the majority. Land reform was proposed, for example, but implementation faltered.[135]

The failure to improve the delivery of government services to the countryside led to the failure of land reform. The challenge of implementing land reform overwhelmed the provincial civil service and the president did not ensure that its capability was adequate to meet the requirements of the job. Moreover, land reform was not a solution by itself – there simply was not enough land to go around (de Dios 1993, 19).[136] A real commitment to rural prosperity needed to be backed up by the development of infrastructure. Instead, large urban, rather than rural, construction projects were given priority, offering large kickbacks to the regime's Manila-based cronies. The failure to develop rural infrastructure was a principle reason for the growth of the income gap under Marcos's leadership, and it is one of the primary causes of different patterns of wealth inequality between the Philippines and Indonesia.

Ultimately, the wobbly commitment to rural development reflected a consistent political rationality. Marcos was faced with the dilemma of establishing political foundations for a regime that

---

[134.] As a further means to consolidate control, a referendum in 1975 gave Marcos the authority to appoint all provincial and local officials whose elective terms expired in December 1973.

[135.] The reform of rice lands, decreed in 1975, exempted holdings of seven hectares and less, thereby excluding 67 percent of the total rice lands (Montes 1992, 43). Although the regime is criticized for ignoring the poor, its land reform program was more extensive than that of any previous Philippine government.

[136.] With rapid population growth, the land frontier had been reached. Thus the land to-the-tiller principle would not help all sections of the rural poor. Moreover, considering

had little actual power. The president needed to create interests that could be tied to the fate of the regime. The government bureaucracy did not have a distinct political orientation, and the military traditionally did not entertain strong political ambitions, so the president looked outside the state to create his own social base. Although the rural poor made up the majority of the population, accommodating their interests would have precipitated a reaction from the landed elites. The president was never confident enough to challenge the landlord classes directly, or the protectionist system that supported large business interests.[137] Export-oriented policies had limited social constituency. Exporters were either heavily subsidized or too small to organize. In general, the peasants, workers, and owners of small businesses were not sufficiently well organized to serve as an adequate support base.

As a result, the regime had to grapple with the need to neutralize or win over the landowners and big urban business interests who were tied to import substitution or natural resource extraction.[138] Since it was the elites who mattered, Marcos decided that instead of pursuing policies to sustain broad-based popular support, the shortest path to finding a social foundation was to create a rival elite. As part of constituency building, Marcos extended citizenship to ethnic Chinese Filipinos. As citizens, the ethnic Chinese were able to play a more open and positive role in the nation's economic life.

An exception in Southeast Asia, the Philippine business class was deeply entrenched and native, with a long tradition of representing their interests through formal organizations.[139] Always cautious, Marcos avoided direct confrontation with this, the region's most outspoken and independent business

---

the government's fiscal resources, land reform could only be achieved through confiscation. Only a major social upheaval would facilitate such a policy.

[137.] Members of the landed classes could be bought out one by one, but the class itself could not be directly challenged.

[138.] A distinction between public and private does little to clarify the Philippine business class, which typically uses the state to enhance private accumulation.

[139.] Because the grip of politicians is always tenuous, Philippine business groups learned to stand on their own. As early as the 1930s, the National Economic Protectionism

community. Therefore, mobilization of mass support against old wealth or wide-scale confiscation was avoided.[140]

The Role of Foreign Credit

Circumventing entrenched interests was not easy. Considerable resources had to be diverted to create an alternative elite. These resources were available in the form of cheap foreign capital, which removed the restraints, allowing the president to build a social base for the regime and thus circumvent resistance from established interests.[141]

Believing that martial law allowed the government to surmount domestic political constraints, the international donors were willing to pour foreign savings into the Philippines. The president's technocratic advisers were adept at telling the donors what they wanted to hear, allowing the president to put basic reform issues on the shelf and still collect funds from foreign sources, without having to worry about developing a broad domestic constituency. From 1974 to 1983, the debt grew at 23.9 percent annually. The rate of foreign financing between 1950 and 1972 was only $326 million from the World Bank, but increased to $2.6 billion between 1972 and 1981 (Montes 1992, 27). The availability of outside funding meant that the president did not have to pursue fundamental reforms. The donors saved the president from making difficult political decisions, such as tax or land reform.

Association advocated the interests of Philippine businesses. A powerful lobby with grassroots organizations up to the city level, it waned as import substitution was phased out, and was replaced by the Philippine Chamber of Commerce and the Philippine Chamber of Industries. These were later merged in the Philippine Chamber of Commerce and Industries. This effective business lobby pursued legislation to increase their control over the domestic market through tariff walls and import controls.

[140.] Only direct political rivals had their wealth confiscated, for example, the Lopezes and Jacintos.

[141.] The state has consistently failed to collect real property taxes from the landlord classes. Landlord domination of the legislature consistently prevented any reliance on landed wealth for taxes. From the early 1950s, until the first Marcos administration in 1968, vested interests in Congress successfully blocked new revenue measures. Government reserves between 1963 and 1966 averaged 10 percent of gross national product (Doronila 1992, 111). Marcos did not have to worry about deriving support from this group or using their resources to run the government. Massive infusions of foreign funds allowed the regime to build support without actually collecting taxes. The international donors were ready to fill in, so that the absence of a constituency did not initially lead to regime failure.

Control Over the Budget

Funds flowed in through the central government over which Marcos retained final budgetary authority. Often the president's ministers could convince him to change expenditure allocations even without consultation with the affected ministries. It became normal practice for the president to require, for example, ministries to attain a 10 percent savings in their current budget. "The funds thereby saved were used for special projects, notably those of the First Lady" (Montes 1992, 33-4).

Privilege

Besides the outright dissemination of funds, the president issued exemptions to favorites. Control of the fiscal system allowed Marcos to develop a system of exemptions for selected concerns. Conflicts over fiscal policy could be resolved by ensuring that affected parties were compensated so their support was assured. Consistent with the regime's narrow political foundations, the president had enough power to hand out exemptions; he could bend the rules although he did not have enough power to challenge vested interests.

An ad hoc committee was designed to hear pleas for exemptions, but the president even circumvented this mechanism, often making decisions independent of the committee. The tariff reform program promoted by IMF was subjected to presidential exemptions. Tariff rates were reduced in accord with IMF guidelines, but numerous decrees exempted specific organizations from customs duties. To maintain donor support, broad macroreforms advocated by the donors were announced, but exemptions helped avoid alienating powerful domestic constituencies. For example, the government's tariff liberalization program called for public hearings before rates were changed. Many firms waited for the public proclamation of the tariff schedules before announcing their objections. The president could then strike a deal with the aggrieved party to amend the promulgated decisions in response to complaints. The result was that tariff reform existed on paper only, satisfying the donors, but the anticipated benefits of a more competitive economy were never experienced.

The greatly expanded level of public spending was used to cement loyalty. Public works contracts, government procurement, industrial incentives, and subsidized credit were funneled to supporters. Graft accounted for only a small part of total accumulation by cronies, more important were the creation of monopolies, direct interventions, and grants of exemptions or exclusive privileges.[142] Direct interventions occurred in food marketing, fertilizer production, labor export, gambling, and pornographic film distribution. Control over the two most important export crops – sugar and coconuts – was given to cronies. Presidential decrees gave tariff and tax exemptions or exclusive rights in a wide range of industries, including livestock, television imports, peroxide, sugar milling equipment, and cigarette filter production. High financial leveraging allowed regime favorites to build business empires and to take financial risks that others would avoid. Thus, both direct interventions and easy credit allowed cronies to move into lucrative areas more easily than competitors.

Government Corporations

Since the public sector was able to attract foreign funds and to control them, the president also created national corporations that did not report financial statements and were not audited. The Philippine National Oil Company is an example. Again political rationality motivated the policy choice. Public corporations were designed to supplant the old business conglomerates with those controlled by the new business elite, therefore they were managed by regime cronies. The public corporations were set up to evade auditing, budgetary, and civil service regulations and were given to friends to run.

Between 1975 and 1981, the number of government corporations increased from 65 (47 parents and 18 subsidiaries) to 212 (92 parents and 129 subsidiaries). In 1975, the national government had 541,640 regular workers (excluding the military) while the corporations employed 94,032. The corporations accounted for 14.8 percent of the combined force. By 1979, 676,525 regular government workers were employed by the government

---

[142.] The Board of Investments reserved certain industries as priorities for rationalization. Members of the martial law coalition were often the principle beneficiaries of the exemptions. "For example, the construction industry incentives were enacted when the company of Rodolfo Cuenca, a Marcos associate, became deeply involved in overseas construction projects" (Montes 1992, 38).

and 132,551 by government corporations. The corporate share increased to 16.4 percent. Salaries for workers in corporations also increased dramatically, from ₱9,479 to ₱13,706, making them 91 percent higher than the salaries of government personnel.[143] This distribution of largess assured the president the loyalty of managers and employees.

Consultation With the Private Sector

A major casualty of the president's strategy of gaining support through the particularistic dissemination of privilege was the consultative process with business. It lost all integrity as direct appeals to the president consistently overturned cabinet decisions. Consultation with the technocrats also suffered, becoming perfunctory. Whereas sector and industrywide representation and participation in decision making was minimal, private self-interested representation was welcome. The dissemination of privilege fostered the need to ensure secrecy, rather than openness. The process was further undermined as decision making became ad hoc. Coordinated consultation with the private sector was aborted, ideas could originate at any stage of the regulatory process from representatives of any group.

Consultation under Marcos was not with the leaders of industry as representatives of their sector, but with individuals as representatives of their firms. This, for example, contrasts sharply with Park's principle of not meeting with private sector leaders as representatives of their firms. Marcos met with individuals, always ready to cut a deal. Thus, consultation was dominated by the need to protect individual interests rather than the need to ensure the general well-being of the private sector. "This protection of individual interests also involved the need for advanced information about government intentions. Again, access to information tended to be individual, based on kinship and other close ties" (Montes 1992, 33). So while Park was attempting to build a general social consensus and to establish that the same rules applied to all, Marcos applied the rules to firms and

---

[143.] Report submitted by the Special Presidential Reorganization Committee to the President of the Philippines, 2 September 1981 (de Guzman et al. 1988).

individuals selectively. The quality of the decision-making process further declined because the press was excluded from knowledge about economic decisions, again in sharp contrast to the Republic of Korea or Taipei,China where economic journalism flourished despite the ban on political dissent.

Since the business community could not trust the president, Marcos had little way of knowing that his policies were failing while causing massive damage. Consider again the contrast with the Republic of Korea where the government targeted exports in consultation with exporters. There, decisions had ultimately to be legitimated by a market test, an export yardstick. Marcos's interventions had no market test and were often not publicly discussed. The more he was cut off, the more he depended on his cronies. Unable to obtain feedback about the success of policies, the president probably could not estimate the depth of discontent and the extent of damage his policies caused.

The Road to Ruin: High Investment for Low Returns

The damage to the economy as a result of martial law was considerable.[144] By 1980, the economy began a tailspin with five consecutive years of negative growth. From 1983 to 1986, per capita income fell 18 percent (Dohner and Intal 1989, 187). Gross domestic savings, as a percentage of gross domestic product, went down from 23.4 in 1971/80, to 16.2 in 1985 (de Dios 1993, 61). Total investment expenditure fell by 50 percent. The shift in credit toward the public sector to support the losses of the two state banks severely constrained opportunities for domestic firms. Because of their implicit government backing, cronies often took excessive risks, and, in the 1980s, due to the worldwide recession, massive amounts of public funds were needed to rescue their operations. These bailouts occurred at a time when international funds were harder to come by.

[144.] "The net effect of these policies on the economy can be summarized in a single figure: the incremental capital-output ratio. In order to raise the annual national output by one dollar, the typical Pacific Asian country had to invest two dollars. Indonesia, hobbled by inefficiency and corruption spent four dollars. India, with worse inefficiency and corruption, has recently been spending six dollars. The Philippines in the early 1980s was spending nine dollars" (Overholt 1986, 1146).

It was only after the bailouts of 1981 that business opposition to the regime became vocal. The preferential treatment meted out to the cronies aroused strong hostility from the traditional interests being crowded out. To make matters worse for noncrony rivals, the government and the cronies also threatened to move into the few remaining lucrative sectors. Still, because traditional businesses often benefited from protection that could be revoked at the president's pleasure, they could not challenge Marcos too overtly. Finally, when the political crisis, triggered by the assassination of Senator Benigno Aquino in 1983, shut off short-term credits and precipitated a severe balance of payments crisis, many business leaders aligned with the opposition to the regime.

To explain the economy's poor performance in the early 1980s, regime officials typically cited the examples of other developing nations. But the ratio of total debt to income in the Philippines was considerably greater than that of its counterparts in the Association of Southeast Asian Nations (ASEAN); it fared poorly even compared to some of the largest Latin American borrowers (de Dios 1988, 83). Many of the regime's problems arose from the need to bail out the firms with close connections to the dictatorship. This suggests that politics – the regime's weak political base – was key to the build-up of unsustainable debt. As the private operations of cronies failed, the government had to take over their assets, along with those of the failed state corporations.[145]

Market forces did not step in to correct the poor choice of investments by cronies. The standard economic assumption that in a market system those with higher valued needs would acquire the assets of less efficient firms did not apply. Private capital would not touch the enterprises of cronies and, as a result, many of the investments ended in receivership by the state banks. Since crony firms arose because of their political connections to the regime, they were not attractive to outsiders who did not have access to the privileges, loans, exemptions, and favorable legal outcomes

---

[145.] "To a significant degree, the higher level of government spending was bound up with the rescue or 'bail-out' of firms with close connections to the dictatorship. Further, from 1981 to 1983, government equity investments (subsidies) in nonfinancial public corporations outstripped the infrastructure share – from 36.3 percent to 46.4 percent of total capital outlay. A common scheme was to pump equity investments as government financial contributions into public corporations. During the period, 13 such corporations averaged 3.8 percent of GNP which were eventually financed through foreign borrowings

that made those firms viable and that determined their ability to compete. Domingo Guevara explains how cronies could drive out their competitors. Guevara claims, Radiowealth, his firm that assembled radios and television sets folded when a crony, Benedicto, was allowed to import, tax free, the same products. Another of Guevara's businesses was driven under because of unfair competition when the government allowed favorites to import finished cars, while Guevara was required to manufacture 50 percent of his car's parts locally. His franchise for the assembly of Volkswagen cars lost its value (Rivera 1994, 173).

Firms owned by cronies qualified for loans because the national government guaranteed the loans, not because the projects were viable or efficient. The loans from international sources were then used to legitimate the businesses because the regime could say the loans demonstrated that the firms were worthy. Foreign banks, because they were assured repayment by the government, had no reason to screen the domestic banks.

The Philippines invested more and grew less than its neighbors. The investment pattern tended to favor capital intensive industries, neglecting the country's comparative advantage in labor intensive activity. Low real interest rates that channeled low cost funds into the hands of favorites encouraged capital intensive industries and methods. The purchasers of capital equipment often benefited from handsome kickbacks paid by suppliers.[146] Overinvoicing and overpayment opportunities led Philippine state firms to buy unique and expensive machines and to misdirect resources toward purchases that expanded opportunities for sidepayments. The acquisition of expensive machinery often poorly reflected the firm's market potential and the nation's comparative advantage. In the end, industrialization did not foster development as these capital-intensive industries generated only limited employment and growth. But most tragic, the costs of failed firms were socialized and were experienced by the entire population.

---

and became part of the country's external debt" (de Dios 1988, 86-7). "By 1984 and 1985, government aid to state owned financial institutions absorbed almost 2 percent of GNP" (Dohner and Intal 1989, 186).

[146.] A nuclear plant built in the Philippines cost three times more than a similar plant built in Pusan in the Republic of Korea by the same firm, Westinghouse.

The regime's outstanding export success was sending labor overseas where construction and contract labor growth boosted the service export share of the economy from 2.5 to 6 percent of the gross domestic product. Philippine factors of production were, in effect, more productive outside than within the country. This encouraged a national loss of confidence.

Moreover, when investment produces limited growth, incentives to save or keep capital in the country are diminished. A comparison of the total inflow of funds with the financing needs for the current account deficit and reserve accumulation indicate an outflow or capital flight of about $3.6 billion from 1971 to 1980, or roughly one third of the increase in total external indebtedness (Dohner and Intal 1989, 172). As the system's vulnerability became apparent, the quick accumulation of wealth dominated long-term investment strategies as cronies realized that a change of regime could jeopardize many of their property rights.[147]

The Donor Puzzle

In the case of the Philippines, the verdict is clear: The era of cheap foreign money allowed the dictatorship to consolidate its rule. The crisis of the dictatorship coincides with the harsher conditions imposed by international lenders, which eroded the regime's independence and its ability to sustain cronyism.

The Philippines ranked high among countries signing standby agreements with IMF – 18 agreements between 1970 and 1984 (de Dios 1988, 116). A number of World Bank projects, such as the Tondo Foreshore Housing project, were conspicuous vehicles of corruption. Crony bailouts were countenanced,

---

[147.] IMF identified the root cause of the Philippine's economic imbalance as the low level of savings and investment. Growth in the Philippines averaged only 1.5 percent, well below the 7 percent regional average. National savings, as a proportion of gross national savings, averaged only 18 percent over the past 7 years — 15 points below the average for Southeast Asia. The IMF representative reported, "The key to explaining disappointing growth performance in the past lies in the behavior of savings and investment". By the logic applied here, another reason can be offered as the cause of low investment in the Philippines. Among countries in the region, it performed lowest according to standards of governance. Critical information was reserved for regime insiders, hence, profits were expatriated rather than saved.

blatantly corrupt activities were sanctioned.[148] Why, then, did the international donors continue to give the regime their seal of good housekeeping throughout the 1970s despite repeated violations of conditionality?

The Marcos regime learned how to appease the World Bank's ideological bias in favor of technocracy and its rigid neoclassical religion that emphasizes macrofundamentals while ignoring the institutional environment. Viewed in terms of macroeconomic variables, the Philippines initially seemed to be doing well. The country's failure to achieve growth was essentially microeconomic. But with the macroeconomists in charge, the banks underestimated the microeconomic elements of resource allocation.

Cronyism as a System

Impersonal market transactions need a system of property rights enforced by neutral third-party referees. If such a neutral contract-enforcing structure exists, parties to an exchange will be indifferent about whom they do business with, providing the same commodity is available at the same price. Martial law compromised the neutrality of those Philippine institutions that supported impersonal exchanges between anonymous trading partners. This interference had a political motivation. To buttress a regime that did not enjoy the support of the nation's elites and lacked power or vision, a broad agenda for change might have been adopted. Instead, political leadership resorted to cronyism by making the executive branch the source of all economic privileges.

Marcos hoped that by concentrating wealth among his followers, he would be able to withstand political opposition, and that by controlling the distribution of assets, he could apply leverage on political opposition. The property rights that ensured the regime's political support, however, ultimately increased the economy's vulnerability to the international recession and debt crisis of the 1980s.

[148.] A number of World Bank projects were in fact also vehicles of corruption of political showcases, such as the so-called "toilet village". "There were many instances when the more `irrational', `inefficient', at times blatantly corrupt, aspects of the dictatorship were countenanced or accommodated by these institutions, particularly its net lending operations and crony bailouts" (de Dios 1988, 121-2).

Cronyism, generally considered to be an extreme form of corruption, is in fact a discrete economic system. It is the allocation of rents to elites according to their loyalty to individuals in power. Clientalism or personal relationships with regime officials determines who benefits from the distribution of these rents. The characteristics of cronyism digress from many of the assumptions, in the economic textbooks used by the donors, about how markets function. To understand why cronyism interferes with an economy's responsiveness to market indicators, making it less capable of change in the face of crisis, consider the full scope of the microeconomic distortions that arise.

The success of the liberal trade and monetary policies, the so-called "Washington consensus" of the 1980s advocated by international donors, rests upon a number of assumptions concerning the stability of property rights. Donor commitment to macroeconomic reforms is based on the economists' assumption that when property rights are clearly specified it should not matter to whom they were originally allocated. In other words, as long as markets exist that allow those who can realize the value of a right most effectively to obtain it from those to whom it was originally allocated, efficiency will result. This assumption allows donors to look the other way when questions of political economy and distribution arise. Structural adjustment packages conducted with delinquent borrowers usually assume that once the macrobarriers to trade are eliminated, the ideal of efficient market allocation will prevail. Only when the transaction costs from the subsequent transfer of the right exceed the potential benefits of its exploitation will the original allocation prevent efficient utilization.

However, this assumption rarely applies to the economies of developing nations. Consider, for example, those economies, of which the Philippines is a classic example, in which cronyism is prevalent. In these economies, leaders use political authority to erect transaction costs to reduce the range of possible exchanges to those groups that will support the leader politically.

Under cronyism, the ruler grants access to property rights in exchange for political loyalty. Open bidding for property rights, a basic presumption of macroeconomic reform, could compromise the system of patronage. Motivated by political considerations, rulers might chose to restrict market access to all but their chosen clients, regardless of considerations of efficiency in allocating and enforcing rights. Transaction costs are deliberately introduced to give economic advantages to groups enjoying political power so that anonymous traders will not trade on the basis of the most favorable price. Instead political connections determine the choice of partners, exchanges, and investments. Political power overrides economic competition to become the coordinating mechanism of the market, as nonprice factors determine the ownership structure of firms and influence the performance of sectors.

One way rulers can constrain market forces is by acquiring control over the judicial system as Marcos did. If the legal system is not distinct from the political system, then contracts may not be enforced. When contract enforcement depends on political will, inefficiencies in the original distribution of property rights will not be corrected. Another method to prejudice the outcome of economic competition, in favor of the ruler's favorites, is to create a capricious regulatory regime complemented by administrative hurdles that require executive intervention to surmount. Marcos also did just this by creating an administrative maze that only he and a couple of close advisers could navigate.

When judicial and administrative obstacles emerge, the risk of contract nonenforcement increases, creating uncertainty that reduces the value of the property rights of those groups that cannot access the ruler's goodwill. When judicial autonomy is compromised, more efficient producers will not risk outbidding the ruler's cronies, allowing the ruler to allocate and enforce rights. This means that under cronyism many economic opportunities or feasible trades will be foregone. Many profitable projects will be driven out.

In the case of the Philippines, an array of tactics to dissuade economic competition were at Marcos's command. Sanctions against the random diffusion of economic rights included denying the original right holder future deals, denying the buyer adjacent rights or essential information, and refusing to buy goods or services from the unwanted interloper. The armory of weapons at the president's hands to discriminate against the winners of market competition are well documented and are exemplified in the proliferation of presidential decrees and letters that endorsed particular interventions on behalf of the president's friends. This included setting exchange, wage, and interest rates; food pricing; and rent controls. Low interest credit granted to favored corporations, and duty and tax exemptions were likewise distributed on the basis of favoritism. The president encouraged entrepreneurs to position themselves for continued government protection so he could control who won. Monopoly and monopsony power was distributed through decrees that gave cronies control over basic commodities, such as coconuts, sugar, rice, wheat, feed grains, tobacco, meat, and fish.[149] In total, 230 firms became dependent on government guarantees, but many of the subsidized firms floundered and had to be bailed out or taken over by the government.

The limits of loyalty-based rights became especially salient after the recession of 1981 when investors did not materialize to bail out the interests of failing cronies. This forced the government to step in to reinforce the regime's economic props at the cost of crowding out noncronies. The economy was sent into a tailspin.

Further problems or inefficiencies with cronyism arise when deals depend on the backing of a particular official. If that official comes under attack, then the contracts of clients will unravel, even if the client has been entirely law abiding.

Thus, the inefficiencies associated with cronyism transcend those associated with corruption. Under cronyism, users with higher valued needs will not buy out the rights of regime insiders who fail. As a result, efficiency-enhancing deals, upon which macroadjustment packages are predicated, will not occur. The inability to trade loyalty-based goods reduces their liquidity. The economic value of such rights declines, while the value of being a crony increases. This explains why properties put on the auction block will not attain their anticipated market value when regimes attempt to privatize without assuring a rule-based system of property rights. In such cases, insiders will dominate the bids because they alone can use political power to defend and nurture their acquisitions.

The need for secrecy under cronyism is another reason such assets underperform. Drawing attention to profits may arouse the ruler's cupidity. Opponents of the regime, especially, must keep

---

[149] Sugar producers were deprived of between P11.6 billion and P14.4 billion from crop years 1974 to 1983. Coconut farmers were paid 9 to 15 percent less by the United Coconut Mills, the private milling and marketing company controlled by Eduardo Cojuangco, the holder of a monopsony in copra purchasing (de Dios 1988).

their assets hidden. Not being able to capitalize effectively on their assets reduces liquidity, thereby reducing the number of property rights that can be openly traded. Thus cronyism reduces liquidity of the economy.

Cronyism has additional drawbacks, which do not figure in standard economic calculations. It enjoins the ruler to become the biggest crony – the wealthiest and biggest capitalist in the country. But when the ruler is the biggest investor, other investors will be reluctant to come forward.[150]

While recipients of the ruler's goodwill may have to make contributions to the ruler's re-election, or offer shares to family members of the ruler, their obligation inevitably goes beyond mere payoffs. They must become stalwart supporters of the regime for they know that political defeat may lead to a redistribution of property rights and the confiscation of their gains. In other words, they must support the regime to the death, whether it is right or wrong. This heightens the stakes of political competition. Recalcitrance dominates relations with the outside, moderation becomes less feasible as defeat may mean the redistribution of assets or even death. Again the Philippines' case bears this cycle out. Within the region during this period, violent opposition to the ruling regime increased only in the Philippines. Revolutionary opposition intensified as the regime continued to violate the human rights of its opponents far longer than its neighbors in East Asia. The murder of principal opponent Aquino exemplifies the high stakes implied by a possible regime change.

When regime opponents have lost their property as a result of political rivalry, the expectation of renewed confiscation when power again changes hands means parties will dig in and fight it out to the death rather than allow regime change to place their wealth at risk. Because a challenge to the status quo implies a possible redistribution of property rights, moderation toward dissent will seem too risky. Thus, under cronyism, political dissent is likely to seem more dangerous and will be more severely

---

[150.] "Former President Marcos was probably the biggest capitalist in the country before his overthrow, in the sense that he held large shares in a number of major companies through dummies and investment companies . . . He is alleged to have obtained most of these shares through extortion or as payment from the companies that benefited from his favors" (Kunio 1988, 70).

punished than when property rights are allocated by impersonal market forces.

Ultimately, cronyism produces political instability. To get access to rents produced by property rights, excluded groups must focus on gaining political power. This explains why the Philippine business community welcomed the opposition after 1983. Since it was necessary to be a member of the martial law coalition to enjoy property rights fully, the opposition ultimately had to overthrow the government to gain access to the economic rents it was denied.

Thus numerous reasons exist for why corruption and cronyism are not the same and have different consequences for the economy. Ignoring political variables, economic forecasts rarely predict the full range of economic uncertainty that exists under cronyism. Standard economic analysis was powerless to anticipate the full impact of political risks on economic outcomes in the Philippines.[151]

The Same, Again . . . And Again

Autonomous systems, such as the economy or the administrative bureaucracy, depend on the validation of mutually subscribed laws among the citizenry. Marcos came to power in a society in which societywide processes did not enjoy societywide approval or agreement. Parochial norms prevailed. Societywide processes, such as law and the macroeconomy, were captured by private interests under the congressional system that Marcos overturned. As a result, Philippine society lacked a consensually validated mission. Reciprocal recognition among social actors was undermined by the vast inequality of conditions. With the possibility of collective self-realization denied, competing interests lacked any overarching ethical community. The result was a disparate plurality of antagonistic interests. Philippine society had

---

[151.] Cronyism as an economic system also can help to explain the performance of Indonesia's economy. In addition to family members, Indonesia's major capitalists depend on close relations with President Suharto. Liem Sioe Liong obtained a number of monopolies and government privileges that allowed him to build the country's biggest business empire that included steel, real estate, cement, cars, and trading. Bob Hasan built his empire in shipping, manufacturing, trading, and construction from a logging concession he obtained from the president (Kunio 1988, 72).

no secular institution that could generate a consensus about goals that transcended the competition of individual interests.

The abolition of Congress did not bestow upon government "an almost absolute power in the field of economic development" (Bello et al. 1982, 27), as the champions of authoritarianism had hoped. Its replacement by one man's personal domination over the legal, administrative, and economic systems made the formulation of socially validated political objectives impossible. Existing institutions lost their normative justification. When the law becomes subservient to a single individual's ambitions, and functions as a justification of that individual's or group's seizure of power, it has no normative justification.

Thus, martial law did not create a social order based on communally shared ethical assumptions. Instead massive skepticism was encouraged about the legitimacy of any social action. Many critics say that the personalized and particularistic political traditions of the Philippines were beyond any leader's or government's capability to transform. Nevertheless, similarly personalistic systems were transformed by institution building in other East Asian nations. In none of East Asia's successful transformations do we find leadership that encouraged growth by wrecking social institutions in order for all social action to depend on the political will of the leader. In Hong Kong, Malaysia, the Republic of Korea, Singapore, and Taipei,China, leadership created institutions and administrative capability that could carry out the objectives of policy independently of the leader's personal action. As a result of the failure to create effective institutions that ensure bureaucratic capability, the Philippines remains the land of great slogans.

Land, electoral, tax, and administrative reforms were all on the table when Marcos came to power, and they remain there. Time and time again the perennial issues become the subject of legislation that is never fully implemented, like the president's land and administrative reform projects. Ideas rage like sudden brush fires. Filipinos have an expression for it, *ningas kugon* – much flame, but quick to fizzle out.

Indeed, the fundamental inequality of conditions undermines social consensus making it difficult for the Philippines to repeat the success of Japan, the Republic of Korea, or Taipei,China. However, the Marcos years have led Filipinos to agree on one thing: Social consensus must be found in a functioning pluralism, making the country's development particularly complex. Political progress will be necessary to facilitate economic order. The idea that political liberty can wait for economic growth cannot apply to the Philippines. Here donors and government must work twice as hard. Economic development will require simultaneous political development.

Marcos's experiment with constitutional authoritarianism is often viewed as a departure from the country's democratic traditions, but it was not a departure from the country's patrimonial traditions. The Marcos regime can be viewed as the summit of those traditions. The same highly personalized style of politics that undermined the efficiency of Philippine democracy, ultimately undermined the efficiency of Philippine authoritarianism. That failure underscores that a nation's governance capabilities are independent of regime type. A highly personalized autocracy will function as poorly as a highly personalized democracy. A failure to develop institutions that channel social goals into collective capabilities will undermine any regime, either democratic or authoritarian. While many draw the lesson from the Marcos experience that authoritarianism does not improve policy performance, the Philippines' case suggests a broader message: That the fundamentals of good governance may be independent of regime type. When a government's relationship with society is based on patron-client relations rather than measurable performance, social cohesion and good governance will be paralyzed, regardless of what type of regime is selected. The course for future donor action in the Philippines is clear. Donors must directly support political development if they hope to see stable economic growth.

CHAPTER NINE

THE STATE'S ROLE
IN EAST ASIAN DEVELOPMENT

Hilton L. Root and Barry R. Weingast

In the conventional "neoclassical" view of the state and economic development, two types of government exist – strong and weak – with the latter usually given better grades for promoting economic performance (Klitgaard 1991). Strong governments, we are told, generally choose interventionist strategies for development. In Latin America, these are associated with populism, import substitution, regulatory manipulation of markets, and substantial and, typically, unsustainable redistributive goals (see Dornbusch and Edwards 1991).

Alternatively, the neoclassical view champions weak governments that foster growth by leaving markets alone. The minimalist state is touted for doing no more than providing a stable macroeconomic environment and a strong legal system, enforcing a system of private property rights and contract law. In this conventional language, *strong* versus *weak* inadequately explains a government's ability to foster or hinder economic development in East Asia. In this region, strong, not weak, states enabled the private sector to make a major contribution to growth.[152] Moreover, strong states attracted the highest level of foreign investment.

These observations challenge the conventional view. Recent assessments of the positive contributions of activist governments in East Asia to economic growth advocate the need for a strong state if economic development is to be achieved (see Campos, Levi, and Sherman 1994; Johnson 1982; Wade 1990a, 1990b; Evans 1992). How are we to reconcile the conventional view of a strong state as an obstacle to economic development, with the revisionist's advocacy of state activism?

Weak Governments

The inability to enforce property rights, or even many of its own laws, handicaps a weak government. Because of the legal inadequacy of a weak state, its interventions are based, not on rules, but on administrative or executive discretion; this results in corruption and opportunism rather than supervision. In fact, insufficient legal clarity is often intentional, thus facilitating random interventions by political authorities.

Although weak states respond to interest groups, they often cannot enforce bargains made with important constituents. Interventionist rules typically cannot be consistently enforced. As a result, reform measures, property rights, and contracts are not durable because the state lacks the means to implement and maintain them.

When states are too weak to control their own officials, agents of the state may act independently of one another. Thus, a policy of reform may be announced by part of the government, while another part blocks its implementation. The inability to enforce rules reduces private business activity unless some important actor of the state, such as the president's family or inner circle, intervenes (for example, Indonesia under Suharto or the Philippines under Marcos). Political power is needed to defend property rights when the impartiality of the legal system is jeopardized or when the rules are themselves inadequate.

[152.] The region's weakest states, Indonesia and the Philippines, were the region's poorest economic performers.

Bureaucrats in a weak state learn to use their power and access to information to extract value from proposed economic activity rather than to promote that activity. With corruption flourishing at all levels of government (Shleifer and Vishny 1993), the deal-making authority of leadership becomes essential.

Not being able to enforce the minimal conditions that are necessary to maintain markets, such as private property rights or a given set of regulations, weak governments can rarely sustain competitive markets. Instead networks of individuals with special connections to the political regime are needed to sustain trade. Inevitably, officials of weak governments are likely to collude with select, but powerful, private groups to extract the nation's resources. A weak state easily becomes a predatory state.

Strong and Unlimited Governments

In contrast to weak governments, strong and unlimited governments have too much power. Lacking constitutionally defined limits, they are likely to be both interventionist and confiscatory. Being able to alter rights and markets at will, they are incapable of making a credible commitment to private sector development. To induce participation in markets, they must offer protection in the form of monopoly rights, trade protection, or guild or trade-union privileges. The exercise of unlimited political discretion allows them to promise excessive benefits to one group to win their support. This, in turn, creates political risk, reducing economic investments and undermining the possible outcomes of reforms. The irony is that due to their unlimited power, no contract with the government or of interest to the government is secure. A strong but unlimited state has much in common with a weak state: both are likely to become predators of private sector wealth.

Strong but Limited Governments

The third type of state is not only strong enough to establish and maintain property rights, but is constitutionally prevented from violating these rights. This state must have an administrative structure that keeps the economic and political activities of regime officials separate. The state must not only be strong enough to adopt rules that are suited to sustaining a strong, competitive private sector, but it must also be strong enough to prevent itself from responding to the inevitable political forces that arise to monopolize access to the marketplace. Only this type of state will ensure the survival of open markets with competitive access.

Strong but limited states have often been mistakenly referred to as minimal states because, in comparison with the interventionist state, they directly provide a relatively small number of goods and services. But the term *minimal* gives the impression of weakness, which is inappropriate. These states must instead be strong enough to withstand the inevitable political pressure on government to intervene in markets. Hong Kong is perhaps a perfect example of such a state in which "positive noninterventionism" protects the market from pressure groups, rent seekers, and unscrupulous officials. Japan, the Republic of Korea, Singapore, and Taipei,China are all examples of states that accepted limits on their discretion over private sector profits. All adopted mechanisms to separate the political and economic functions of government, and protected property rights and the right for private parties to contract. These regimes did not have to be paragons of political development. To attract the energy or capital necessary for economic growth, they only had to be more effective in sustaining markets than the majority of developing nations.

Implications

Distinguishing strong but limited government from the conventional perspective that identifies only weak and strong government helps us to make sense of the advantages of each, and the contradictions between them. In the conventional view, the two types of strong states are not distinguished. A state that carries out and maintains massive interventionist policies, such as import substitution or the subsidization of a highly unionized urban workforce, is confused with a strong but limited state that plays a neutral role in the allocation of rents and subsidies. As a result, strong but limited states are able to foster equitable growth, while strong but unlimited states often promote social and regional inequality. More importantly, champions of the strong state rarely identify the attributes of the state that are essential to protect markets. As noted earlier, both strong unlimited and weak states are prone to plunder the markets. What conventional wisdom calls a *weak* state is not weak in the sense above, but rather a strong state that can maintain the market, providing the necessary public goods while resisting capture by interest groups.[153] In varying ways, the successful Asian regimes can be distinguished from many of the developing world's economically less successful regimes because they possessed strong but limited states.

The challenge to the conventional wisdom launched by the new champions of state activism (Robert Wade, Alice Amsden) also fails to distinguish between the two types of strong states. While they raise reasonable doubts about the earlier neoclassical view, they do not explain why some strong states promote economic development while others pursue policies hindering it. After all, the majority of countries that pursued the activist policies they advocate experienced negative growth along with exacerbated social inequality. Even if we take the arguments of the new statists' findings at face value – that these states have made a direct and significant contribution to economic growth – they have done no more than show that this role for the state is feasible, something long known.

But why have some strong states promoted growth rather than other political goals? The conventional view offers little help. By contrast, the example of East Asia's successful regimes suggests that states are strong when critical and durable limits channel government behavior into activities compatible with economic development.

Achieving Strong But Limited Government

The development of strong but limited government depends on the existence of institutions that make it in the interests of political officials to abide by limits on their power. In many reform environments, the desire to create strong but limited government often drives leadership to increase the executive's discretionary power. Both Gorbachev, in the former Soviet Union, and Yeltsin,

---

153. Capture theory is a theory of regulation where an industry that is regulated can benefit from its regulation by "capturing" or gaining control of the regulatory agency involved. This can occur because of political influence; superior technical knowledge that forces the regulatory agency to depend on the industry; appointees being selected from the regulatory industry or the possibility of future positions in the industry, and the agency's need for recognition and informal cooperation from the industry. So too, interest groups can "capture" a government or state.

in Russia, took this approach. Many in Latin America seem also attracted to it. Reform by mechanisms, such as presidential decree, is a two-edged sword, however. On the benefit side, the reform-minded leader gains the power to design and implement a reform package, eliminating many of the natural veto points blocking reform. On the cost side, all such reform programs can also be undone by decree and hence they are only as good as the paper they are written on.

One task of economic reform must also be to place reform on a more durable foundation by making it costly for political authority to renege on promises once made. As the American federalists realized, durability cannot depend upon altruism. No government should expect public service to attract only god-like figures who always serve the public first before serving their family or friends. Institutions must be designed so that political actors have incentives to maintain and preserve the system, while carefully delineating where their power to intervene in private economic activity begins.

A government's commitment to market-led growth requires the design of appropriate government institutions that ensure clear boundaries between the private and public, and that protect both property rights and agreements with the business sector. The assurances that such boundaries are in place will expand the investment horizons of investors so that sustained long-term growth can begin.

CHAPTER TEN

THE SEARCH FOR GOOD GOVERNANCE

"I know what time is," said Augustine of Hippo (5th century AD) "but if you ask me, I cannot tell you." Good governance, a much sought after precious commodity, similarly evades definition. It arouses the sharpest disagreements and inspires the greatest introspection. Social welfare depends upon it, yet no one agrees on its definition. Some nations believe it to be too subjective to be discussed with outsiders. Other governments believe it to be too volatile a topic to be discussed even among citizens. Some governments are willing to discuss governance, providing the word is not mentioned in the discussion. Some assume their own experience provides the universal thread, while others believe their case is unique, its evolution impenetrable from the outside. Yet today it is obvious that beliefs and assumptions must be put aside and a dialogue opened, as progress toward world development clearly hinges on progress in good governance.

The definition of good governance is intellectually complex. It must give equal account to the particular and the universal. The abstract and the concrete must be blended. Leadership must be balanced by institutions. Accountability by autonomy. Transparency by respect for the proprietary nature of information. Democracy by meritocracy.

Governance is also politically sensitive. The most normative of all development concerns, governance rarely figures in the dialogue of donors with borrowers or in the concepts of economists who mediate much of that dialogue. The development banks do not support a full-time staff who specialize on the topic, yet all have policy papers documenting that governance is essential.[154]

Although development cannot exist without good governance, economic theory offers no easy measure. Economists know more about how to distinguish good from bad policy, than about what distinguishes well administered from poorly administered policy. Although they have reached a consensus on the essential macroeconomic fundamentals, exactly how these are to be implemented is a quite different matter. In fact, economics as a discipline may be poorly equipped to advise on governance. Whereas the strength of economics is what it owes to science, governance is a time-honored craft, its practice owes much to judgement and wisdom.

So far, most proselytizing about governance takes place among international organizations dominated by the experience of the donors, most of whom are Western nations. Japan was the only Asian nation to participate in the pronouncement of the Development Assistance Committee of the Organisation for Economic Co-operation and Development (see OECD 1995). In this document, no reference was made to the recent experience of contemporary Asia, but many statements elevated the Western path to be the universal prototype of development. The inability to distinguish between regime type and good governance reduces the document's applicability to Asia where good governance thrives amidst political diversity. Excellent examples of economic development supported by good governance in which regime construction diverges greatly from Western models can be found in the recent history of East Asia.

What do we know now, after undertaking a study of the East Asian experience, that Max Weber did not know? The most universally admired sociologist did not anticipate the capitalist development of East Asia, so hopefully this study will offer some fresh insights, while defining some parameters that persist despite particulars.

[154.] However, until recently governance has been beyond the usual range of prescriptions that characterize the dialogue between governments and their constituencies, and donors with developing nations.

The Lessons

First, we have learned that good governance is not synonymous with good policy. The ability to formulate appropriate policies is essential, but good governance implies a further step. It refers to the ability of a government to deliver what it promises, to implement the policies it chooses. The existence of good policies does not ensure that the government has the capability to carry out what has been proposed.

Good governance is not synonymous with good institutional design. The charters of national development banks are similar throughout the world. Some work well, while others function as the exclusive reserve of regime cronies. The Nigerian constitution mimics that of the United States. Good design is necessary, but not sufficient.

A distinction between the process and outcome of policy making is critical. The process, rules, and mechanisms of policy making should be predictable, although the policies may vary according to circumstances. Thus, stable processes, unstable outcomes.

Good governance does not imply expanded state economic intervention. As exemplified by Hong Kong, strong and effective government is essential to maintain a liberal trade regime.

A standard definition of an apolitical bureaucracy includes the notion that policy formulation is the job of elected officials and implementation the function of career bureaucrats. The experience of East Asia, however, suggests the need to modify this definition. It is both unrealistic and does not identify the damaging effects of politicization on policy outcomes and government performance. Although continuous close contact between politicians and administrators violates the strict definition of an apolitical bureaucracy, civil service influence in policy making should not be confused with politicization. In most developing countries, a complete separation of political and administrative spheres is not practical. Administrators often play a large role in the decision-making process because of the general shortage of expertise in civil society.[155] Consider the contrast of Malaysia and Singapore with the Philippines. Malaysia and Singapore experience considerable bureaucratic input into policy formulation, yet politicization of the bureaucracy has not led to significant distortion of economic policy making. Whereas the Philippines, reputed to have the most politicized bureaucracy of the countries in this sample, has the lowest level of civil service input in policy making. The comparison suggests that the sources of politicization most detrimental to administrative neutrality in developing countries are political intervention in recruitment and promotion, and manipulation of bureaucratic budgets for private advantage.

The relative autonomy of the state from interest group pressures does little to explain the variance in national economic performance. Economic interest groups are not by themselves harmful to prospects for growth. Business groups can also be the motivation for changes that improve national productivity. A more important key to the introduction of economic policy reform is the construction of mechanisms for effective communication between the state and private sector. Appropriate consultative mechanisms that integrate the business community into the policy process contributes more than insulation to successful economic transformations.

A fundamental difference exists between development based on political will and state power, and that based on institution building. As the contrast between the Philippines and Indonesia, and the other countries in the study suggests – the latter is sustainable while the former is not.

Paternalistic and hierarchical social traditions prompt the chief executive in most developing countries to become personally active in the decision making of collaborating officials and agencies. By contrast, the most successful East Asian rulers endowed their governments with a core of neutral competency. They designed organizations to function on a universalistic, rather

---

[155.] In Western views of democracy, the roles of politicians and civil servants are sharply delineated. The politicians chosen by the people formulate the policies, the bureaucracy implements. The inadequacy of this traditional dichotomy of politics and administration has been recognized by many students of development (Sayre 1964, 224).

than particularistic, criteria that utilized rule-bound, rather than discretionary, methods for conducting government business. Precedents and rules were introduced that replaced favoritism with merit and that supplanted personal preferences with impersonal codes as a prescription for behavior. In essence, they designed institutions to substitute merit and neutrality for patronage and dependency, so that government would be more responsive to general interests.

The sphere of neutral bureaucratic competency cannot be created entirely on the basis of formal rules. No amount of formalization will protect bureaucratic autonomy if top leadership will not gain political benefits as an outcome of stable economic policies. Therefore institutional design by itself does not explain bureaucratic performance.

In East Asia, the need to establish broad coalitional foundations was the motivation for leadership to create mechanisms for the technocratic formulation of policy. The institutions to ensure technocratic neutrality worked when top political leadership derived key coalitional support from economic policies that provided broad-based economic growth (Campos and Root 1996). Political motivation to enforce neutrality is critical. A political system featuring economic patrimonialism did not lead to gross inequality and inefficiency in Malaysia because political competition was based on being able to deliver equitably distributed growth. Indonesia's Suharto defended his technocratic team to assure international donors of a stable macroeconomic policy framework, while fighting the spread of communism at home. Chang Kai Shek, in Taipei,China, courted the support of the native Taiwanese by providing economic opportunities based on growth. The Republic of Korea's General Park had to demonstrate the effectiveness of a noncommunist path to industrialization and military security. Lee Kuan Yew had to ensure Singapore's economic viability despite international skepticism and the imminent danger of communist insurrection.

Thus in each case, external motivations derived from the need to build broad coalitional foundations for regime survival, explain the commitment of regime leaders to neutral economic policy making. In each case, civil service neutrality was politically valued because the alternative, a dysfunctional bureaucracy, could impair business confidence. Lack of business confidence would undermine the government's ability to sustain growth, which in turn could cause the collapse of the ruling coalition. By contrast, despite a constitution that guaranteed the integrity of the civil service, neutral competency did not emerge in the Philippines, instead political leaders routinely intervened behind the scenes in ad hoc ways to aid particular clients. Protected from left-wing contestation, leadership in the Philippines made its bid for coalitional support by catering to a narrow elite whose parochial concerns provided little motivation for top political leaders to defend the technocratic basis of economic policy making. In short, economic policy making cannot be protected from political opportunism merely through the erection of formal structures: external political motives will determine whether those structures work and if they will be created at all (Qian and Weingast 1995).

This study also suggests the value of an analytical framework that views improvements in organizational and institutional arrangements as a source of productivity increase. Growth theory normally assumes an accounting formula where productivity increase is sought mostly in the introduction of new technology. The governance perspective offers an alternative viewpoint of economic development in which institutional arrangements directly influence the productive capacity of an economy. As institutional framework can increase the gains to knowledge and information acquired through learning so that dependence on the personal will of a strong leader is minimized. Once acquired, institutional capacity can help government play a catalytic role in the promotion and coordination of social objectives, both growth and equity.

The Ingredients of Economic Policy Successfully Applied:

Structural Adjustment and Good Governance

Beginning in the early 1980s, the World Bank undertook worldwide structural adjustment lending in a wide range of borrowing countries that had acquired unsustainable debts. Generally introduced to prevent a balance of payments crisis, structural adjustment involved a set of medium-term policy and institutional reform packages, including the opening of trade and exchange rates, reducing domestic regulation, improving public sector efficiency, and increasing the efficiency of the mobilization of domestic resources through the rationalization of expenditures.[156] These reforms promised to restore macroeconomic balance and improve microeconomic efficiency in countries where debts became unsustainable. The adjustment packages were often initiated to prevent the threat of foreign exchange shortage considered by many macroeconomists to be the most critical constraint on growth.

The reform packages were viewed as appropriate and noncontroversial methods to overcome unsustainable debts attributed to interventionist industrial policies. Underlying the adjustments was the hope that once distorted microeconomic incentives resulting from intervention were eliminated, the price system would function more effectively. The reforms prioritized "getting the prices right" so that investors would receive accurate information with which to assess scarcity. The expected outcomes of the adjustment exercises were investment and technological advances made in response to market signals by individual economic agents. Unfortunately, the anticipated investment did not occur in a number of the countries that undertook adjustment.

Political Feasibility

Among the underlying reasons why structural adjustment failed to produce the anticipated results is the absence of both political feasibility and governmental capacity. The absence of political feasibility has many components. The failure to gain support through broad participation in the negotiations is one difficulty that can often be addressed by making the policy dialogue more effective.

An understanding of the political foundations of most developing countries is critical to explanations of the political vulnerability of the adjustment packages. Interventionist policies were welcomed by postindependence governments as ways to consolidate political support. Expanding the state's economic role provided the government with resources to reward followers.

[156.] Structural adjustment often had to be combined with short-term macroeconomic stabilization, a combination of fiscal, monetary, and exchange rate policies, which in many cases had already weakened support for the government by mobilizing interest groups. Stabilization comes first as a way to reduce high inflation, escalating fiscal deficits, and widening the balance of payments deficits. Stabilization provides the foundation for growth, adjustment provides the impetus.

While rewards could take many forms, the availability of discriminatory legislation, tariff protection, price supports, and direct fiscal and financial transfers all encouraged rent seeking and favoritism. The resulting patronage, nepotism, and corruption allowed the state to be captured by narrow, private interest groups. Once captured, governments were unable to deliver policies that benefited the entire population. The problem was not simply excessive budgetary deficits; public goods were provided without any concern for equity or growth. Capture by interest groups made the governments' ultimate stability suspect, which in turn reduced the investment horizons of would-be investors. Governmental change often meant a reversal of property rights. Under conditions of political instability, short-term investments with quick returns that could easily be exported were preferred to long-term commitments that could be held hostage when governments changed. If the underlying cause of instability – the absence of broad coalitional support for government – is not addressed, structural adjustment does little to alter the calculations of investors.

Imposing structural reform can be deceivingly simple. Trade and exchange rate policies can be changed by an executive decree that affects one or two government ministries.[157] Such decrees, the outcome of agreements between the multilateral donors and the borrowing country, were often negotiated behind-the-scenes with little participation of the parties that would be affected by the changes. Although simple to enact, the reforms are difficult to sustain. Imposed by administrative fiat, structural adjustment could just as easily be overturned.

One reason adjustment programs lacked political feasibility is that they entailed sacrifices from groups not generally included in the negotiations. The first wave of reform packages were conducted without the participation of opposition groups, often without effort to inform the press, parliament, labor unions, or other potential sources of opposition. The groups affected often learned about the adjustment after the programs were signed and

---

[157] Some elements of adjustment packages, such as privatization, are administratively complex, requiring cooperation of several government agencies, labor unions, parliaments, and even the judicial system.

delivered, making the governments politically vulnerable once the consequences became visible. Often opposition took time to materialize as the effects of the reforms were not immediately apparent. More open negotiation would not reduce the underlying causes of opposition but could help identify possible means to reduce friction. The groups that stand to lose from restructuring are likely to offer organized resistance, nevertheless, appropriate compensation for losers, safety nets, sequencing, and coalition building can always be improved through more effective dialogue (Nelson 1989).

The vulnerability of the packages cannot be correlated to the types of regimes that undertook the reforms. In fact, many countries subjected to adjustment lack mechanisms by which economic policy can be opened to dialogue. The existence of mechanisms to promote policy dialogue with constituent groups does not correlate with regime type. In this regard, democratic developing countries tend to be no different than nondemocratic regimes. Parliaments of young democracies often have limited capacity to analyze policy content. Governments dependant on particularistic relations with interest groups generally lack mechanisms for broad participation in sector or economywide decision making regardless of whether they are classified as democracies. By contrast, East Asia's high performing economies exemplify the role of institutions for effective policy dialogue. Leadership typically constructed mechanisms to bargain with representatives of those functionally relevant groups whose consensus would be necessary for economic policy to succeed. Policy acceptance attained through institutionalized dialogue reduces the need for coercion in implementation.

Another factor that played a major role in determining the sustainability of adjustment packages was the degree of income inequality. During adjustment, countries that suffer from severe income inequality – real or perceived – often experience political polarization. Adjustment packages become contestable on charges of intensifying perceived inequalities. Income inequality heightens the danger of violent social reaction prompting the application of coercion to enforce the bargain, which in turn may jeopardize government legitimacy. Here again East Asia has important lessons to convey. The high performing East Asian economies grew while adhering to policies that reduced income inequality during growth. As a result, policy innovations, and macroadjustments, in particular, were less likely to result in social polarization. Even more important is that because of shared growth governments did not need structural adjustment in the first place, because they had not acquired unsustainable debts by buying the political support of narrow interest groups. Debts were linked to national development programs that had broad constituencies so that resources were not dissipated in satisfying narrow, but well organized, groups. The regime's ability to promote well-rounded growth provided the legitimacy needed to surmount the rise of such groups.

Political vulnerability of adjustment packages, then, is due both to the manner in which the packages are negotiated and the degree of social polarization that precedes the negotiations. When it is perceived that some groups will benefit more than others, the reforms become politically contestable. In an unstable political environment, investors understand that what was enacted by administrative fiat can easily be overturned. Aware that the reform bargains often lack extensive social, or even political, support, investors hesitate. In fact, the hesitation was often justified because a number of the governments that undertook adjustment were overturned.

In effect, governments that suffered unsustainable debts also suffered from political risk. Adjustment packages rarely addressed the causes of political risk. Moreover, the packages addressed only the choice of economic policy while neglecting the government's ability to implement those promises.

Capacity to Implement Reforms

The second reason adjustment falters is the absence of state capacity. Governments often lack the administrative capability to enforce reform packages in a fair and consistent manner. In cases where the bureaucracy was known to be corrupt before adjustment, the expectation was that adjustment would be circumvented. A number of examples will illustrate the expectations. Governments may have agreed to across-the-board reduction of import barriers but then exempted some favored firms from reductions. Divestiture of publicly owned firms might benefit regime insiders, thus nullifying the expectation of competition. Increased tax rates can be selectively collected. Permits and licensing requirements can be moved to different levels of administration rather than eliminated. Regional licensing authorities can emerge to do what national authorities once did. Rationalized expenditure and investment programs can be monitored by regime supporters, thus nullifying the intended neutrality of the adjustments. The reform packages can be negotiated by technocrats who have limited social or political support.

Where public administrative capacity was weak and where professional neutrality was lacking, adjustment did little to supplant the sources of weakness. Typically, governments could not effectively carry out the reforms, even after agreeing to the reform packages. Implementation might fail because bureaucracies lacked autonomy from interest groups, agencies lacked oversight, and judicial systems had no autonomy from political power. In other words, poor governance distorted the outcomes of adjustment just as the outcomes of government economic intervention were distorted by poor management. When structural adjustment does not correct failures caused by unsound development management, the adjustments fail for the same reason the original interventions fail. When either political feasibility and governmental capability are lacking, adjustment packages lack credibility and groups react by defending the status quo.

Promises, Promises, Promises

The East Asian case demonstrates that market friendly approaches are as dependent on state capacity as are the policies they purport to replace. Governments that are unable to deliver policy neutrality will fail to benefit from undertaking structural adjustment for the same reason they failed to implement state-led strategies effectively. The laissez-faire model, upon which structural adjustment is predicated requires a state that can provide political and procedural predictability on the basis of legal and administrative autonomy from interest groups. When neutrality, consistency, and accountability in the public sector is lacking, even after the adaptation of the liberal reform packages, infrastructure, human capital, and technological and managerial capabilities will not receive adequate investment from the private sector. Adjustment packages fail when governments lack the credibility to persuade the private sector that the packages will not ultimately be reversed due to political uncertainty.

Expectations generated by perceptions of government capability are a key to the success of economic policy. Policies designed to promote economic development are in effect promises. The benefits will be seen down the road but the costs are often up front. If the necessary ingredients to fulfill that promise are lacking, then economic actors, either groups or individuals, will wisely not anticipate success and will behave in ways that are likely to undermine the intended outcome. In East Asia, governments signaled their commitment to growth through a wide range of commitment mechanisms that included communication devices based on councils and the maintenance of bureaucratic integrity. When business anticipates capricious or biased behavior by government, it will not invest. Labor will not accept sacrifice and discipline. Families will not invest their time and money to educate their children. Populations in developing countries have heard many promises. Without attention to the quality and capacity of government, structural adjustment packages are just more of the same.

Governability and the Legitimacy of Government:
Why Shared Growth Matters

One unique feature of East Asian development is that in contrast with other documented cases of economic growth, East Asia has experienced relatively low levels of income inequality. Moreover, wealth was most equally divided in the countries that grew the fastest.

In preindustrial Europe, it was perhaps possible to have growth without equity. But the legacy of Karl Marx has made any such pattern politically unsustainable. Communism's historic mission was to make development without equity an anachronism. Today, unequitable growth presents political dilemmas that are probably insurmountable. Conversely, sustainable growth cannot benefit one ethnic group in the same polity at the expense of others. The example of Malaysia has demonstrated that until ethnic quarrels are resolved, high-level development must wait.

Income distribution does matter. When inequality is too high, governments must concentrate on distributive issues rather than general social welfare. Income equality allows leaders the space to pursue policies that are economically rational and distributionally neutral. When equity is absent, growth may invite destabilizing political conflicts, as often occurs in Latin America. Philippine President Fidel Ramos stated the connection very bluntly during the 10th anniversary of the Edsa Revolution that overthrew Marcos. "We may undergo revolution again and again if we do not strengthen our country economically, if we do not manage growth so that it will bring social justice and better lives to the poor." The president warned that upheaval will occur if social inequality is not reduced (Mesina and Lacson 1996).

Today, the distributive consequences of public policies often determine the success or failure of strategies and the tactics for reform. Policies that seem to have a negative impact on the welfare of the many have little chance of being sustained. The rub is that initial conditions seem to matter enormously.

Some countries are praised for pragmatic leadership. But the presumption that some leaders are less rational than others misrepresents the problem. In all countries, the success of leadership is measured by its ability to stabilize competing demands of the population, thereby maximizing its duration in office. Regime longevity requires leadership that can access support and resources often at the disposal of some section of the polity.

How does leadership acquire its vision or predilection for pragmatism? Why are some leaders willing to put economic growth first? Ferdinand Marcos of the Philippines was not less pragmatic than the Republic of Korea's Park or Singapore's Lee. The policies of Marcos were politically rational – he believed he could rule by balancing the interests of the powerful elites who had traditionally dominated the nation's policies. The policies of Lee and Park similarly were pragmatic. They had to cope with an environment that was not dominated by elites, so to survive politically they worked to ensure that growth was equitably divided.

Leaders, like Lee, Park, or Chang Kai Shek, who followed a technocratic path were not more pragmatic than their elitist counterparts. When political rationality is best served by catering to narrow coalitions, technocrats will be ousted in favor of agents of the rich and powerful. The fact that some countries are more technocratic than others is a reflection of the regime's political foundation. Technocratic rationality prevails in regimes that build their political support or gain their legitimacy from the promise of shared growth. But when only a few seem to benefit, populist outrage may arise to kick out qualified economists. Good policies matter, but gaining a consensus to achieve growth is a political question. We know much more about the relationship of economic variables than about the interaction between economics and politics.

Technocrats can solve some of the macroeconomic issues but not the more complex political issues of gaining support for policies. When countries experience large discrepancies in the original distribution of wealth, distributional issues will determine the acceptance of economic policy. A government that can credibly commit to shared growth can diffuse the pressures to focus on distributional issues, and can focus instead on policies that benefit the economy. However, when social class differences are too vast for society to coalesce around policies that produce growth, redistributional conflicts may lead to regime failure. When the lack of consensus caused by great disparities in power and wealth cannot be overcome by education or entrepreneurial skill, a unifying set of economic policies will be difficult to formulate. The majority will find itself locked in a struggle with the privileged few and policies will be judged and supported according to their redistributive impact. Thus great inequality will color all economic policy making, preventing rational economic policies from gaining social consensus.

The Philippine case highlights the political hazards that occur when economic interests of the elite diverge from those of the majority. Policies that enhance global economic indicators can be condemned as mere "trickle down". Others are criticized for "selling the country to foreigners". The expectation that a policy will intensify inequality will make implementation politically divisive despite the policy's intrinsic economic merit. If the expectation cannot be dispelled that some will gain at the expense of the majority, the policy will become politically unsustainable.

When initial social conditions are highly·unequal, distributional concerns will constrain policy choices. This explains why liberalization came earlier in the People's Republic of China than it did in India, where the existing vast inequality of conditions was not eliminated. Disparity of initial conditions also explains why economic policy making has been more technocratic in Malaysia than in the Philippines. The new, recently configured *bumiputera* elite in Malaysia still sees itself as having more to gain from an expanded economy,[158] than the Philippine elite whose interests diverge so dramatically from those of the majority that it sees technocratic rationality as a threat to its interests.[159]

Countries that suffer from wide income inequalities find it difficult to attract investment. There is always the lingering fear that the reformers will be pushed out of power in favor of someone who will cut the price of rice. Income inequality is one of the reasons why the liberal reform agenda in India and the Philippines is often under attack. When reform is given little chance of success because of the inevitably of social conflict, political coalitions in favor of reforms will be difficult to sustain, sealing the development trap, and ensuring the status quo.

Social equality increases the gains to be had from education. In an egalitarian society, social distinctions derive not from class or social origin but more generally from educational attainment. The marginal benefits of additional education are greater when education, and not family membership, is the primary source of one's status.

Vast class and economic differences also compromise the possibility of procedural justice. Corruption of the justice system would matter less if the economic capacities of individuals were alike, but when justice is for sale, the small group that dominates the distribution of wealth will also dictate the decisions of the judicial system. Land reform floundered in the Philippines, where the lawyers of landholders defeated the valid claims of the peasants before judges who were also landlords, who depended on law enforcement officers who were landlords as well.

Equality and Bureaucracy

In many developing countries, the effectiveness of modern management techniques in bureaucracy is deterred by the persistence of traditional notions of social status and paternalism. The application of modern bureaucratic principles requires a system of hierarchy based on merit rather than on social status.

[158.] The new business elite is comprised of government-connected capitalists, created by the increased government intervention in the economy under the new economic policy.

[159.] A divergence of interests may eventually occur in Malaysia once the new class of wealthy bumiputeras is consolidated. But now, that class sees its interest as being best served by a strong economy.

Equality of social condition makes it easier to introduce recruitment based on impersonal measurements of merit. Similarly, government workers must reject preexisting social roles in favor of roles predicated on performance standards to ensure the functioning of the bureaucracy. When social and economic inequalities are rampant, personal advancement will inevitably be associated with social power and influence, personal pull will always be perceived to prevail over merit.

The Philippine experience suggests that the pursuit of technocratic aims depends on the recognition of the equality of all stakeholders and that the use of public administration to attain personal patronage benefits is likely to be influenced by the preexisting inequality in society. For example, in the Philippines, social status undermines bureaucratic standardization and imposes personalism in its place. Personalism may have many faces: nepotism, high-level patronage, preferment of proteges in temporary positions, the creation of emergency or confidential positions at lower levels, pro forma performance ratings, or favoritism in reclassification of positions. As a result of such compromises of standardization, patron-client relationships dominate, engendering administrative factions or cliques. When a citizen enters an office one learns that "first come, first served" does not apply. Instead, a personal follow-up often occurs after papers are moved from desk to desk. Short cuts and go-betweens are necessary to attain routine objectives. When civil service entrance exams are given, they focus on general, rather than specialized, content allowing for maximum discretion in the selection of candidates. With a pool of hundreds of formally qualified individuals, personalized standards can be applied. Similarly, formal education is valued above up-to-date competency. A premium is often placed on expensive master of business administration degrees, especially valued in the Philippines because they facilitate social discrimination.

Malaysia offers a compelling contrast to the Philippines by demonstrating how relatively egalitarian social conditions may be a precondition for modern management techniques to take root in a society. Among Malays, the official-citizen relationship does not reflect a fundamental social inequality of social conditions.[160] A democratic ethos allowed the government to inculcate modern management techniques successfully. Within the civil service, the same rules apply regardless of the officeholder's status as citizen.

To promote this ethos of egalitarian treatment, Malaysia has introduced a Best Client's Charter (1993) requiring government agencies to formulate goals and to allow the agency to monitor how effectively goals are pursued. The Charter affirms that an agency's willingness to assist a client depends upon existing rules, not a civil servant's volition. The citizen need not play the role of supplicant but is instead viewed as a client who can demand a recognized level of service. As a result, favorable action from a public official does not create a personal debt for the recipient. In addition, the existence of a client's charter that specifies work norms, standards, and procedures thwarts government workers from soliciting bribes to expedite approvals of licenses or permits. Although a similar effort to develop a customer orientation based on a system of rules is recognized as urgently needed in the Philippines, it has not been introduced. There, instead of clearly stated rules that apply to all, the applicant's background is likely to determine the quality of the bureau's response.

As this discussion suggests, the persistence of vertical affiliations may have broad consequences for development. Robert Putnam has observed that civic engagement is reduced when society is organized vertically into pyramids of patron-client relations. "The uncivic society" is typically characterized by the absence of "horizontal relations of reciprocity and cooperation". Vertical structures intensify social cleavages, Putnam concludes, whereas horizontal relations breed "honesty, trust, and law abidingness" (Putnam 1993, 111).

Thus the performance of public institutions in East Asia raises important questions about the relationship of the equality of social conditions and the emergence of bureaucratic norms. However, the casual relationship between the two is not well understood.

[160.] Just as in the Philippines, some "Malaysian administrators are strong believers in the legitimacy of status differences and in the superiority of some men over others". The colonial policy of recruiting members of the ruling class to fill the ranks had the tendency to reinforce those status differences. Nevertheless, a considerable influx of Malays from ordinary backgrounds has occurred since independence, so that today, "In Malaysia the higher civil service can be considered to be more representative of Malaysian society than in many developing countries" (Puthucheary 1978, 72).

Max Weber's ideas on this topic are still the place to begin. He presumed a close correlation between bureaucratic rationality, that is, technocracy, and the leveling of a priori social status. But Weber was never explicit about which came first, or about how level the playing field must be at the outset, or about the role of leadership and political feasibility in ensuring that technocratic priorities are maintained. Whereas Weber assumed that bureaucracy would overtake and level social differences, the experience of developing nations in East Asia suggests a more nuanced pattern.

One presumption upon which modern bureaucracy rests is that citizens will interact as equals, not as patrons or clients, governors facing petitioners. A modern bureaucratic state replaces vertical relations of authority and dependency with neutral, rule-bound, decision making. However, where fundamental equality of social conditions is absent, bureaucratic norms can be overtaken by highly personalized relations of dependency. Citizens become petitioners, hoping to win favors from government on the basis of personal connections. Bureaucratic neutrality is quickly dissipated once personalized interventions by the strong and well connected take precedence over the rights of citizens to equal treatment before the law. When citizens perceive that rules are made to be broken, the civic mindedness of others cannot be assumed, social trust withers, civic reciprocity is forfeited. When citizens can no longer distinguish private from public realms of action, a basic pillar of the modern state has crumbled. There are also economic costs of a personalized system of public administration. When bureaucracy does not perform a neutral role, uncertainty increases for investors, as administrative risks are added to ordinary business risks.

Equality of social conditions helps establish the basis for a shared moral vision of the rights and responsibilities of citizens to each other. When individuals enjoy equality of social conditions, they are more likely to share the same opinions or to interpret events in the same way. This facilitates the establishment and enforcement of the norms of governance. When equality of social conditions facilitates the adaptation of coherent societywide programs, consensus on policy making will be easier to attain. Individuals will find it easier to play interchangeable economic roles. The principle of equality, by making it easier for different strata to hold interchangeable opinions and perform interchangeable roles, makes it easier for the polity to adopt policies that enjoy mutual consent.[161] As Tocqueville pointed out about democracy in America, "Equality of condition does not of itself produce regularity of morals, but it unquestionably facilitates and increases it" (de Tocqueville 1960, 216). Self-enforcing economic relations based on a shared vision of moral responsibility are an important component of economic development. An often unacknowledged achievement of Lee Kuan Yew's Singapore was the forging of a unified culture amidst ethnic diversity. Shared social understanding reduces transaction costs, thus increasing the range of possible economic interactions (North 1990, 42-5).

The rise of East Asia raises very difficult questions about how much progress in public administration can be achieved without social revolution: How much can be done through institution building? What is the relationship of institution building to social development? Does bureaucratic rationality reflect the degree of social transformation, or does it require that social transformation has already taken place? These questions pose a fundamental analytical and operational challenge to the progress of development management.

The Right Kind of Corruption:

The Korean Paradox

Corruption scandals in East Asia make worldwide headlines. When former President Roh Tae Woo (1988-1993) was arrested for raising $650 million in corporate contributions for a personal slush fund, the *Los Angeles Times* (Watanabe 1995, 1) featured a front page article on the Republic of Korea's "Culture of Corruption".[162] The message was that East Asians do not adhere to international business standards: Traditional attitudes to money and favors have yet to be reconciled with economic development.

[161.] Tocqueville pointed out in his *Democracy in America* that when democracy is introduced into a country that is still struggling with vast social inequality, individuals are unlikely to share the same opinions about the world (de Tocqueville 1960, 191-2). When equality of social conditions prevail "It is in vain that wealth and poverty, authority and obedience, accidentally interpose great distances (de Tocqueville 1960, 192).

[162.] Chun Doo Hwan (1980-1988) was charged with collecting an even greater slush fund of $900 million.

Such patronizing critiques of the East Asian tigers often appear in the press of industrialized countries. Exhorted by international organizations to avoid corruption, developing country authorities also find reason to gloat over the mishaps of East Asia's high performers. They can point to the scandals as proof that East Asians are no more politically or economically virtuous than others. More regrettably, many draw the lesson that rampant corruption does not impair development. For example, the *Far Eastern Economic Review* concluded "As the hundreds of millions of dollars former South Korean Presidents Chun Doo Hwan and Roh Tae Woo siphoned off for themselves should remind us, executive corruption – however lamentable – need not be a barrier to development" (Editorial 1996, 5). Both perceptions fail to identify how the pieces of the puzzle – high growth and political corruption – fit together.

Koreans were shocked by the size and extent of corruption that sent their two former presidents to jail in November 1995. Smaller scandals have tarnished the reputation of political parties in Japan, Malaysia, and Taipei,China. Why despite the scandals are business environments in East Asian countries rated as relatively clean by corporate executives who conduct business internationally. How can these scandals be reconciled with the fact that these countries have grown more quickly than other developing countries without contaminating their reputation for a conducive business environment? Although business people insist that corruption increases business risk and uncertainty, why does it not drive investors away from East Asia?

To see why corruption did not have a debilitating impact on economic confidence, consider one of the most irksome sources of uncertainty in business calculation – a capricious and opaque regulatory environment. Government bureaucracy is the primary beneficiary of that uncertainty as it both administers the regulations and gains side payments for steering business through the regulatory maze.

In many developing countries, bureaucratic posts with limited salaries are typically awarded to political followers because political parties do not have other resources to allocate. Politicians will look the other way when their supporters abuse public responsibilities to enrich themselves from state coffers. Once the bureaucracy is bloated with political appointees, the pool of money available for salaries shrinks, increasing the appeal of nonsalary supplements. Patents, licensing, local regulatory codes, import-export schedules, and tax programs all provide opportunities to use public office for private enrichment. Business has no way to anticipate the resulting uncertainty, delays, and unforeseen expenditures from manipulation by the gatekeepers of an opaque regulatory regime, as bureaucrats become specialists in the multiplication of nuisances that only they can contain. Contrasted with lump sum, up-front payment to a political party, which can be anticipated and amortized, this kind of graft causes apprehension because the investor never knows where the next demand will come from or how much will be requested. Recourse to the courts is rarely available in the battle against corruption as judges are likely to be political appointees.

Reducing the costs often associated with bureaucratic venality is the first clue as to why corruption in the Republic of Korea and Taipei,China did not impair investment. The administrative reforms of the late General Park Chung Hee (1961-1979), eliminated many of the sources of bureaucratic abuse. Administrative structures are highly centralized, and licensing for large investments is dominated by a single agency that reports directly to the president. General Park kept his bureaucracy small, limited by an exam-based recruitment process. Merit, not patronage, is the basis of recruitment and promotion within the bureaucracy; independent boards that administer exams determine bureaucratic career paths. Despite the growth of venality at all levels of the political system, the administrative mechanism he introduced and institutionalized have hardly changed and are not implicated in the scandals.

Comparable to the Republic of Korea, small bureaucracies in relation to gross domestic product are a typical feature of governments in East Asia's high performers. For example, Japan's bureaucracy is smaller than in other member countries of the Organization for Economic Co-operation and Development. Among the high performers, lines of authority are highly centralized, redundant functions are limited. Fewer bureaucrats mean fewer hands in the till. Also, typical of the high performers, investment screening is usually conducted at the top and controlled by one agency. Procedures are streamlined and publicly documented.

Another potential source of business uncertainty is unstable macroeconomic, monetary, and trade policy. Governments in developing countries have considerable discretion over the banking system as independent central banks rarely exist. Governments may inflate the currency by printing money to hide deficits. They may ration scarce credit or change the policy mix of credit allocation in favor of small- and medium-sized firms at the expense of allotments to large enterprises. The unpredictability of such actions, however, impairs business calculations, and is viewed as one element of risk. Labor relations can be another source of policy unpredictability. For example, when the opposition in the Republic of Korea came into power in the National Assembly in 1988, it immediately proposed a law to allow political activity by labor unions. Business became alarmed, offering the incumbent Democratic Liberal Party an opportunity to tighten the screws on reluctant contributors.

East Asian business people report that they rarely receive quid pro quo for campaign contributions. As one Korean company president reportedly said, "For all the money we give, we receive benefits only 10 percent of the time". Those who paid were treated more or less the same, paying for fair treatment, not special treatment.[163] Those who refused to pay, however, found that they did receive special treatment: harsh tax assessments, denial of credit, and the loss of government business. Special treatment, then, was more likely to be meted out as punishment for those who resisted the normal way of maintaining a stable business environment. This may sound like an ordinary protection racket, but it operates quite differently.

Companies are persuaded to support the dominant incumbent party in Japan, Malaysia, the Republic of Korea, and Taipei,China to ensure the continuity of policies that promote capital investment. In effect, when business people in these countries give money to political parties, they do so to ensure regulatory benefits and policy outcomes that they value [164] and to prevent something they don't like – sudden, unpredictable changes in the rules of the game can devastate investors in any country.

---

[163] Roh's defense has been that he received donations – ruling money – and that he never swapped favors.

[164] The ruling party receives over 90 percent of the legally donated money.

Although democracy is linked in many minds with greater government accountability, politicians extract more money from business, especially in Taipei,China (since 1989) and the Republic of Korea (since 1988) as democratic institutions are consolidated. Why does policy stability cost more with democracy? Opposition parties may offer an altered policy mix that may not be favorable to business, as well as changes in the application of rules and regulations. Economic regulations in developing countries tend to be very general, inviting new applications that are, in effect, policy alternatives. For example, regulations that allow government to subsidize loans to industries may not specify the size or activities to be funded. To avoid these risks, incumbents request more money to keep challengers at bay, while inventing innovative ways to raise funds from the firms whose interests would be endangered by a change of regime.

The Republic of Korea provides an example of the escalating costs of political support during the consolidation of democracy.[165] The structure of government, including presidential oversight of important functions, has changed little since Park's death in 1979. The president's office still controls the prosecutor's office, police, and tax authorities, allocation of credit, and major investment projects. However, the costs extracted by political parties have escalated dramatically since Park because the political system has become more competitive. Politicians need larger slush funds, they must campaign longer and harder, public projects have to be secured by larger kickbacks.[166] The party in power can charge more for protection from policy change, allowing Roh Tae Woo to amass

---

[165.] Taipei,China's KMT is beset by a different set of problems. Because small- and medium-sized enterprises dominate the private economy, it is more difficult for the party to raise large contributions, than for Korea's Liberal Democrats. As a result, since 1989 the KMT must provide private rather than public goods, such as a sound policy environment, to garner constituent support. The result is a less consistent regulatory environment than Korea and the danger that democracy will undermine technocratic decision making in favor of the private and ad hoc distribution of regulatory benefits to narrow interest groups. Since small firms are less capital intensive, they worry less about the overall coherence of the framework. Another danger to consistent policy making in Taipei,China and the Republic of Korea is the growing power of regional constituencies that must be courted with projects (Rampant Corruption 1995, 22-67).

[166.] In developing countries, Korea included, candidates are not easily distinguished by issues, but by personalities, which means building personal networks that are costly to construct and maintain. Elections are very expensive to run because participants at all

a secret fund of $650 million from 1988 to 1993.[167] Nothing fundamental has changed – administrative state structures are unaltered – but a change of party implies the possibility to investors of a change in the rules even after their investments have been made. As a result, more insurance from political uncertainty can be sold.

Such insurance is valued by large firms with considerable fixed assets, whose capital intensive activities are less mobile, and more easily held hostage to changes in the regulatory environment. Therefore, such firms will depend more on stability in the political marketplace and they are willing to pay for that stability, which explains the close relationship between Korean chaebols and the Liberal Democratic Party. That relationship is analogous to the relationship of railroad tycoons and political parties in the United States during the nineteenth century.[168]

Thus corruption, an impediment to attracting capital everywhere, has not held back East Asia's high performers. Self-enforcing limits on corruption exist because parties have incentives to keep firms that make capital investments healthy.[169] To secure political survival, the party leadership in turn promotes technocratic guidance of the economy, and provides a clean bureaucracy to prevent the dissipation of private sector profits by dozens of side payments.

---

levels of the electoral process, including the voters, want money to participate. The cost to incumbent parties of maintaining power include staff salaries, payments for drivers, office upkeep, and the ubiquitous gifts to be distributed at funerals, weddings, and anniversaries. Therefore, white envelopes with cash must always be on hand. Meetings of all kinds generally require dinner for participants. One Korean political staff person reported his routine operating expenses are usually five times higher than monthly salary and legal contributions combined. Dinners for as many as 30,000 people are reported in Taipei,China.

[167.] The elections since 1988 have generally been too close to call in advance. Due to the increased risks of opposition victory, opposition leader Kim Dae Jung received 2 billion won from Mr. Roh to secure political protection.

[168.] Unlike bankers, once the tracks are laid, the railroad companies cannot get up and leave to shake off unfriendly policies. A banker's assets are mobile allowing easy exit from unfriendly states. The assets of the railroads are not mobile. Hence, firms resort to voice – rather than exit – finding a more hospitable environment. Similarly, large firms in Korea that have invested heavily in plant and equipment cannot get up and leave. Small firms can more easily shift their product mix to accommodate changes in the rules or in market conditions.

[169.] As a percentage of economic growth, even at the margins, the sums involved in kickbacks and contributions are trivial, but because they are highly concentrated in the hands of top party leadership, they arouse strong sentiments.

Campaign contributions are part of a system that includes the creation of a business environment conducive to long-term investments. When political party leaders, rather than a particular politician, receive the contribution, the party implicitly assumes responsibility for policy outcomes. To warrant continuous collection of contributions, the party must show success in policy implementation. The economic benefits of good policies then accrue to the firms, and the political benefits to the parties identified with the policies. The system has endured because a continuous stream of private sector profits ensures a continuous source of funds for the party. Both growth and political stability are maintained.

Large campaign contributions reflect the high involvement of the state in the economy, which also allows politicians to punish noncontributors. Therefore, the solution to political corruption seems to many to be greater liberalization. But decontrol may weaken the incentives for political leadership to oversee bureaucratic corruption, opening business to a new form of uncertainty that the political system was once able to reduce. While reducing opportunities for bribe taking and cutting the benefits of contributing to the party, decontrol may also make it more difficult to identify and persecute wrongdoers. It may weaken party discipline and result in more personalized corruption at the agency and lower government level. The new risks can be contained only by an enhanced legal framework that includes independent courts, administrative oversight, and checks and balances between branches of government. Competition is needed between levels of government, as well as between local units of administration. Such changes imply the need for a new generation of state builders in East Asia. The work of economic development is never over.

Regime Type Does Not Provide a Clue

The economic and social record of Asia's experiments in democracy are ambiguous.[170] Equality in the distribution of income

---

[170.] Democracy is defined here as the political process by which the adult population has freedom to elect top leaders.

has been a feature of those economies that grew most quickly in East Asia. They were generally not democracies. By contrast, India and the Philippines, Asia's oldest continuous democracies, and Pakistan and Thailand, the sporadic democracies, post the weakest social indicators in their respective subregions. In these countries, democracy has not provided transparent or predictable policy environments and has not ensured the integrity of the public sector. Despite ranking high in the provision of political freedom, government in these countries often lacks effective oversight mechanisms and is bottlenecked by corruption and patronage.

Lacking accountable, transparent, and predictable procedures for the implementation of policy, the region's democracies have not reduced inequality in the distribution of income, education, or health. Their poor performance on achieving growth with equity suggests that the existence of procedural democracy alone does not ensure responsive systems of policy formulation and public administration. The primary sources of corruption in the system of public administration are popularly elected politicians.

Political systems that allow some the right to compete for public office do not necessarily lead to wider participation in the policy-making process in Asia. The lack of an accountable public-private interface is the source of persistent criticism by both domestic and international businesses operating in India, Pakistan, Philippines, and Thailand. Key variables of growth – access to the policy-making process, a transparent regulatory environment, or the availability of information to the general public – are not guaranteed by the existence of electoral competition. The region's democracies often lack grassroot accountability for program performance, a result depriving the beneficiaries of programs the opportunity to improve the design and implementation of projects targeted to increase local welfare.

In effect, the evidence from Asia suggests that good governance is independent of regime type. The capacity of Asia's democracies for consistent and accountable policy formulation and implementation is independent of the process that determines governmental succession. Participatory development must extend beyond the election of public officials to accountability for the implementation and performance of economic policy. Democracy should not be an excuse for the poor performance of government personnel or for the weak performance of government projects.

Predictability Grounded in Institutions

The path to democracy is still largely uncharted territory in the social sciences. Even less is known about the sequencing of reforms to consolidate democracy. From the experience of the Republic of Korea and Taipei,China, we can observe that institutions developed by leadership to coordinate cooperation can prepare citizenry for the transition to democracy, while ensuring the continuity of responsible policy making. Ranked as hardened authoritarians only ten years ago, they are now among the region's democratic leaders. Only in Indonesia and the Philippines, under Marcos, was progress toward democracy weak. Dominated by the will of an individual political leader, institutions did not mature and new leaders with political experience and constituent support did not emerge. A connection emerges between institutional deepening, learning, and successful political transitions.

Once the world could be divided into autocracies and democracies, but the East Asian case suggests the irrelevance of these categories. What distinguishes the authoritarian regimes from each other is as great as what divides them from democracies. There is as much variation within the categories as between them. Many democracies are weak on the protection of rights, some so-called autocracies do much better. Hong Kong's experience confirms that the rule of law is distinct from democracy. The Philippine example confirms that personalized forms of interaction will undermine autocracy and democracy alike. The integrity of the public domain in a highly personalized dictatorship will not differ significantly from that of a highly personalized democracy. This leads us to one of the most salient lessons of the ongoing Asian miracle study.

A transition from family-based to rule-based trust is critical for an open society to flourish in the context of democratic institutions. That trust cannot be attained simply by the introduction of elections.

The missing link between liberal politics and liberal economics is the level of institutionalization and the degree to which political sovereignty and economic ownership are distinguished by rules, practices, and norms. An independent judiciary and public service depend on a broadly accepted normative framework and the existence of a social constituency that prioritizes public sector integrity.

Although the Philippines traditionally has had a strong private sector, the accumulation of wealth and status was not through open participation, equal opportunity, and free disclosure of information, but more generally through networks of kin and personal connections. When kinship is the basis of trust, economic opportunity depends on the proper social connections. A world of private or family-based enforcement mechanisms cannot guard against a Hobbesian struggle of all against all, in which force ensures the exchange of goods and services.

For the full effects of the price system to work and generate what Frederick Hayak has called "the extended order", the system of public administration must be sharply distinguished from the system of economic ownership. Conflicts of interest must be explicitly barred by the constitution. Those who are guardians of the public trust must be guided by a concern for the stability and continuity of the state. They must not partake in the private profits that accrue to entrepreneurial activity by using public information for private gain.

Economic liberalization will not produce long-term growth unless it is supported by institutions, practices, and norms that sharply distinguish the interests of the state from the profits of entrepreneurial effort. When the leaders of the state seek the same profits as the business sector, conflict will result, as in the Philippines under Marcos, and in Indonesia on the eve of the succession of Suharto. Institutions must be designed to prevent politicians from using their authority to personalize both the material and political benefits that can be derived from their access to the rents created by state intervention in the economy. The economic benefits of policy making must not accrue to the officeholder, but to the policies or to political parties identified with those policies.

The successful Asian regimes found their own way to achieve the separation of politics from entrepreneurship. There is great institutional diversity in approaches confirming the observation that good governance is a blend of the universal and the particular, the concrete and the abstract. Despite the particular mechanism chosen, until the separation of public office and ownership is institutionalized, business will not trust government to lead or coordinate development. The quintessential contribution of Lee and Park for the development of their nations is that both affirmed that the path to wealth must not be through government service.

By crafting mechanisms to limit government discretion, spreading information openly, enforcing property rights of all citizens equally, and ensuring the predictable conduct of public business, Lee and Park created the conditions for trust among anonymous trading partners.

When institutional predictability is lacking, continuity of leadership can be a substitute, as in the case of Indonesia. But stability is not the key to the Asian miracle because it does not help us to distinguish how the tigers were different from Mobuto in Zaire or Marcos in the Philippines, both of whom ruled for more than 20 years and clustered around them an extremely wealthy cohort of loyal followers. Relationship-based trade can be a functional substitute for rule-based contract enforcement, but it fails the test of predictability and gives rise to uncertainties that will reduce the horizons of private sector investment. The region's high performers stand out among developing nations because of their creation of institutions that generate reliable expectations about how contracts will be enforced. When relationships with regime officials are the basis of contract enforcement, a consistent set of expectations will not be generated and business confidence will falter. Predictability grounded in institutions, rather than stability grounded in persons, is key.

The transition from a network- to a contract-based society is the critical component of the East Asian miracle that links it to the great universal themes in the sociology of development begun by Max Weber. That transition also suggests that the core of the Asian miracle is not uniqueness, but universality. Certain Asian leaders, led by the imperative to nurture cultural nationalism, insist on particularistic qualities to explain East Asia's rise. This study does not dispute the importance of nationalism to a nation's collective psyche, but it asserts that nationalism can also be affirmed in the adherence to, and celebration of, universal principles of good governance.

Democracy in an Asian Mirror

Much can be learned from the rise of industrial Asia about the link between the polity and the economy. But that experience is usually misclassified in outdated categories that stir political passion while providing little insight. Western observers, for example, often comment on the absence of familiar social and political institutions to suggest that somehow East Asia didn't get it right. Some see in the rise of industrial Asia a reason to extol the virtues of authoritarian rule. Yet there is little evidence outside of East Asia that authoritarianism compliments growth. Public rhetoric in East Asia often insists on the primacy of Asian values. Nationalism, not truth, benefits from this assertion, which deprives Asia's economic achievements of their universal relevance.

One way to misapprehend the relationship of the political to the economic order is to think in categories that are too big. The biggest and most enticing category is the term democracy; it is usually pitted against authoritarianism, just as states are pitted against markets, and capitalism against socialism, as alternative paths of development. These big categories – that dominate contemporary thinking about historical change – offer little insight into the forces that have transformed the global economic environment since World War II. The democracy-authoritarianism split tells us little about how democracy works or about how different institutions influence economic outcomes.

Democracy, the selection of leaders through competitive elections, is often practiced at the same sites where property rights, the rule of law, free markets for goods and services, and human rights are protected. Therefore democracy is sometimes construed as a necessary condition, a preserver or guarantor of a liberal economic order. Asia's experience of democracy suggests the need to rethink this correlation. Effective economic outcomes and the holding of elections coincide among developed countries not because those countries use elections to constitute their governments, but because institutions exist in the political system to ensure limits to governmental authority.

No matter how it is constituted, if powerful enough to create property rights, government can also confiscate those rights. Elections, therefore, must be buttressed by a panoply of countervailing institutions to prevent the abuse of power. These countervailing institutions needed to ensure a transparent and predictable environment for economic policy making do not exist among all countries holding multiparty elections. For example, Asia's democracies feature less effective communication between the state and the private sector than the nondemocracies, many of which designated formal mechanisms to integrate the holders of economic property rights into policy making. Many nondemocracies appoint technocrats to conduct macroeconomic policies and allow freedom to contract according to consistent rules that are the same for all citizens. Such rules, and the councils in which they are deliberated, represent explicit limits on the discretion of government over economic policy. By contrast, in many democracies a capricious and interventionist regulatory framework allows those who win elections to overturn the property rights of those who lose.

Whereas the standard definition of democracy, the choice of government through multiparty elections, sometimes stands in as the definition of accountable government, many avenues exist for democratically elected officials to avoid accountability. The most obvious – very familiar to one Asian democracy, the Philippines – is the constant switching of parties, making party labels meaningless. Accountability is enhanced when politics is dominated by a party that depends for its legitimacy on being able to produce socially desired outcomes. When policies fail in Malaysia, the Republic of Korea, Singapore, or Taipei,China, the public can identify the party responsible, but not in the Philippines where citizens bewail the general corruption of politicians but cannot identify any responsible group or party. When parties are no more than vehicles to enable an individual or group to capture power, accountability for policy outcomes is blurred. The path to democracy of the Republic of Korea and Taipei,China was paved by state institutions that held those who control the levers of power accountable for the results of policy. When elections were introduced, strong party identities were already established, making party leaders accountable for policy outcomes so that elections become an opportunity to throw the rascals out.

In India too, a functioning democracy has evolved that does not have to justify itself by being able to provide economic development. In fact, apologists claim India's political maturity is one reason for economic difficulties. The two are unrelated. Democracy in India failed to provide basic security for economic rights. Indeed, civil liberties were protected – citizens express any opinion they choose – but firms needed government licenses to make even routine decisions about where and how much to invest.

In Pakistan, despite a constitutional legacy that provides checks and balances, in practice laws can be amended, and civil servants transferred by executive action. Budgetary allocations can be modified without parliamentary consent, the census can be called off and local elections delayed largely due to political considerations. The enactment of thousands of exemptions to the commercial code allows government to provide selective benefits to firms. Protection, sometimes offered to one particular factory within a given sector, distorts competition. When laws change according to who is in charge, no one's property is secure and in the absence of limits on the power of elected officials, political contestation often takes a violent course.

Weak inputs into policy making, discretionary regulations, and the capricious enforcement of property rights help explain why in social indicators Asia's oldest democracies rank lower then many nondemocratic counterparts. In the United Nations' ranking of 173 nations according to human development, the Philippines ranks 99, Pakistan 132, India 135, and Bangladesh 146, lower than many of their more authoritarian Asian counterparts. Indonesia at 105 performs worse than the Philippines but it started at a much lower level, and it outperforms most South Asian democracies (United Nations Development Programme 1993). The rankings of Asia's most venerable democracies alongside the world's most notorious dictatorships in providing social welfare allows several simple but compelling generalizations to be stated: The existence of institutions to make politicians responsible for outcomes cannot be assumed by the existence of procedures for popular participation in elections. The existence of multiparty elections tells us little that is meaningful about the characteristics of the political systems that are market preserving. Unfettered government discretion over economic decision making fails to bring about social or economic development in democracies and dictatorships alike.

The missing link that unites democracy with economic performance is liberalism. Although liberalism is not a term typically found in the language of donor organizations, it is the key to what distinguishes those countries that succeed economically from those that fail. Governance, however, which has become a common term of reference among development specialists, is the bridge to liberalism that will allow international organizations to alter the course of economic change among both democracies and dictatorships.

The definition of governance that has become most broadly accepted by those international organizations whose business is economic development, such as the Asian Development Bank and the World Bank, includes measures to ensure an accountable, predictable, and transparent policy environment. This definition, which includes procedures to ensure that rules governing property rights are fairly and impartially enforced, limits the arbitrary use of state power, hence its essence is liberalism.

Perhaps the greatest surprise of Asia's political development is that states with democratic procedures sometimes develop liberal institutions less quickly than their nondemocratic counterparts. If multiparty elections do not necessarily generate a liberal economic order, then East Asian leaders should not apologize for failing to develop Western political institutions during the transition to a market economy. Instead of pursuing democracy as an end in itself, by campaigning for good governance, donors may be getting something they treasure even more, a firm foundation for democratic practice.

APPENDIX A

INSTITUTION BUILDING

FOR DEVELOPMENT

The outcomes of broadly similar reform packages have varied significantly across countries. Governance, the capacity of the institutional environment in which citizens interact with each other and with government agencies, is one of the factors underlying these variations. Hence, getting the policies right may not, by itself, be sufficient for successful development. Good governance is required to ensure that governments actually deliver the promises to their citizens.

The experience within Asia does not establish any direct correlation between the type of political regime and rapid economic and social development. Successful development has taken place in countries with different political systems. Within the region, it is the quality of governance, not regime-type, that seems to be associated with the differences in economic performance.[171]

Evaluations of project performance in developing countries indicate the importance of the nonpolitical, functional components of governance. Separate evaluations conducted by both the Asian Development Bank and the World Bank reveal that even when

---

[171.] A general definition of governance used by the World Bank is "the manner in which power is exercised in the management of a country's economic and social resources for development". This definition was designed to extend beyond the capacity of public sector management to the rules and institutions that create a predictable and transparent framework for the conduct of public and private business, and to accountability for economic and financial performance (World Bank 1991a).

projects are narrowly focused, success is often dependent upon the overall capacity of public administration.[172] Well-designed programs are important, but so is the ability to implement them. This ability cannot be predicted from regime type. Implementation capability reflects three fundamentals in the strategic interactions between citizens and government officials. These fundamentals – accountability, transparency, and predictability – determine the performance of economic policy.

The Essentials of Development Management

Accountability

Accountability refers to the imperative for citizens or key broad-based elites to make public officials responsible for government behavior and responsive to the needs of citizens.[173] Accountability at the microlevel implies that government structures are flexible enough to offer beneficiaries the opportunity to improve the design and implementation of projects. Similarly, outcomes of macropolicies affecting the economy as a whole ultimately depend on the support and cooperation of those groups affected. This may necessitate some degree of citizen representation, ranging from narrowly conceived consultative committees to a broadly elected legislature.

Accountability also means establishing criteria to measure the performance of public officials, as well as oversight mechanisms to ensure that standards are met. The litmus test is

---

[172.] Background papers for the Asian Development Bank (ADB 1994b) *Report of the Task Force on Improving Project Quality* concluded that a number of projects that were technically sound fell short of their potential because of problems in implementation. These failures indicated that weaknesses spread through the public sector will diminish the impact of even narrowly focused ADB projects, increasing costs for both borrowers and lenders alike.

This project survey confirmed earlier findings of a World Bank study conducted in November 1992, which similarly cited implementation as a critical component of project performance. That study (World Bank 1992a) called for rethinking project design to account for the influence of implementation capability on project outcomes.

The importance of implementation became especially clear to the World Bank in connection with structural adjustment lending, where it was recognized there was a need to create an enabling environment in which the macroreforms could be anchored (World Bank 1992b).

[173.] For example, most East Asian regimes had a high degree of participation of local leaders in policymaking.

whether private actors in the economy have procedurally simple and swift recourse for redress of unfair actions or incompetence of the executive authority. Lack of accountability tends, in time, to reduce the state's credibility as an economic partner. This can ultimately cause even autocratic regimes to fail, since they are rarely able to sustain the confidence that leads to long-term, growth-enhancing investment from the private sector.[174] In short, accountability can curb sovereign risk.

Accountability must also include the existence of mechanisms to evaluate the economic and financial performance of public institutions. Economic accountability relates to the effectiveness of policy formulation and implementation, and efficiency in resource use. Financial accountability covers accounting systems for expenditure control, as well as internal and external audits.

Transparency

Transparency refers to the availability of information to the general public (including rival elites), and clarity about government rules, regulations, and decisions.[175] Thus, it both complements and reinforces predictability. Ensuring transparency is difficult because the generator of information alone may know of its existence, and therefore can limit access to it. Hence, the

---

[174] The risk of confiscation, favoritism, or capricious enforcement of policies characteristic of autocratic rule will generate uncertainty that can reduce private sector initiative. The irony of autocracy is that the leader's claim to be above the law reduces the state's credibility as an economic partner, and undermines the willingness of citizens to take risks and engage in wealth-enhancing activities.

[175] A comparison of uniform tariffs and multiple tariffs will illustrate the point. With a uniform tariff, merchants know exactly what payment is required. In contrast, multiple tariff rates offer customs officials discretion over the classification of the goods, and thus provide a basis to supplement their private income. Although a good case can be made for multiple tariffs from an economic point of view, a developing country that offers discretionary interventions to underpaid officials has opened a Pandora's box, regardless of how compelling the argument for multiple rates may seem. When bureaucratic capability is in doubt, the uniformity of tariffs at very low levels would reduce the possibilities for corruption, as well as rationalize economic decision making. Similarly, inconsistent foreign investment laws subject to different interpretations can create uncertainty among potential investors. The successful East Asian regimes combine transparent rules for protecting, registering, and taxing property rights, with effective company laws. As a result, the legal rights to contract and maximize the income or return on assets are guaranteed. Many countries offer variable rates for imported automobile registration. Complex standards for assessing rates allow for personalized negotiations and side payments between importers and officials.

citizen's right to information must be supplemented by legal enforceability. Broadly restrictive laws that permit public officials to deny information to citizens, for example an Official Secrets Act, should provide for an independent review of claims to confirm that such a denial is justified in the greater public interest.

Access to accurate and timely information about the economy and government policies can be vital for economic decision making by the private sector. Such data should be freely and readily available to economic agents on the grounds of efficiency alone. While this is true across all areas of the economy, it is especially relevant to information-intensive sectors, such as finance, in general, and capital markets, in particular.

Transparency in government decision making and public policy implementation reduces uncertainty and can help inhibit corruption among public officials. To this end, rules and procedures that are simple, straightforward, and easy to apply may be preferable to those that provide discretionary powers to government officials or are susceptible to different interpretations. However well-intentioned the latter type of rule might be in theory, its purpose can be vitiated in practice.[176]

Limits on the principle of transparency may sometimes be necessary. Such limits should be mindful of the distinction between information as a commodity, and information as a process. For example, intellectual property rights may need to be protected to encourage innovation and invention; but decision making on the establishment of intellectual property and rights, thereto, (that is, to whom they are granted and why) should be transparent.

Predictability

Predictability refers to the existence of laws, regulations, and policies to regulate society, and their fair and consistent application. It is dependent upon a rule of law that encompasses both well-defined rights and duties, as well as mechanisms to enforce laws and settle disputes in an impartial manner. The state and its subsidiary agencies must be bound by, and answerable to, the legal system, as must private individuals and enterprises.

[176.] For example, a uniform tariff rate (where merchants know exactly what customs duty payment is required) may be preferable, on this ground, to multiple tariff rates that offer customs officials discretion over the classification of goods.

Rule-based systems of rights are essential for economic actors to plan investment decisions. A predictable regulatory framework enables firms to calculate the return on their investment. On the other hand, regulatory uncertainty raises the cost of capital by increasing the risk of investment.

Predictability can be enhanced through appropriate institutional arrangements. For example, it has been argued that an autonomous central bank could lead to more predictable monetary and exchange rate policies. Many governments face the challenge of regulating money supply while pursuing expansionary fiscal policies to encourage investment. In such situations, if monetary policy is too accommodating, inflationary pressures can put investor confidence at risk, thus defeating the very objective of the fiscal policy. In some countries, managing the fiscal deficit may be made more difficult by compulsions to bail out a politically manipulated banking sector. By granting greater autonomy to the central bank, government can signal to investors that macroeconomic policy will be prudent and sound. Insulating economic ministries from political pressures can have similar benefits.[177]

Balancing the Extremes

Although the three elements of good governance – accountability, transparency, and predictability – tend to be mutually supportive, in general, accountability must take priority over transparency. The need to balance accountability with the independence of central bank officials illustrates this relationship. The experience of the central banks of both Germany and the United States suggests that to ensure accountability, fixed terms and transparent rules for personnel turnover, as well as rules that will prevent the abuse of power, such as prohibitions against the appointment of relatives, are all essential. A supervisory board,

---

[177.] Central banks must be able to signal to investors that macroeconomic policies stabilize fiscal deficits and resist the political clout of vested interests. Independence insulates the bank from pressures to use monetary and exchange rate policy irresponsibly or to endorse loans to regime cronies or uncompetitive parastatals. Hong Kong's commitment to predictable macropolicies was affirmed by pegging its currency to the American dollar thereby removing any basis for concern that local politics would motivate opportunistic monetary policies. The independence of financial ministries from political opportunism can have the same beneficial effect of an independent central bank.

perhaps composed of representatives of private banks from different regions, is one way to establish effective oversight procedures. An adjudication system is important as a final resort in disputes over questionable behavior.

Transparency also requires careful balancing. One can anticipate a number of situations in which parties may choose not to enter a negotiation for fear of exposing their position to public hostility or for fear that rivals will gain advantages from the public exposure of private information.[178] The limits of transparency must respect the need to prevent the disclosure of private information that can compromise the position of key partners to an agreement.

Although conceptually the three elements of governance indicated above tend to be mutually reinforcing, accountability is the ultimate safeguard of transparency and predictability. In general, transparency and predictability cannot be ensured without institutions that impose accountability. As noted, while predictability requires financial decision making by a politically independent bureaucracy, agency accountability to the communities targeted by their policies is needed for balance.[179]

Devices to achieve accountability must subject officials to constituent oversight, and they must impose a standard to measure agency performance. Without the requirement to be accountable to affected groups, agencies may become self-interested entities that place agency interests over those of their constituents. Transparency and information openness cannot be ensured without legal frameworks that balance the right to disclosure with the right of confidentiality, and without institutions that accept

---

[178.] In diplomacy, it is generally accepted that transparency is temporarily suspended when negotiating concessions from parties to an agreement may require delaying public exposure of the terms under discussion until the reactions of parties directly privy to the agreement are registered. Another trade-off is between transparency and innovation. Transparency between bidders for existing public utilities to supply new capacity requires specifying the type of plant. However a bidder may resist precise specification when innovative solutions are being considered. Changes in exchange rates represent another area in which premature exposure could invite behavior that undermines the policy. Students of international relations acknowledge that transparency does not always increase cooperative behavior between political rivals.

[179.] For example, the independence of finance ministers from political pressures must be balanced by the need to be consistent with the commitment to constituents on political issues.

accountability. Predictability in the functioning of the legal framework is helpful to ensure the accountability of public institutions. At the same time, predictability also requires transparency, because without information about how similarly placed individuals have been treated, it may be difficult to ensure adherence to the rule of equality before the law. Transparency facilitates accountability, participation, and predictability of outcomes.

Part two: Providing the Institutional Framework

Building an effective public sector that can provide the necessary physical infrastructure, and promote equity and social justice requires administrative capacity. Because politics will influence the outcome, the criteria for institutional reform in one country may be different from what works in another.

The politics of reducing all budgets by 10 percent – macro adjustment – vary significantly from those of moving 10 percent of the budget of one government bureau to another, as in public sector management. Although measures to stabilize the economy through price and trade liberalization require considerable technical capacity, they are not complex administratively. A small circle of nonofficials – technocrats in a few key ministries who have the backing of top leadership – is needed. Most importantly, the political costs of such liberalization can be diffused. Because the initial temporary costs of macrostabilization are spread over much of the population, coordinated opposition focused in a legislature or among powerful interest groups may not be as focused as opposition to changes in public sector management.[180] For example, in many developing countries, civil service reform may require the cooperation of a range of government ministries that may have divergent points of view. The sweeping institutional

---

[180.] The political risks of public sector reforms are greater than those of monetary reforms. Monetary policy is the prime example of a socially neutral policy. When the consequences of tight monetary policy are estimated by means of counterfactual analysis using a macro–micro model, the incomes of all groups are found to fall in roughly equal proportion. Workers bear the consequences of tight monetary policy, but they find it difficult to draw a clear connection between monetary policy and their situation. There are delays between the monetary measures and firm failures, not all firms fare equally poorly. All stabilization measure carry risks, but those risks may be lessened by emphasis on measures which are relatively neutral with respect to income distribution in the short term. (Haggard, Lafay, and Morrison 1995, chapter 4, 49-58).

changes that accompany financial sector reforms, rationalization of state enterprises, or the restructuring of social services may require cooperation of the legislature, courts, and local governments. The costs of such reforms are highly localized, imposing permanent losses on specific, often well-organized interests. The combination of well-organized resistance and the need for broad governmental coordination makes the politics of public sector reform more difficult than adjustment of the monetary system. To avoid a direct confrontation that may weaken the government's resolve, fiscal reform that affects all sectors of the economy equally can be a good place to begin the process of public sector renewal. An effective fiscal system establishes the foundations of responsive government.

Building Government Capacity

A critical issue for public sector management is the need to endow government with the administrative capability and revenue to offer essential public services. Inevitably, the provision of indispensable public goods and services requires an increase of tax revenue or the transfer of funds from one agency to another. In some cases, expanding the state's capability necessitates eliminating commitments to parastatals and to large public bureaucracies or, at the least, enhancing the efficiency of the concerned enterprises. Such public sector reform cannot be achieved without opposition from one highly mobilized interest group or another. Initiating measures to enhance the efficiency of the concerned enterprises is often the best way to begin.

To compensate for rampant tax evasion, governments in developing countries devise tax regimes that allow considerable official discretion in assigning rates. But, expansive tax powers that are capriciously applied drive private firms into the informal sector. Deprived of these tax revenues, governments cannot provide basic services, such as law enforcement. Failing to collect what citizens owe, governments often depend on parastatals for revenue. The result is that the impoverished government has few benefits to offer firms that cooperate in the disclosure of profits.

Throughout the developing world, a large informal sector has developed in response to the state's failure to provide basic services. To induce firms to play by the rules, positive incentives must be given to encourage them to become licensed operators in the formal sector, and thereby provide tax revenues. This, in turn, will increase government's ability to perform its functions better.[181] Reform must begin with the elimination of the dangers of arbitrary taxation and discretionary standards for licensing by unaccountable government officials, who often operate in overlapping administrative jurisdictions. Tax rates should be consistent and should not unduly burden economic activity, forcing enterprises into the informal sector.

A government's ability to implement projects successfully or undertake reforms depends in large part on its institutional capacity to conduct public business. Failure to provide effective public sector management undermines the credibility of reform initiatives. When credibility is lacking, firms will act in the expectation that government will not be able to sustain growth, and will only make short-term investment decisions. When government fails to provide adequate property rights or the necessary infrastructure, industry responds by failing to provide the necessary investment, shrinking tax revenues and reducing growth.

The key to sustaining a growth equilibrium is to convince the parties whose cooperation is necessary that they will gain more by postponing present consumption in order to enjoy greater long-term benefits. Leadership must provide assurances that the benefits will not be eroded by corruption or by the rent seeking of powerful elites. Thus microlevel reform of the public sector, including the civil service, is a fundamental component of economic reform. Unless the government's ability to protect property rights and ensure a level field for all players is established, individuals are unlikely to sacrifice present consumption for increased investment.

---

[181] In some Asian countries, for example, India, Philippines, and Sri Lanka, wage employment in the urban informal sector grows faster than in the formal sector. This deprives the government of revenue and deprives the producers of legal protection. "In India, twice as many jobs have been created in the unorganized manufacturing sector as in the organized" (United Nations Development Programme 1993).

Improving Accounting and Auditing Procedures and Statistics

Improvements in auditing and accounting procedures are the first line of reforms that governments must undertake to ensure responsible performance of management tasks. Improved financial accountability often requires improved accounting and auditing practices, compliance with financial management standards, and financial accountability assessments.

Audits are fundamental to accountability and are a necessary component of public sector performance.[182] An independent audit system strengthens expenditure control by monitoring and evaluating public expenditure programs for effectiveness and performance. A mechanism to review and act on audit results is critical.[183] So, too, are reliable accounts – their absence has been a major constraint to efficient public sector management. Another issue of great concern is the allocation of budgetary expenditures within and between sectors.

One area that is often overlooked is the relationship between capital and recurrent expenditures. Appropriate fiscal approaches are needed to ensure that borrowers consider maintenance costs when they contemplate capital investments. Many projects fail when they are funded without reference to a government's ability to ensure project upkeep. In extreme cases, investment will be deterred by the difficulty of evaluating profits when official accounting is inadequate to calculate statistics for inflation.

Renewing the Civil Service

Improving the productivity of the civil service is perhaps the most elusive transformation that a reform-minded government

---

[182] Financial accountability refers to the duty of anyone who handles public funds or goods to respond publicly to others for the manner in which the duties have been performed. Accountability can be enhanced when an independent auditor examines a paid invoice and counts the money returned. Audits should entail a publicly presented or independently verified report.

[183] Development agencies can help by providing funds to train accountants and auditors; upgrade professional standards by imposing a code of ethics and disciplinary procedures; modernize procedures; and finance career development through the support of teaching and research and by making materials more accessible.

must undertake. A professional and accountable bureaucracy that can enforce the rules and ensure standards, competition, and property rights is critical to encouraging private sector confidence that liberalization can succeed. Clear career paths and adequate compensation are vital. Efficiency at lower levels requires mechanisms to evaluate performance so that promotion is based on achievement. Such incentive systems are key to improving staff productivity. Performance improves when compensation is explicitly linked to successful administration of programs. For instance, incentives should include linking the possibility to upgrade skills with successful program implementation.

Rare is the country not concerned with reducing corruption. Yet, corruption is responsible for reducing the economic prospects of a number of countries in the region. Some strategies for corruption control are more effective than others. Countries must design and adopt national procurement rules that emphasize transparency and open access. Simplifying procedures and reducing the number of unproductive staff will also decrease the scope for corruption, as will creating effective oversight mechanisms. The links between agencies within the bureaucratic structure must be clearly defined.

A number of additional questions should be raised. What are the monitoring criteria within the agency? Does a criterion exist for external oversight? Have political authorities endowed agencies with mechanisms such as hearings, investigations, and policy pronouncements, which serve as guides to regulators? How are the views of constituents transmitted to overseers? How do constituents express dissatisfaction to overseers? Do alternatives exist to the explicit monitoring and evaluation of agency administration? Do mechanisms exist that allow overseers to judge agency success without directly evaluating agency decisions?

The region features many examples of oversight mechanisms that are successfully institutionalized to prevent government agencies from serving their own interests. Singapore and Hong Kong offer outstanding examples of independent agencies that monitor and prosecute abuse, and report directly to the highest executive authority. Japan has developed an independent agency that supervises the various government agencies and sets the criteria for recruitment and salaries. In the Republic of Korea, the fear of executive censorship has motivated departments to set up their own penalty committees to evaluate abuse among members.

Corruption control requires tailor-made solutions that can be designed by policymakers familiar with what has worked elsewhere. Appropriate design of an oversight system depends on a case-by-case evaluation of what is feasible in a particular environment. A body with oversight capability is critical, but where to lodge that body will depend on what institutional patterns are already established.

Creating a Coalition for Change

Public sector reform is a political process that requires broad coalitional support. This process is made particularly difficult by its dependence on the cooperation of groups that stand to lose the most from the reforms. Firms, politicians, bureaucrats, and, oftentimes, organized labor may combine to block reforms of the public sector to prevent the loss of rents. Meanwhile, those who stand to benefit from the reforms are either unorganized, for example consumers, or are unwilling to incur present costs that might lead to future benefits. Fearing a loss of support, politicians may hesitate to implement policies needed to reform the public sector. Even when reform is mandated, government officials at all levels can undermine its implementation.

Good policies by themselves are insufficient if doubts about the quality of public sector management undermine social support for the policies. A reform that cannot be credibly implemented, however well designed, inspires little support and may, in fact, arouse strong opposition from those groups upon whom the regime depends. If groups perceive that the regime cannot credibly commit to the implementation of policies designed to spur growth, they will prefer the status quo of no growth. When uncertainty exists about a regime's ability to implement a policy or about its very survival, it is rational for players to defend present wealth against uncertain future benefits.

The equitable distribution of future benefits resulting from growth depends on the quality of economic management. Entrenched administrative corruption, or fears that the sacrifices and benefits will not be broadly shared, will cast doubts on successful implementation, which in turn undermines citizen support for reform. These doubts focus on the fear that the old regime's insiders will benefit most from the reforms. It is therefore critical for public sector reform to precede liberalization. Without an efficient public sector, liberalization is in doubt from the outset.

Such doubts will shift the investment horizons of the private sector away from long-term capital intensive commitments toward short-term projects with immediate payoffs.

A Legal and Regulatory Framework for Development

Legal reform has two dimensions: revising the laws and restructuring the court system. Revising the laws involves upgrading the legal capacity to sustain the level of contract writing required by modern business practices. Restructuring the court system involves protecting the independence of the judiciary[184] and offering commercial litigants a forum for the efficient resolution of disputes.[185]

An appropriate legal framework is one of the institutional characteristics necessary for the effective operation of a market economy. The legal system must protect private property, regulate its exchange, and register titles to facilitate transfers, thus ensuring that property can be used as collateral. This results in the enhancement of credit and liquidity in the economy. The efficiency of the legal system is one of the important determinants of the depth and liquidity of capital markets.

In addition, a legal framework is needed to enforce contracts, reduce the costs of bankruptcies, and set competition policy, including the rules for entry and exit of sectors. The law must also establish the accountability of public authority. Laws must be effectively communicated to all citizens, and mechanisms must exist to change rules that are no longer adequate.

Political opponents of the regime must be entitled to equal protection under the law for their rights and property. Accordingly, the rule of law must not apply simply to commercial law. When

---

[184.] Independence of the judiciary includes: (i) independence, impartiality, and freedom from outside pressure, influence, and corruption; (ii) an open process for selecting judges based on competence and integrity and involving opinions outside the executive; (iii) security of tenure for judges; (iv) implementation of judicial rulings; and (v) public credibility of the courts.

[185.] Bankers and lawyers in one developing member country of the Asian Development Bank noted that the high court lacks personnel with commercial training. The level of judicial competence is reported to be much higher in civil and criminal, rather than commercial, law. The training of high court judges in commercial matters is widely called for. Another solution suggested by interviewees was the establishment of private adjudication in commercial matters supported entirely by the private sector.

citizens are not defended from the abuse of state power they will be unable to defend their property rights.[186] Private firms must be able to protect themselves from opportunistic behavior of government-run operations.

The ability of lenders to cope with the inevitable information asymmetry implicit in all credit relations is influenced directly by the efficiency of the legal system. A dysfunctional legal apparatus undermines the confidence of economic actors in the enforceability of agreements, thereby increasing economic uncertainty. The interest rates needed to compensate for risk partly reflect the confidence of both parties in the level of recourse provided by the legal system. By determining the ease with which lenders can attach the borrowers' assets in the case of default, the perceived efficiency of the legal system will determine the willingness of lenders to provide loans. The legal system also influences the ability of firms to finance themselves by offering equity.

Explicit legal liabilities and responsibilities must bind political and administrative authority to follow rules that are transparent to economic decision makers. Uncertainty with regard to contract enforcement impedes investment and trade. The importance of rules that are objectively applied is that property rights will become more liquid as their protection becomes more universal. Uncertainty about the future enforcement of rights and contracts undermines the ability of firms to assess risks. The optimal amount of trade and investment will not occur when property rights are not clearly defined and explicitly enforced.

A forum to reach honest and efficient judgment is necessary for contracts to be enforceable. Especially important is whether the legal system is distinct from the political system. The absence of judicial independence limits exchange to personalized networks. It makes political favoritism in the distribution of resources inevitable and difficult to reverse while preventing the expansion of anonymous trade between third parties.

---

186. The rule of law must include: (i) the fair and public hearing of all criminal charges; (ii) due process, including the concept of innocence until proven guilty, no arbitrary searches or seizures, the right to make a full defence, and the right to review of conviction; (iii) competence, integrity, and impartiality of lawyers; (iv) prosecution of government officials, particularly for violations of others' rights; and (v) public access to legal and juridical services (free legal assistance where necessary).

In countries that do not distinguish between the political and judicial functions of government, the rights of privileged insiders can be maintained because rulers both allocate and enforce rights. If the legal system is not distinct from the political system, contracts may not be enforced so that there is little incentive for more efficient producers to attempt to outbid the ruler's cronies. Loyalty to regime leadership becomes the basis of property enforcement. A good with a value dependent on the strength or weakness of ties to regime insiders is difficult to price and trade. Blocked entry and exit results, ultimately reducing the economic value of loyalty goods.

Productivity is impaired when a nation's economic resources are not open to competitive bidding. The limitations of loyalty rights become especially salient during periods of abrupt economic change.[187] The absence of public information, in turn, reduces credit opportunities and restricts the market for loyalty-based rights. When uncertainty arises because the property rights of all citizens are not equally enforced, adjustment to economic change will be impaired; trade among owners of goods and services will be restricted.[188] In the absence of clearly defined property rights that can be defended by a third party referee, markets may not allocate resources to the users with the highest returns.[189]

Rights based on clientalism are not tradable since the rights clients hold are based on their relations with a member of the regime. Potential users of such rights or privileges cannot signal, either by purchase or bribe, the value such rights represent. To get access to rents produced by loyalty rights, excluded groups

---

[187.] In the same way, the privileges held by members of Nomenklatura in the Soviet Union created rents that could not be bid away because the rights could only be used by another member of the party.

[188.] American banks will not give a good interest rate to a firm without seeing the books. Organizations like the Securities Exchange Commission were created to make information widely available so a thick liquid market could exist.

[189.] This lack of liquidity due to enforcement problems was one of the reasons the Philippines failed to respond as well to the oil shocks of the 1970s as did neighboring countries. Since the profits of Marcos's cronies were hidden, contemporaries knew who held a right, but not how much rent could be extracted. Thus efficiency-enhancing deals, like those made in neighboring nations to reduce economic inefficiencies, were not made in the Philippines. When shifts in wealth among individuals occur after the original allocation of the right, those who benefit from the shift, but who are not politically connected to the regime, cannot signal their newly acquired ability.

must focus on gaining political favor. Thus, the absence of a rule-bound system of property rights invites the use of lawless means to gain economic advantage. The politically excluded might divert resources toward overthrowing the regime to gain economic opportunity.[190] Both stability and growth will be impaired.

In sum, markets in countries that do not distinguish the political from the judicial system will not allocate resources to the users with the highest returns. Exchanges will be limited to bidders who possess political connections to defend their property rights.

Transparent and rule-bound criteria for business licensing must ensure that firms will be protected from harassment by regime insiders seeking competitive advantages for their own enterprises. When the legal system works only for friends of the regime there are few incentives for businesses to seek formal registration. An informal sector will result that can add to lawlessness.

Because informal producers function in the shadow of the law, they generally cannot register their property, and they do not have access to formal grievance-settling mechanisms. As a result, they often resort to extralegal methods, including force, to resolve disputes. Inevitably they must break some law in order to operate, providing authorities with justification to confiscate or impound their property. Lacking formal titles to property, informal producers have no collateral when seeking credit, so they depend on narrow familial circles for finance.

Creating a transparent regulatory environment, which in turn makes formal registration an advantage rather than a burden, should increase the willingness of firms to operate formally, increasing the state's revenue base. Once dependent on collecting taxes from a functioning and formally registered private sector, government should become more accountable and willing to satisfy a constituency other than itself. Thus reforming the legal

---

190. The economists' assumption that trades will not be consummated until all gains are exhausted will not operate when the legal system is inoperative. This theory assumes that property rights of all citizens are protected by the legal system. The consummation of all feasible trades depends on the protection of property rights. Thus, in the absence of a legal system to protect property rights, not all economic assets and rights are liquid, and therefore cannot be freely traded as commodities.

environment will make liberalization more sustainable by increasing the size of the formal sector. Building a broad tax base will enable government to provide equitable and accountable policy enforcement mechanisms, a virtuous circle that will reduce the political causes of economic conflict.

Technical assistance is needed to teach informal operators how to access formal sector services, and to prepare documentation that would facilitate gaining access to credit. The goal is not to suppress the initiative of the informal sector, but rather to assist informal producers to join the mainstream of development. The approach for providing capital to microlevel enterprises must be combined with attention to the legal foundations of microenterprises. Unless the property rights of microfirms are clearly established in a functioning legal system, those firms may fall prey to protection rackets. Their operations will need either extralegal protection or patronage from regime insiders in order to prosper.[191]

Careful attention to local circumstances and institutions is critical for work on legal reform. For particular interventions or laws to be effective, studies must be conducted to determine whether the legal system is operational and whether laws will be implemented.[192] Approaching legal reform from the perspective of economic reform can be more effective than seeking to reform a ministry of justice or the court system directly. One can often find advocates of legal reform in ministries concerned with economic performance.

[191.] "The Asia Foundation reports that small and medium-sized enterprises in Indonesia sometimes falter due to their weak legal foundations. The effectiveness and efficiency of the judiciary in commercial litigation is important to the development of small and medium-sized enterprises, which generally lack political connections. Without more access to justice, small and medium-sized firms will be limited to transactions with firms or individuals whose reputations they can verify through personal channels. Moreover, without judicial recourse, they can be exploited by larger firms with political connections." Conversation with Steve Parker, chief economist of the Asia Foundation, with reference to the Foundation's project in Indonesia: "Participation, Policy and Micro-Enterprise Development", 1995.

[192.] The *International Herald Tribune* quoted the claims of a Japanese manufacturer that ill-defined labor laws caused both disputes and corruption among Chinese government officials. "The major problem is that while the basic laws concerning workers have been set, implementation is up to the judgment of regional authorities" (Quint 1994). The implication of this inconsistency is that bribes were sometimes necessary to prompt officials to either overlook or enforce the laws. The firms had no recourse to the courts to settle these disputes.

Among the reform options to be explored are the rationalization of obsolete rules, and, where the legal system is bottlenecked, commercial arbitration, and alternative private dispute settlement mechanisms.[193] Judges in business law and basic economic analysis of economic and business fields require training.

Transitional economies present a special set of issues; rules that originated under socialism allow conviction for crimes that are normal business practice in a competitive economy. Such rules promote arbitrary enforcement. Also, transitional economies present the challenge of enterprises in which the rights and responsibilities of management are ambiguous, making the transfer of ownership particularly problematic.

Sam Rainsy, the finance and economics minister of Cambodia, put the case for legal reform bluntly at the 1994 meeting of Asian Development Bank's Board of Governors, "We want a market economy, but we need to put laws in place. Without laws, we will have just a jungle economy . . . The international donor community should help us, advise us, push us to establish a transparent and enforceable legal system" (*Reuters Daily News Digest* 1994).

Participatory Development

A broad consensus exists among practitioners that accountable governance and economic performance depend on mechanisms that allow constituents to participate in the policy-making process. The nature of these connections may vary significantly from country to country, and any attempt to link economic progress and political development must be mindful of the vast divergence of political forms that have flourished in the region. The coexistence of significant economic development alongside vast political diversity sets Asia apart from other developing areas. A definition of participation that respects the region's uniqueness and considerable achievements must be appropriately broad.

[193.] The former British colonies, such as India, offer access to arbitration, but not private adjudication.

Participation is necessary for government to make informed choices while allowing social groups to protect their rights. The memo of the Organisation for Economic Co-operation and Development on participatory development stresses five components (OECD 1995).

(i) Consent. In democratic theory, consent is viewed as the foundation of government legitimacy. A mature democracy is one in which the governed can withdraw their consent and participate in a peaceful replacement of one government by another. However, the history of democratic transitions does not offer any sure or direct route to this level of participation, and there is no consensus on the appropriate sequencing of steps toward mature democracy. Most argue that nations must find their own way.

(ii) Accountability. Participation is a way to ensure the accountability of government. Mechanisms must be in place to ensure that government actors serve the public rather than their own interests. Accountability requires information openness, transparency of decision making, and oversight mechanisms sustained by independent judiciaries. Participatory development contributes to accountability by empowering groups, communities, and organizations to negotiate with and influence state officials and institutions. A strong civil society can monitor and reduce unaccountable behavior by government.

(iii) Representation. Representative government, which implies parliamentary procedures and multiparty elections, is often defended on the terms of accountability. However, skeptics question whether it can credibly guarantee accountability without a host of supporting mechanisms that are rarely found in developing nations. Moreover, the choice of mechanisms for representation, and the universal merit of multiparty elections raise issues considered outside of the purview of most donors, because they involve the choice of political regime.

(iv) Appropriate Policies. Participation can assist a government to formulate appropriate policies, and can thereby enhance the efficiency and sustainability of programs. The region features a wide variety of successful participatory mechanisms.

(v) *Human Rights.* Participation can contribute to the protection of individual and group rights. The relationship between participation and human rights, however, is complex. Human rights violations may originate in participatory forums in which majorities can dominate minorities.

While acknowledging that regime-specific linkages between economic performance and participation arouse considerable controversy, the experience of the region indicates that participation is critical for reducing information asymmetry between the private and public sectors (Campos and Root 1996). In fact, East Asia stands out among all developing regions for its successful use of participatory forums to reduce information asymmetry in the economic policy dialogue. As part of a commitment to economic development, participatory development can be promoted as a means of creating avenues for the efficient exchange of information between the state and public sector.

The transparency of government decision making is critical for the private sector to make sound decisions and investments. Freedom of the press contributes to information symmetry or openness, but, alone, does not ensure the exchange of relevant information between the state and civil society.

The publication of reliable audited accounts is critical for the development of capital markets.[194] There is a distinct advantage for firms to conform to standard auditing and accounting procedures. However, if firms fear that disclosure of assets could invite confiscation or extortionary levels of taxation, such information will be withheld. The actions of government are part of the risk calculation that influences private sector decisions; therefore, a competitive private sector requires accurate

---

[194.] Arbitrary relations between banks and clients are a consequence of financial markets that lack transparency. The famous "behest" loans under Marcos or "memo" lending in Indonesia are examples. When disclosure and accounting standards are poor, the lender lacks the means to adequately evaluate the risks or creditworthiness of clients. Instead, reputation or government guarantees become the criteria for borrowing. The guarantees by the state of nonperforming assets in effect socialize private losses, passing the costs along to the population at large. Thus, the lack of transparency in the banking system inevitably reinforces privilege and reduces equity by redistributing the responsibility for private risk to society.

information about government regulation.[195] Firms will not take risks when information about the regulatory environment is opaque or when the actions of officials are unpredictable.[196] Governments that play by preannounced rules will foster trust upon which conditions of information openness depend.

Capital markets depend on information openness. The existence of publicly available information reduces information asymmetry, thereby reducing interest rates (North and Weingast 1989). Since the government is often a debtor, the existence of effective capital markets can reduce the costs of supplying basic public services.[197] When the government borrows less, the private sector is not crowded out of credit markets. However, when the information environment is uncertain, the public may refuse to part with their savings or may choose not to save.

Corruption or cronyism will impinge upon the development of capital markets by intensifying information asymmetry. Corrupt or arbitrary action by government officials enters the calculus of business by inducing the need for secrecy. Firms will hide assets when profits are the result of special arrangements or behind-the-scenes deals.

Government too must have access to accurate information from the private sector to make effective economic decisions and to draft effective policies. The principal barrier to such information flows from the private sector is the danger of a government behaving opportunistically. The solution lies in the design of institutions to reduce the likelihood of opportunistic behavior by government officials. Institutions must be designed to increase the opportunity costs of predatory behavior to government.

The successful East Asian regimes developed structures that reduced information asymmetry between government and the

---

[195] One aspect of this problem is fair contract conditions in public procurement. But this is probably the most difficult type of contracting to control by oversight. Nevertheless, the Bank can help to establish procurement guidelines and procedures that can be assessed from the perspective of competition and transparency.

[196] This does not mean that officials should be barred from making decisions on the basis of new information, but rather that the criteria upon which those decisions are based is predictable.

[197] Recurrent services should be provided from taxation. Only capital assets should be financed out of loans. External current account deficits to finance investment are regarded as healthy compared to those that fund consumption.

private sector by binding the government to rule-bound decision making. Japan, Malaysia, the Republic of Korea, Singapore, and Thailand developed an effective government/private sector interface consisting of consultative committees with real input into the policy process.

These committees, or deliberation councils, induce private sector cooperation with the regime while making it more difficult for the government to renege on agreements or rules once they are agreed upon. The business councils were highly valued by the government because they opened lines of information sharing between the private and public sectors. By including the relevant parties in the discussion, the councils increased the capacity of government to achieve consensus on policy directives. The possession of accurate sources of information about private sector needs allowed government to help business coordinate activities.

The gains from cooperation contributed to a bargaining surplus that could be shared among all firms in an industry.[198] The institution was stable because it served a fundamental requirement of regime legitimacy.[199] The councils were politically valued by the leadership, which depended upon private sector support to make the regime's commitment to growth credible. Thus the private sector had self-enforcing assurances that the government would not deviate from the consultative process when formulating economic policy.[200]

[198.] Councils allowed government to assist industry to achieve collectively desired goals that firms on their own might not otherwise attain. An export drive is an example of how a council can reduce the costs to individual business of undertaking the necessary investment in information. At the outset, knowledge about international markets may be too costly for individual firms to acquire, but when that knowledge is pooled an entire industry can benefit.

[199.] This is where the standard confusion over industrial policy arises. By coordinating private sector investment, Japan's Ministry of International Trade and Industry created a bargaining surplus for the firms that participated in the process. Getting the firms that benefited most to share the bargaining surplus with those firms that faced the highest costs of adjustment added value to council membership. When the Ministry tried to direct industry where it should go, i.e., pick winners, it often failed. Success occurred when industry capacity was expanded by planning that involved synchronizing contracts. The harmonization allowed independent producers to provide the increased capacity without government's direct involvement in the costs of the expansion. Standardization of new products was also facilitated by council deliberation (see Campos and Root 1996).

[200.] The importance of information in development is emphasized in *Asian Development Outlook 1994* (Asian Development Bank 1994a, 46-7).

The same institutions that facilitate dialogue between the regulators and the regulated also serve as safeguards against corruption. The most effective oversight is derived from open participation in rule making.[201] In East Asia, the actions of bureaucrats were open to the scrutiny of the entire council, making it difficult for officials to secretly arrange behind-the-scenes, sweetheart deals for preferred clients in the private sector.

Thus, the East Asian example suggests that, if properly designed, councils will increase the level of accountability, transparency, and predictability in policy formation, while insulating the bureaucracy from pressures of individual firms or powerful individuals. The benefits of mobilizing cooperation and coordinating investment – which is made possible by effective information flows between the private and public sectors – cut across sectors and firms and are independent of regime type.

Strengthening Civil Society

A strong civil society is necessary to nurture and support an open, competitive economy. An active civil society offers the best hope of finding solutions for social problems. Bringing government closer to the people by expanding the capability of municipal and local government is the first step.

Decentralizing and Empowering Local Government

Decentralization is usually discussed in its purely political context, with the questions: How will political power be divided up? What will be the political consequences for already constituted interests? Rarely do politicians consider the economic consequences of decentralization. Even where decentralized units of government have registered outstanding economic performance, that performance was often an unwitting consequence of the political struggle for control over resources, not of conscious design.[202]

[201.] Steep penalties for corruption cannot substitute for an open and transparent information environment. Transparency is a necessary condition in the fight against corruption.

[202.] This seems to have been the case for American federalism and for the more recent Chinese decentralization (Qian and Weingast 1995).

Research is needed to help identify the characteristics of decentralization that are market-preserving and that can enhance economic performance so that political decision makers will be alerted to the economic consequences of their choices.

A sound legal formulation for decentralization that stabilizes intergovernmental revenue flows while allowing comparative advantage to determine regional economic choices is the key to capturing the maximum economic benefits from decentralization. It may also be a key to political stability in a number of countries. During decentralization, a critical issue is whether financial accountability of different components of government can be accurately assessed so that regions can benefit from policies that produce a tax surplus.[203]

Permitting opportunities for local governments to raise funds, through taxation or borrowing, renders local governments more accountable for the fiscal and financial consequences of local policies. When localities are constrained to compete between themselves, they will experience the costs of inefficient policies directly and will not, for example, want to bail out failing industries endlessly.

For the full market-preserving qualities of decentralization to be realized, central authority must be able to prevent local governments from using their regulatory authority to erect local trade barriers. Prohibiting trade barriers among regions will prevent jurisdictions from off-loading the costs of unsound policies on their neighbors.

In some economies, including the People's Republic of China, a legal framework to sustain fiscal federalism is critical to long-term political stability. Formulating firm legal foundations for fiscal federalism may be a crucial step toward expanding the participation of regions in the national policy-making process. A

[203.] Devising a systematic division of total public resources is critical to successful decentralization. In the absence of a coherent constitutional structure, individual local governments will opt to maximize their own receipts to the detriment of the whole. Designing a revenue responsibility trade-off, while the capacity of local government is dramatically increased, are the twin challenges of decentralization. Regional governments must not receive responsibilities without the resources or authority to execute them. To prevent this danger, the managerial capacity of the provinces must be built while the coordinating capacity of the center is expanded.

formal process of representation in which tax revenues are exchanged for representation might increase tax yields and economic performance at the same time.

Decentralization also has important consequences for regional economic cooperation. Regions may find themselves part of trading networks that transcend national jurisdictions, as in the case of Northern Thailand's relationship with Myanmar, Lao People's Democratic Republic, and southern sections of the People's Republic of China.

Decentralization has another advantage: it allows for pilot procedures or experiments.[204] The cost of experimentation and the ease of getting a consensus can depend on shared social understandings or norms. Social experiments can more easily be undertaken locally and success can then be copied by neighbors. Although models do not ensure followers, they do help. The best argument that can be made in favor of good governance is the economic success of those countries that practice it.

Concentrating on a sample region that can produce a demonstration effect may help overcome the lack of confidence that goes with economic failure. Special economic zones that generate demonstration effects can counteract the typical excuses for failure. Demonstration effects can also counterbalance the power of vested interests who, to protect rents, will often argue a given reform cannot work here. However, even powerful interests have difficulty arguing with success.

For decentralization to work, the active involvement and widespread participation of the local community is indispensable. Nongovernment organizations can help to foster patterns of social cooperation while being a focal point for the generation of norms of active citizen participation (see Putman 1993).

Working with Community or Nongovernment Organizations

The proliferation of nongovernment organizations (NGOs) in many countries offers both borrowers and lenders an added

---

[204.] Although development in East Asia was centrally administered, the region itself was a decentralized system of competing jurisdictions. These multiple and competing polities had a common defense administered largely by an outside power.

capability to engage civil society in program formulation and implementation. The range of issues in which NGOs can be particularly helpful include tackling poverty, reaching the poor, empowering marginal groups, challenging gender discrimination, and delivering emergency relief.[205] Some of the responsibilities for the micromanagement of projects can be shifted to NGOs – they can operate as consultants, shareholders, and as the eyes and ears for project managers. In addition, their involvement will enrich the policy dialogue.

Expanding Project Level Participation

There are merits to moving beyond poverty alleviation defined strictly in terms of social and economic rights, to an expanded definition that includes empowerment and participation. Participatory development must not be limited to the support of elites who dominate the production of goods and services. Rather the focus should be on supporting local tendencies that contribute to greater participation and good governance. This requires a deepened policy dialogue with partners, both within the government and society.

Participation can and should be brought into the program design process, regardless of the recipient's regime type. Opportunities for participation should include all aspects of the development process, including project planning and evaluation, as well as strategy formulation. Participation must not be viewed as a substitute for a rational policy environment, but rather as a vital complementary element. While a focus on participation will increase the workload of project managers, the gains can be considerable. A number of development organizations have reported that by reaching out to diverse elements they gain respect

---

[205.] NGOs help to increase the access of project managers to information known by the poor (knowledge of local customs or ecology) that is needed for project success; to mobilize and structure the collective action of targeted groups; and to channel the resources of the poor or of local groups into the project (for example, using credit pooling). NGOs must avoid being absorbed by the functions and authority of the professional elites of international donor organizations. NGOs may be vehicles of decentralization but not necessarily of democratization, as their decision-making structures may be elitist and hierarchical. They may represent the participation of interested minorities within regions rather than the general, broadly defined concerns of the local population.

and increase legitimacy. Fostering participation reduces suspicion and increases credibility.[206]

Program managers must recognize opportunities to promote local participation that arise from their special country circumstances. The experience of a number of practitioners on expanding participation suggests that the variations across countries are enormous. There is no paradigm. Rather, approaches to participation must be compatible with local customs and behavior. Practitioners must be encouraged to use what works. Although efforts at defining regional best practices are valuable, second-best solutions, tailor-made to the environment, may work best.

NGOs offer opportunities to expand local involvement. Focus groups managed by NGOs are sometimes the best ways to reach the poorest segments of the population. The extensive use of workshops and forums can help. Forums provide opportunities for groups that do not usually get together to meet. The membership of these groups should include a cross section of the population that includes women, youth, and the elderly. Human rights abuses may be disclosed once a forum for discussion is established, although the abuses were never discussed before. In this sense the economic development process can contribute to political openness by forming a network of relationships in which controversial information can be conveyed.

Local participation should occur early in the strategy-making agenda, ideally even before sector-level interventions are considered. Projects should be designed so that those targeted to benefit will be able to participate at all stages of program design, implementation, and evaluation. Collegial discussion over how a program can be designed will facilitate implementation without detracting from the program budget. First, the scope of work should be done in collaboration with the borrowers. After initial discussion with targeted groups, program managers should be prepared to go back to the drawing board to assess the project's

---

[206] A point often made at the monthly "Participation Forum" conducted by the United States Agency for International Development. A summary of the monthly meetings are disseminated over the INTERNET.

final design. Participation makes it necessary to respond to issues that may not have been anticipated at the outset, and thus suggests the desirability of phased programs, rolling designs, and flexibility.

Promotion of participatory approaches should begin in avenues that are not likely to seem political and that are not of immediate concern to entrenched powers. Usually a wide range of policy issues are possible. Looking for an entry is preferable to imposing an agenda from the outside. For example, a representative of one country refused to discuss civil service reform on the grounds that it constituted political interference. But when the question of poor implementation of projects was raised, the official replied that help to reduce delays would be welcome and conceded that delays often resulted from internal disagreement between ministries and between local and central authorities over who had responsibility for what. In effect, while conceding that poor linkages within the bureaucracy cause poor program implementation, he was offering an entry point to discuss civil service reform.

Increasing the capacity of civil society to articulate problems that require public assistance will enhance the development process. One of the long-term objectives of participatory approaches is to assist local communities to define problems, assess alternatives, and design viable programs, as well as manage, implement, and evaluate their own needs. Making communities collectively responsible for benefits and losses is a critical component of participatory development, and involves innovative mechanisms to allow localities to participate in the fiscal benefits of programs.

A point of access is needed to initiate engagements at the community level – a local NGO or political leader is important. Inevitably reform means the focus must be on strengthening local alliances and networks. This includes building alliances with senior policymakers and bureaucrats who can benefit by promoting the reform agenda. Identifying promising local officials is helpful because they are often in office for a longer period than their central bureaucratic counterparts and, because they live in the area, have a higher level of commitment. These alliances must evolve into networks that extend beyond government into private interest groups.

Equity or Poverty Reduction

Despite the region's exceptional economic performance, Asia contains the world's largest population of poor people. The incidence of poverty remains as high as 45 percent in some of the slower growing economies, and, in general, the number of poor has been increasing. This increase poses environmental, health, and, ultimately, political hazards to the region's overall economic prospects. Poverty strains health, nutritional, and educational services, as well as intensifies gender discrimination and environmental degradation. It is also one of the root causes of political instability and regime failure.

A commitment to equity gives government the latitude in the policy dialogue to resist pressures from narrow interest groups and to concentrate on strategies that provide broadly dispersed, long-term benefits. Unlike those in South America and Africa, East Asian regimes established their legitimacy by promising shared growth. The promise of shared growth made it possible to resist the demands of narrowly constituted interest groups, which would have resulted in long-term, deleterious consequences for economic expansion.

When equity is established, less behind-the-scenes lobbying will occur and government can focus on policy reforms that will make everyone better-off. Equity lowers the returns of lobbying. For example, broad-based social support allowed the governments of the Republic of Korea and Japan to ignore radical labor union demands without the risk of regime failure. By appealing to a broad constituency, the goal of growth enhancement dominated the selection of economic policies. As long as the benefits of that growth were perceived to be widely distributed, the government could resist buying the support of organized labor with privileges that could restrain overall productivity. It is for this reason that East Asia's high performers ranked among the least indebted of all developing countries during the oil-crisis years. East Asian leaders did not have to buy the support of powerful urban interest groups by subsidizing urban consumption through foreign loans.

The recent experiences of growth in East Asia suggest a high positive correlation between growth and income equality. The fastest growing economies also registered the most equitable distribution of wealth. Thus Asian development diverges from standard economic observations that link the early stages of growth with expanding income inequality. Unfortunately, not all countries grew as quickly or as equitably. Much of the success in Asia can be related to efforts by government to encourage rural prosperity.

Fostering Rural Development

Poverty tends to be diffused through the rural sectors in much of Asia, for example, in the Philippines 70 percent of all poor families live in rural areas (ADB 1991). Markets often work poorly in these areas because equity and information are closely correlated. The groups most lacking in information about market opportunities are generally the poorest. To help villages overcome their remoteness from national marketing channels, governments can foster programs to reduce the imperfect and asymmetric information available to the poorer sectors of the population living far from capital cities.

The East Asian high performers all made special efforts to reach farmers by developing mechanisms to increase the access of the rural population to product, land, and credit markets. Rural operators were introduced to alternative technologies, information about prices, national and international markets, and new varieties of seed. Government helped by certifying market information, promoting competition, enforcing contracts, and designing and enforcing quality standards.[207] Producer and consumer groups were organized to benefit from collective credit, while purchasing and selling under name brands.

East Asian leadership recognized that rural programs are not useful unless farmers do well. Bureaucrats who administer farm projects were given incentives to be concerned with the performance of farmers. Compensation was linked to the successful administration of programs.

---

[207] In India, where 70 percent of the population lives in rural areas, rural development is critical to reducing income inequality. The poor make up 28 percent of the rural population, down from 54 percent in the 1980s. Several years of good monsoons and improved irrigation and agricultural projects, debt relief, and better procurement prices account for the improvements. Nevertheless, few consumer goods penetrate rural areas due to inefficient distribution, weak logistics, and a fragmented transportation infrastructure. The expansion of distribution networks to create markets will help to bring the peasant household into the national economy. However, the costs of developing such networks may be prohibitively expensive for private firms.

Special attention must be given to rural credit. Co-guarantees and other forms of group credit help by reducing the costs to bankers of screening loan recipients and enforcing repayment. Groups are organized that will then select members as good risks, screening recipients on the premise that membership will be responsible for each other's payments. Because transaction costs to donors are reduced, loans will be larger when granted to an entire group.

In addition, staff members of financial institutions must be given a stake in the success of programs. Indonesia provides an excellent example: rural banking flourished once local banking units were given authority over loans. Village-level accounting procedures were reformed when the village-level staff were encouraged by a cash incentive system. Volume tripled and 82 percent of village units were profitable after three years.

Ultimately, rural credit must be based on secure property rights. This requires government involvement in land registration, which in turn will increase the rural sector's access to credit. The political and economic weakness of the agricultural sector has significant implications for the ability of leadership to develop coalitions for growth. Bringing the peasant to the market is especially important in the move toward openness because the rural sector offers the strongest potential support for an open economy.

Samuel Huntington was among the first to observe that power based in the countryside will produce more stable political structures and more export-oriented policies. The People's Republic of China offers an excellent example of this logic. During the transition to open trade, the agricultural sector is less likely to oppose liberalization and monetary convertibility. Less capable of disturbing civil peace, rural populations will have difficulty contesting adjustment programs to gain tax relief or subsidies.

The importance of rural reform was squarely stated by the Cambodian finance minister. "The Khmer Rouge are more afraid of peace than war. The only way to win the battle is rural development." He added that in a country that is 85 percent rural, land ownership laws are crucial, and farmers should be given incentives to stay on the land rather than join an exodus to urban shanty towns or be driven by poverty into the arms of the Khmer Rouge. The program to keep people on the land should include flexible exchange rate policies and rural infrastructure development. Making Cambodians self-sufficient in food was vital (*Reuters Daily News Digest* 1994).

In fact, the Cambodian finance minister was repeating a lesson known to all of the region's high performers. Indonesia, Japan, the People's Republic of China, and the Republic of Korea all focused on eliminating rural poverty at the early stages of their development programs.[208] The success of communist insurgency depends on the willingness of the peasantry to harbor guerilla soldiers in their midst. This menace can be reduced by bringing the countryside into the growth economy.

Upholding Standards in the Marketplace

Markets for certain products will not exist without the establishment and maintenance of standards by an outside authority. For example, providing information about increments of quality may be difficult for a seller. Consider certifying the purity or cream content of milk, or the certification of an animal's health before slaughter. An independent agency that can reduce the costs of manifesting quality will increase the market for that product. The agent rewards the attention to quality by reducing the incentives for buyers and sellers to mislead each other.[209] Reducing the variation in quality across sellers should be expected to increase the demand for the product.

As more products, people, and capital enter the market, there is a need for expanded information systems and devices to ensure the quality of goods and the integrity of contracts. Thus, as markets become more complex (with the addition of new activities and products over wider geographical areas) the costs of management increase. These costs are a basic component of market governance and their elimination is not necessarily automatic since the costs of maintaining the market may surpass the benefits that can be

---

[208.] An interest in reducing poverty is not unique to the high performers. India's development strategy has emphasized concern for human resource development, poverty reduction, and equity; however, progress toward improving social indicators has been slow. The Asian Development Bank's analysis of India's poverty reduction efforts reports misallocations and poor targeting, including an overemphasis on indirect subsidies.

[209.] Market institutions evolve more slowly than demand for products and services. For a discussion of the role third parties play in reducing information asymmetry see Klitgaard (1991).

captured by any one seller or producer. A framework for collective action must be established so that the functions are properly performed. When such a framework is costly for independent private firms to establish, then government alternatives should be explored.

Governance is a Dynamic Process

Policy reform can rarely begin from a clean slate. Therefore, reformers must consider the existing environment and propose adjustments. The match between national circumstances and choice of regulatory regime requires constant renewal. The balance between objectives and methods fluctuate continually. External circumstances change, technologies are outdated, administrative systems age. Even the best solutions in one environment may fail in another. Success, ultimately, depends on evolution and learning over time. Through constant fine tuning, in an environment enlightened by institutions that reinforce mutual learning, citizens can help craft the building blocks of an open society.

APPENDIX B

Figure 2: **Composition of Manufactured Exports, 1970 and 1991**

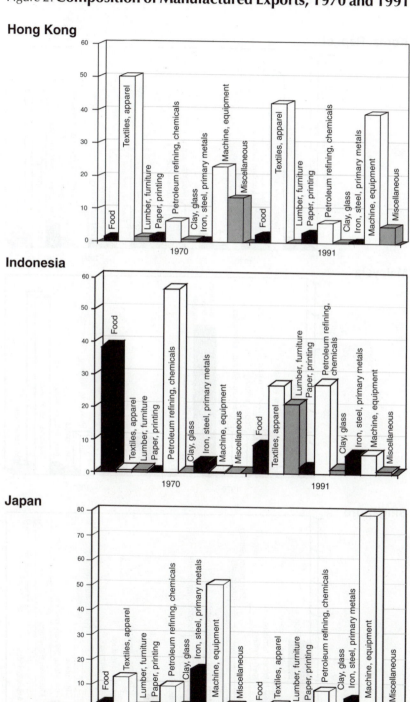

Figure 2: **Composition of Manufactured Exports, 1970 and 1991**

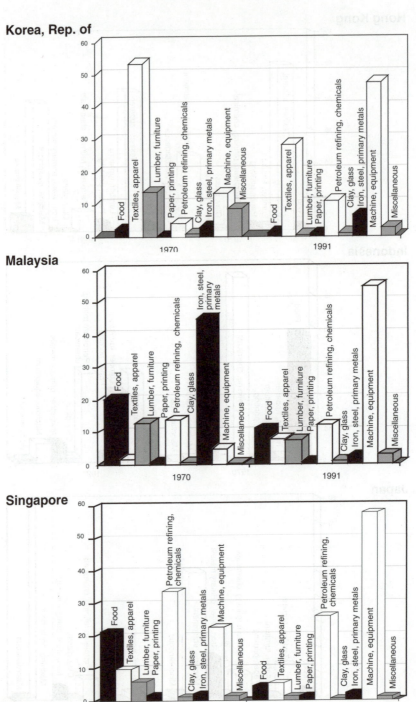

Figure 2: **Composition of Manufactured Exports, 1970 and 1991**

Taipei,China

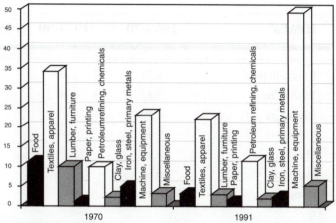

Other Developing Economies

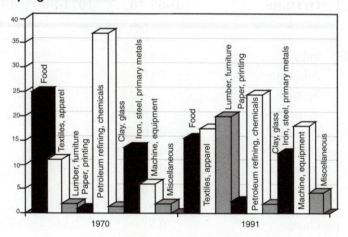

Table 3:

Gini Index[a]

HPAEs[b]	1965-70	1971-80	1981-90
Korea, Rep. of	0.34	0.38	0.33
Taipei,China	0.32	0.36	0.30
Singapore	0.50	0.45	0.41
Indonesia	0.40	0.41	0.30
Thailand	0.44	0.38	0.37
Malaysia	0.50	0.48	0.42
Hong Kong	0.49	0.42	0.39

OTHERS	1965-70	1971-80	1981-90
India	0.40	0.41	
Pakistan	0.37		
Nepal		0.53	
Bangladesh		0.37	
Sri Lanka	0.41	0.35	
Philippines	0.48	0.45	0.39
Argentina	0.43	0.41	0.43
Brazil	0.57	0.60	0.60
Colombia	0.56	0.58	0.51
Chile	0.50	0.53	0.53
Mexico	0.58	0.52	0.53
Peru	0.59	0.57	0.40
Venezuela	0.52	0.53	0.44
Gabon	0.65		
Sudan	0.44		
Zambia	0.49	0.53	
Kenya		0.59	
Average	**0.50**	**0.50**	**0.48**

Notes:[a] Average across all available index values for the period.
       [b] High performing Asian economics
Source: World Bank (1993a)

Figure 3a:

Gini Coefficient and GDP per Capita Growth Rate
(1965-1970)

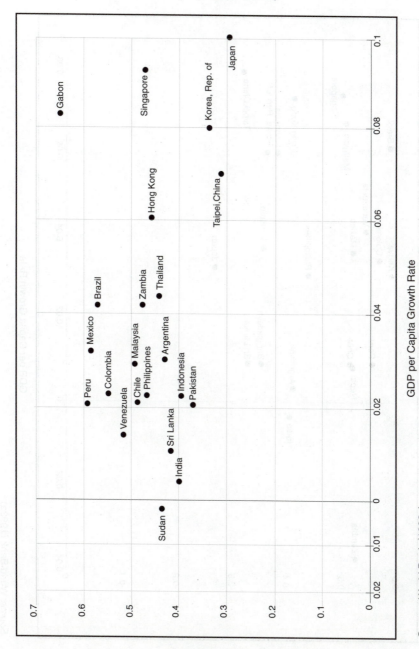

Source: World Bank (1993a).

Figure 3b:

Gini Coefficient and GDP per Capita Growth Rate
(1971-1980)

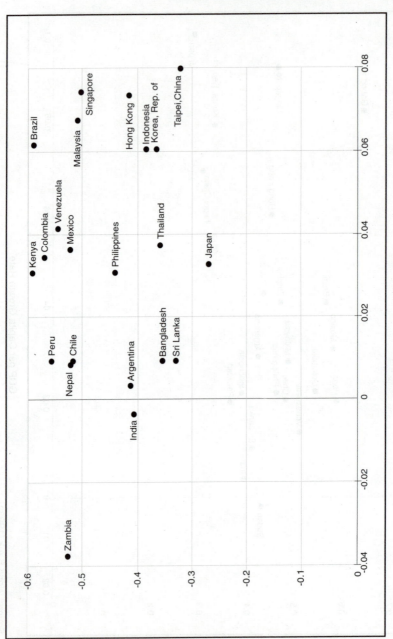

Source: World Bank (1993a).

Figure 3c:

Gini Coefficient and GDP per Capita Growth Rate
(1981-1990)

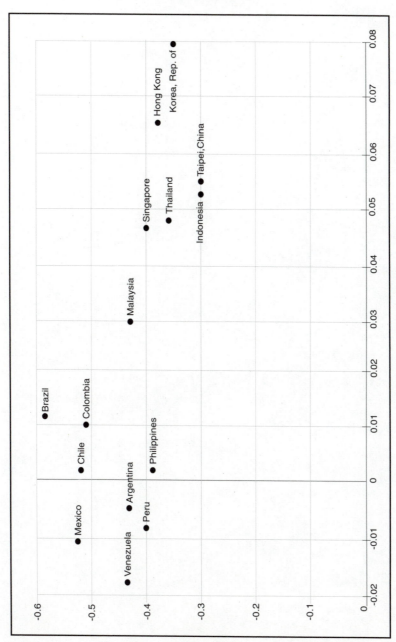

Source: World Bank (1993a).

REFERENCES

REFERENCE LIST

Ahmad Sarji Bin Abdul Hamid. 1993a. *Inculcating Values and Excellent Work Culture in the Public Administration of Malaysia.* Selected Speeches of Tan Sri Dato' Seri Ahmad Sarji Bin Abdul Hamid, chief secretary to the Government of Malaysia. Kuala Lumpur: Institut Tadbiran Awam Negara.

_____. 1993b. *The Changing Civil Service: Malaysia's Competitive Edge.* Malaysia: Pelanduk Publications.

Amsden, Alice. 1989. *Asia's Next Giant: South Korea and Late Industrialization.* New York: Oxford University Press.

Australia, Government of. 1995. *Overseas Chinese Business Networks in Asia.* Canberra: East Asia Analytical Unit, Department of Foreign Affairs.

Asian Development Bank (ADB). 1991. Proposed Loan on Technical Assistance, 6 November:2.

_____. 1993. *Key Indicators of Developing Asian and Pacific Countries.* Hong Kong: Oxford University Press.

_____. 1994a. *Asian Development Outlook 1994.* Hong Kong: Oxford University Press.

_____. 1994b. *Report of the Task Force on Improving Project Quality.* Manila: ADB.

Bello, Walden, David Kinley, and Elaine Elinson. 1982. *Development Debacle: The World Bank in the Philippines.* San Francisco: Institute for Food and Policy Studies.

Bhattacharya, Amar, and Mari Pangestu. 1993. *The Lessons of East Asia: Indonesia, Development Transformation and Public Policy.* Washington: World Bank.

Bowie, Alasdair. 1991. *Crossing the Industrial Divide: State, Society, and the Politics of Economic Transformation in Malaysia.* New York: Columbia University Press.

Burns, John P. 1991. "Hong Kong: Diminishing Laissez-Faire." In *Mini Dragons: Fragile Economic Miracles in the Pacific,* edited by Steven M. Goldstein. Boulder: Westview.

_____. 1993. "China's Administrative Reforms for a Market Economy." *Public Administration and Development* 13:345-60.

_____. 1994a. "Administrative Reform in a Changing Political Environment: The Case of Hong Kong." *Public Administration and Development* 14:241-52.

_____. ed. 1994b. *Asian Civil Service Systems: Improving Efficiency and Productivity.* Singapore: Times Academic Press.

_____. 1994c. "Civil Service Reform in China." *The Asian Journal of Political Science* (December):44-72.

Campos, Edgardo, Margaret Levi, and Richard Sherman. 1994. "Rationalized Bureaucracy and Rational Compliance," Working Paper 105, Institutional Reform and the Informal Sector, College Park, Maryland, USA.

Campos, Edgardo, and Hilton L. Root. 1996. *The Key to the East Asian Miracle: Making Shared Growth Credible.* Washington: The Brookings Institution.

Cariño, Ledivina V. 1992. *Bureaucracy for a Democracy: The Dynamics of Executive-Bureaucracy Interaction during Governmental Transitions.* Manila: University of the Philippines.

Cheong Mei Sui, and Adibah Amin. 1995. *Daim: The Man behind the Enigma.* Malaysia: Pelanduk Publications (M) Sdn. Bhd.

Chu, Yun-han. 1989. "State Structures and Economic Adjustment in the East Asian Newly Industrializing Countries." *International Organization* 43(4):647-72.

_____. 1992. *Crafting Democracy in Taiwan.* Taipei: Institute for National Policy Research.

_____. 1993. "Industrial Change and Developmental State in Two East Asian NICs: A Case Study of the Automotive Industries in South Korea and Taiwan." *Proceedings of the National Science Council 3, No. 2, Part C: Humanities and Social Sciences* (July):203-23.

Council for Economic Planning and Development. 1993. *Taiwan Economy* 198(June).

Dahlman, Carl J., and Ousa Sananikone. 1993. "Economic Policies and Institutions in the Rapid Growth of Taiwan (China)." In *The Lessons of East Asia: Common Foundations of East Asian Success*, edited by Peter A. Petri. Washington: World Bank.

de Dios, Emmanuel S. 1988. "The Erosion of the Dictatorship." In *Dictatorship and Revolution: Roots of the People's Power*, edited by Aurora Javate-de Dios, Peronilo Bn. Daroy, and Lorna Kalaw-Tirol. Quezon City: Conspectus Foundation.

————. 1993. *Poverty, Growth and the Fiscal Crisis*. Manila: Philippine Institute for Development Studies and International Development Research Center.

de Guzman, Raul P., Alex B. Brillantes, and Arturo G. Pacho. 1988. "The Bureaucracy." In *Government and Politics of the Philippines*, edited by Raul P. de Guzman and Mila A. Reforma. Singapore: Oxford University Press.

de Tocqueville, Alexis. 1960. *Democracy in America*, Vols. 1-2, edited by Phillips Bradley. New York: Vintage Books.

Dohner, Robert, and Ponciano Intal, Jr. 1989. "Debt Crisis and Adjustment in the Philippines." In *Developing Country Debt and the World Economy*, edited by Jeffrey Sachs. Chicago: University of Chicago Press.

Dornbusch, Rudiger, and Sebastian Edwards. 1991. *The Macroeconomics of Populism in Latin America*. Chicago: University of Chicago Press.

Doronilla, Amando. 1992. "The Transformation of Patron-Client Relations and its Political Consequences in Postwar Philippines." *Journal of Southeast Asian Studies* 16(1):99-116.

Dunn, Lydia. 1989. "The Role of Members of the Executive and Legislative Councils." In *Hong Kong: The Challenge of Transformation*, edited by Kathleen Cheek-Milby and Miron Mushkat. Hong Kong: The Center of Asian Studies, University of Hong Kong.

Editorial. 1996. *Far Eastern Economic Review*, 29 February.

Evans, Peter. 1992. "The State as Problem and Solution: Predation, Embedded Autonomy, and Structural Change." In *The Politics of Economic Adjustment*, edited by Stephen Haggard and Robert Kaufman. Princeton: Princeton University Press.

Far Eastern Economic Review. 1995. 10 August:37.

Glassburner, Bruce. 1978. "Political Economy and the Soeharto Regime." *Bulletin of Indonesian Economic Studies* (November):24-51.

Gold, Thomas B. 1986. *State and Society in the Taiwan Miracle*. New York: M.E. Sharpe.

Gomez, Edmund Terence. 1990. *Politics in Business: Umno's Corporate Investments*. Selangor, Malaysia: Forum Enterprise.

_____. 1991. *Money Politics in the Barisan Nasional*. Kuala Lumpur: Forum Publications.

Haggard, Stephan, Jean-Dominique Lafay, and Christian Morrisson. 1995. *The Political Feasibility of Adjustment in Developing Countries*. Paris: Organisation for Economic Co-operation and Development.

Hahn, Young-Whan. 1993. *Challenges and Responses in the Development Process of Korea*. Seoul: Central Officials' Training Institute.

_____. 1995. "Bureaucratic Capability for Economic Development: The Korean Experience." Presented at the Regional Workshop on Governance and Development: Lessons of East Asian Experience, Asian Development Bank, April.

Hirono, Ryokichi. 1990. "Economic Development of Singapore and The Role of Social Values." Ms. prepared for East Asian Study Group, Southeast Asia Team.

Ho, H.C.Y. 1979. *The Fiscal System of Hong Kong*. London: Croom Helm Ltd.

Ho Khai Leong. 1992. "Dynamics of Policy-Making in Malaysia: The Formulation of The New Economic Policy and The National Development Policy." *Asian Journal of Public Administration* 12(2):204-27.

Hofheinz, Roy, and Kent E. Calder. 1982. *The East Asian Edge*. New York: Basic Books.

Huntington, Samuel P. 1968. *Political Order in Changing Societies*. New Haven: Yale University Press.

Ida, Toyohiko. 1994. "Who Monitors, Inspects, and Audits the Performance of Administrative Agencies and Public Corporations, and Who Monitors the Monitors, Inspectors, and Auditors?" Ms. prepared for The International Colloquium on Civil Service and Economic Development: The Japanese Experience.

Independent Commission Against Corruption. 1983. *Annual Report*. Hong Kong: Government of Hong Kong.

Indonesia, Government of. 1994. *Repelita VI: Indonesia's Sixth Five-Year Development Plan, 1994/95-1998/99.* Jakarta: Office of the Minister of State for National Development Planning/National Development Planning Agency. Republic of Indonesia.

Jaramillo-Vallejo, Jaime. 1994. *Proceedings of the World Bank Annual Conference on Development Economics.* Washington: World Bank.

Johnson, Chalmers. 1982. *MITI and the Japanese Miracle.* Stanford: Stanford University Press.

Jones, Leroy P., and Il. Sakong. 1980. *Government, Business, and Entrepreneurship in Economic Development: The Korean Case.* Cambridge, Mass: Council on East Asian Studies, Harvard University.

Khoo Boo Teik. 1995. *Paradoxes of Mahathirism: An Intellectual Biography of Mahathir Mohamad.* New York: Oxford University Press.

Kim, Chung-Yum. 1993. "President Park Chung Hee's Economic Development Policy: 1961-79." Ms. presented at Board of Directors' Colloquium on "Lessons from East Asia," World Bank, 25-26 March.

Klitgaard, Robert. 1991. *Adjusting to Reality: Beyond "State versus Market".* San Francisco: ICS Press.

Krugman, Paul. 1994. "The Myth of Asia's Miracle." *Foreign Affairs* (November-December):62-78.

Kunio, Yoshihara. 1988. *The Rise of Ersatz Capitalism in South-East Asia.* Manila: Ateneo de Manila University Press.

Kwame Sundaram Jomo. 1986. *A Question of Class: Capital, the State, and Uneven Development in Malaya.* Singapore: Oxford University Press.

Lal, Deepak. 1994. "Participation, Markets and Democracy." Human Resources Development and Operations Policy Working Paper #20, World Bank, Washington.

Landa, Janet Tai. 1994. *Trust, Ethnicity, and Identity: Beyond the New Institutional Economics of Ethnic Trading Networks, Contract Law, and Gift-Exchange.* Michigan: University of Michigan Press.

Lethbridge, David, ed. 1984. *The Business Environment in Hong Kong*. Hong Kong: Oxford University Press.

Liddle, R. William. 1985. "Suharto's Indonesia: Personal Rule and Political Institutions." *Pacific Affairs* 58(Spring):68-90.

MacIntyre, Andrew, ed. 1994. *Business and Government in Industrializing Asia*. St. Leonards, Australia: Allen & Unwin.

MacIntyre, Andrew J., and Kanishka Jayasuriya, eds. 1992. *The Dynamics of Economic Policy Reform in South-East Asia and the South-West Pacific*. New York: Oxford University Press.

Mahathir Bin Mohamad. 1970. *The Malay Dilemma*. Singapore: Donald Moore for Asia Pacific Press.

_____. 1991. "Malaysia: The Way Forward (Vision 2020)." Working Paper Presented by the Prime Minister at the Inaugural Meeting of the Malaysian Business Council, Kuala Lumpur, Malaysia, the National Printing Department.

Malaysia, Government of. 1993. *Upholding the Integrity of the Malaysian Civil Service*. Contributions by Tan Sri Dato' Seri Ahmad Sarji bin Abdul Hamid and Tan Sri Dato' Mahmud bin Taib. Malaysia: Pelanduk Publications (M) Sdn. Bhd.

_____. 1994. *Dealing with the Malaysian Civil Service*. 2nd Edition. Malaysia: Pelanduk Publications (M) Sdn. Bhd.

_____. 1995a. *Current Good Practice and New Development in Public Service Management: A Profile of the Public Service of Malaysia*. London: Commonwealth Secretariat.

_____. 1995b. *Federal Constitution*. (Incorporating all amendments to 25 June 1995). Kuala Lumpur: International Law Book Services.

McBeth, John. 1995. "Strategic Retreat: Lost Seats in Parliament No Threat to Army." *Far Eastern Economic Review* 18 May.

McBeth, John, and Henny Sender. 1996. "Living Dangerously: Hongkong Bank is Mired in an Indonesian Nightmare." *Far Eastern Economic Review* 29 February.

Meow, Seah Chee. 1985. "The Civil Service." In *Government and Politics of Singapore*, edited by Minxin Pei, Chan Heng Chee, and Seah Chee Meow. Singapore: Oxford University Press.

Mesina, Elmer, and Liza Lacson. 1996. "Ramos: Poverty Will Spark New Revolution." *The Philippine Star*, 26 February.

Milne, R.S. 1987. "Levels of Corruption in Malaysia: A Comment on the Case of Bumiputera Malaysia Finance." *Asian Journal of Public Administration* 9(1):56-73.

Miners, Norman J. 1992. *The Government and Politics of Hong Kong*. Hong Kong: Oxford University Press.

Montes, Manuel F. 1992. *Financing Development: The Political Economy of Fiscal Policy in the Philippines*. Monograph Series No. 13, Philippine Institute for Development Studies, Manila.

Nasution, Anwar. 1995. Recent Developments and Future Prospects of the Indonesian Economy." In *The Southeast Asian Economic Miracle*, edited by Young C. Kim. New Brunswick, New Jersey: Transaction Publishers.

Nelson, Joan M. 1989. "Overview: The Politics of Long-Haul Economic Reform." In *Fragile Coalitions: The Politics of Economic Adjustment*, by Joan M. Nelson et al. New Brunswick (USA) and Oxford (UK): Transaction Books.

North, Douglas C. 1990. *Institutions, Institutional Change and Economic Performance*. Cambridge: Cambridge University Press.

North, Douglas C., and Barry R. Weingast. 1989. "Constitutions and Commitments: The Evolution of Institutions Governing Public Choice in 17th Century England." *Journal of Economic History* 49(December):803-32.

Okimoto, Daniel I. 1989. *Between MITI and the Market: Japanese Industrial Policy for High Technology*. Stanford: Stanford University Press.

Okuno-Fujiwara, Masahiro. 1993. "Government Business Relationship in Japan: A Comparison of Government Styles." Ms., University of Tokyo, presented at the World Bank's Asian Miracle Project Workshop in Hawaii, 29-30 October.

Organisation for Economic Co-operation and Development (OECD). 1995. *DAC Orientations on Participatory Development and Good Governance*. Paris: OECD.

Overholt, William. 1986. "The Rise and Fall of Ferdinand Marcos." *Asian Survey* 26(11):1137-63.

Pei, Minxin. 1994. "The Parasitic State and Transitional Governability." Ms. prepared for the Hoover Institution 1994-1995 National Fellows Program, Stanford, California.

_____. 1995. "The Political Foundations of the East Asian Miracle." Ms., Hoover Institution, Stanford University, and Department of Political Science, Princeton University.

Petri, Peter A. 1993. *The Lessons of East Asia: Common Foundations of East Asian Success*. Washington: World Bank.

Price Waterhouse. 1994. *The Study on Regulation of Private Monopoly in Developing Countries*. London: Price Waterhouse.

Puthucheary, Mavis. 1978. *The Politics of Administration: The Malaysian Experience*. Kuala Lumpur and New York: Oxford University Press.

Putman, Robert. 1993. *Making Democracy Work: Civic Traditions in Modern Italy*. Princeton: Princeton University Press.

Pye, Lucian. 1990. "Political Science and the Crisis of Authoritarianism." *American Political Science Review* 84(1):3-19.

Qian, Yingyi, and Barry R. Weingast. 1995. "Beyond Decentralization: Market Preserving Federalism with Chinese Characteristics." Ms., Hoover Institution, Stanford University, California.

_____. 1995. "Institutions, State Activism, and Economic Development: A Comparison of State-Owned vs. Township-Village Enterprises in China." Manuscript. Hoover Institution, Stanford, California.

Quah, Jon S.T. 1982. "The Public Bureaucracy and National Development in Singapore." In *Administrative Systems Abroad*, edited by K.K. Tummala. Washington: University Press of America.

_____. 1991. "Promoting Accountability in Public Management: The Singapore Case." In *Public Management in the 1990s: Challenges and Opportunities*, edited by Goraksha Bahadur N. Pradhan, and Mila A. Reforma. Manila: Eastern Regional Organization for Public Administration.

_____. 1992. "The Changing Role of Government: Administrative Structures and Reforms." *Proceedings of a Round Table of the Management Development Programme of the Commonwealth Secretariat*. Sydney, Australia, 24-28 February.

_____. 1993a. "Controlling Corruption in City-States: A Comparative Study of Hong Kong and Singapore." Ms. presented at the conference on "The East Asian Miracle: Economic Growth and

Public Policy," Policy Research Department of the World Bank, Stanford University, 25-26 October.

_____. 1993b. "The Rediscovery of the Market and Public Administration: Some Lessons from the Singapore Experience." *Australian Journal of Public Administration* 52(3):320-28.

Quah, Jon S.T., Chan Heng Chee, and Seah Chee Meow, eds. 1985. *Government and Politics of Singapore*. Singapore: Oxford University Press.

Quint, Michael. 1994. "Asia Swims Against Ebb Tide of Asia Investment." *International Herald Tribune* 3 June:15.

Rabushka, Alvin. 1987. *The New China: Comparative Economic Development in Mainland China, Taiwan, and Hong Kong*. Hong Kong: Westview Press.

Rampant Corruption, Technocrats On the Retreat. 1995. *Commonwealth*, September (in Chinese).

Regional Briefing. 1995. *Far Eastern Economic Review*, 31 August.

Reuters Daily News Digest. 1994. 6 May.

Rivera, Temario C. 1994. "The State, Civil Society, and Foreign Actors: The Politics of Philippine Industrialization." *Contemporary Southeast Asia* 16(2):157-77.

Root, Hilton L. 1989. "Tying the King's Hands: Credible Commitments and Royal Fiscal Policy During the Old Regime." *Rationality and Society* 1(2):240-58.

Rüland, Jürgen. 1986. "Authoritarianism at the Grass-Roots: Urban Neighborhood Organizations in Metro Manila." *Asian Journal of Public Administration* 8(1):2-39.

Sayre, Wallace S. 1964. "Bureaucracies: Some Contrasts in Systems." *Indian Journal of Public Administration* 10(2):224.

Scott, Ian. 1986. "Policy-Making in a Turbulent Environment: The Case of Hong Kong." *International Review of Administrative Sciences* 52:447-69.

_____. 1989. "Administration in a Small Capitalist State: The Hong Kong Experience." *Public Administration and Development* 9:185-99.

_____. 1994. "Public Administration in Hong Kong." Ms., University of Hong Kong.

Shleifer, Andrei, and Robert W. Vishny. 1993. "Corruption." *Quarterly Journal of Economics* 108:599-617.

Singapore, Government of. 1991. *Singapore Facts and Pictures 1991.* Singapore: Ministry of Information and the Arts.

Sto. Tomas, Patricia A. 1994. "The Philippine Bureaucracy: A Question of Numbers." *CSC Executive Letter* IV(1).

Suffian Bin Hashim, Tan Sri Mohammad. 1976. *An Introduction to the Constitution of Malaysia.* 2nd edition. Kuala Lumpur: Government Printer.

Summers, Lawrence H., and Shekhar Shah. 1992. "Introduction." *Proceedings of the World Bank Annual Conference on Development Economics 1992.* Washington: World Bank.

Tan, Kong Yam. 1994. "Economic Development and the State: Lessons from Singapore." Ms., National University of Singapore.

Tan Sri Dato' Seri A. Ahmad Sarji. 1994. *The Civil Service of Malaysia: A Paradigm Shift.* Kuala Lumpur, Malaysia: Percetakan Nasional Malaysia Berhad.

_____. 1995. "The Civil Service: A Vision of Excellence." Address to Senior Officers of The Civil Service of the Republic of Zimbabwe, 13-17 July.

Teranishi, Juro. 1994. "Shared Growth and East Asian Miracle: A Comment on the World Bank Study." Ms., Hitotsubashi University, Japan.

_____. 1994. "Sectoral Resource Transfer, Conflict, and Macro-Stability in Economic Development: A Comparative Analysis." Ms., Hitotsubashi University.

Thomas, Vinod, and Yan Wang. 1992. "Government Policies and Productivity Growth: Is East Asia an Exception?" In *The Lessons of East Asia: Common Foundations of East Asian Success,* by Peter A. Petri. Washington: World Bank.

Tien, Hung-mao. 1989. *The Great Transition: Political and Social Change in the Republic of China.* Stanford: Hoover Institution Press.

Transparency International Corruption Ranking. 1995. *Internet Corruption Ranking.* In [World Wide Web]. Available: e–mail: http://www.gwdg.de/~uwvw/ranking.htm.

United Nations Development Programme. 1993. *Human Development Report*. New York: Oxford University Press.

Wade, Robert. 1990a. *Governing the Market: Economic Theory and the Role of Government in East Asian Industrialization*. Princeton: Princeton University Press.

_____. 1990b. "Industrial Policy in East Asia: Does It Lead or Follow the Market?" In *Manufacturing Miracles: Paths of Industrialization in Latin America and East Asia*, edited by Gary Gereffi and Donald Wyman. Princeton: Princeton University Press.

Watanabe, Teresa. 1995. "South Korea's Culture of Corruption." *Los Angeles Times* 23 November.

Weber, Max. 1976. *From Max Weber: Essays in Sociology*, translated and edited by H. H. Gerth and C. Wright Mills. New York: Oxford University Press.

Wei-Ming Tu. 1989. *The Modernization Process in East Asia*. Copenhagen: Museum Tusculanum Press.

Winters, Jeffrey A. 1994. "Indonesian Development: A Missed Opportunity." Ms., Northwestern University, United States.

World Bank. 1990. *World Development Report 1990*. Oxford University Press: Washington.

_____. 1991a. "Managing Development; The Governance Dimension, A Discussion Paper." World Bank, Washington, D.C.

_____. 1991b. *World Development Report 1991: The Challenge of Development*. Oxford University Press: Washington, D.C.

_____. 1992a. "Effective Implementation: Key to Development Impact." Washington, D.C.

_____. 1992b. "World Bank, Adjustment Lending: An Evaluation of Ten Years of Experience." Washington, D.C.

_____. 1993a. *The East Asian Miracle: Economic Growth and Public Policy*. New York: Oxford University Press.

_____. 1993b. *World Development Indicators 1993*. Washington: Oxford University Press.

_____. 1993c. *World Tables*. pp. 348-9 (Indonesia) and pp. 388-9 (Republic of Korea). Washington: World Bank

_____. 1994. *World Development Report 1994*. Washington: Oxford University Press.

Wurfel, David. 1988. *Filipino Politics: Development and Decay*. Quezon City: Ateneo de Manila University Press.

Yusoff, Mohammad Agus. 1992. *Consociational Politics: The Malaysian Experience*. Kuala Lumpur: Perikatan Pemuda Enterprise.

INDEX